SEAN CONNERY

ALSO BY MICHAEL FREEDLAND

Jolie: The Al Jolson Story
Salute to Irving Berlin
James Cagney
Fred Astaire
Sophie: The story of Sophie Tucker
Errol Flynn *(in America:* The Two Lives of Errol Flynn*)*
Jerome Kern
Gregory Peck
Maurice Chevalier
Peter O'Toole
The Warner Brothers
So Let's Hear the Applause: The Story of the Jewish Entertainer
Dino: The Dean Martin Story
Jack Lemmon
Katharine Hepburn
The Secret Life of Danny Kaye
Shirley MacLaine
The Goldwyn Touch: A biography of Sam Goldwyn
Leonard Bernstein
Jane Fonda
Liza with a 'Z'
Dustin – A biography of Dustin Hoffman
Kenneth Williams
André Previn
Music Man: The story of Frank Simon

With Morecambe and Wise – There's No Answer to That

With Walter Scharf – Composed and Conducted by Walter Scharf

SEAN CONNERY

A BIOGRAPHY

Michael Freedland

WEIDENFELD AND NICOLSON, LONDON

First published in Great Britain in 1994 by
Weidenfeld & Nicolson

The Orion Publishing Group
Orion House
5 Upper St Martin's Lane
London WC2H 9EA

A catalogue reference is available from
the British Library

ISBN 0 297 81248 3

Filmset by Selwood Systems, Midsomer Norton
Printed and bound in Great Britain by
Butler & Tanner Ltd, Frome and London

For Beth
The first of a new generation and a new apple of my eye

Contents

ILLUSTRATIONS

Sean and Brigitte Bardot in *Shalako* (Syndication International)
A mature Sean in *Never Say Never Again* (British Film Institute)

Between pp 180 and 181

Poster for *The Hill* (Ken Hyman private collection)
With Ken Hyman, producer of *The Hill* (Ken Hyman private collection)
Connery the golfer (Syndication International)
The glamorous side of golf (Rex Features)
Connery with the Celtic football team, 1967 (Syndication International)
Connery the action man at the 28th Venice Film Festival (Hulton Deutsch)
Sean at a charity evening at the Royal Albert Hall in aid of Muscular Dystrophy, June 1984 (Sport & General)
With Richard Harris in *The Molly Maguires* (Syndication International)
With Audrey Hepburn in *Robin and Marian* (Syndication International)
Connery and Michael Caine in *The Man Who Would Be King* (Rex Features)
Connery with Charles Martin Smith, Kevin Costner and Andy Garcia in *The Untouchables* (British Film Institute)
Receiving his Oscar for *The Untouchables* (Rex Features)
In *The Name of the Rose* (British Film Institute)
With his future bride, Micheline, on the set of *The Man Who Would Be King* (Syndication International)
Sean and Jason in 1988 (Syndication International/Dave Hogan)
Sean and Micheline at the end of Sean's legal action against former financial advisor Kenneth Richards (Syndication International)
With Harrison Ford in *Indiana Jones And The Last Crusade* (British Film Institute)
As the Soviet submarine commander in *The Hunt For Red October* (British Film Institute)
Sean and Edinburgh school children when he received the Freedom of the City, June 1991 (Syndication International/Scottish Daily Record)
Receiving the Freedom of the City of Edinburgh in June 1991 (Syndication International/Scottish Daily Record)

ACKNOWLEDGEMENTS

Sean Connery is a somewhat enigmatic figure. Everybody knows he is an outstanding actor, an undisputed superstar. Some people know that he cherishes his privacy, which does not always fit easily with a man who earns his living by being a public personality.

That being so, the task of thanking people who have co-operated on this biography becomes more difficult than usual. I interviewed more than 100 people for this book on both sides of the Atlantic and in various parts of Europe. They were for the most part frank, always kind, considerate and understanding of the work I had set myself. Many of them, however, spoke on the condition they would be anonymous, a wish I had to respect. So this is a blanket thank-you to a group of Connery associates, friends and colleagues without whom I couldn't have written this book – which I like to think is the most detailed study of the star's life yet published.

But among those people who helped so valiantly are also the following: Ken Adam, Letizia Adam, Honor Blackman, Adrienne Corri, Susan Crosland, the late Roald Dahl, Tony Dalli, Isabel Dean, Alice Faye, Ronald Fraser, Dr Lillian Glass, Walter Gotel, Kenneth Griffith, Charlton Heston, William Hopkirk (whose help assisting me getting the Edinburgh of sixty years ago into perspective was more than simply invaluable; it was remarkable), Ken Hyman, Caroline Hyman, Jerry Juroe, the late Roy Kinnear, Anna Korda, Alex Kitson, Desmond Llewellyn, Wolf Mankowitz, John McLellan, the late Vivien Merchant, Steve Minchen, Ossie Morris, the late Leonard Mosley, Peter Noble, Robert Rietty, Peter Rogers, Iris Rose, Dennis Selinger, Maude Spector, Victor Spinetti, Tom Stoppard, Judy Tarlow, Gerald Thomas, Alex Thompson, Craigie Veitch and Michael Winner.

Just as vital in completing this book was the help of Ruth Mindel, who managed to find people who seemed to have hidden themselves from public life and organised a series of appointments with interviewees that would have been beyond me if left to my own devices. I must thank, too, my son Jonathan who carried out some essential work for me supplementing my efforts in the United States and who constantly makes me an exceptionally proud father, and Stuart Kuttner, managing editor of the *News of the World*, whose office helped with a great deal of background research.

Also, there is my deep appreciation of my editors Allegra Huston and Elizabeth Blumer whose help was invaluable. Neither would I want to forget my agent, Desmond Elliott, always a source of support, advice and wisdom. To them all my thanks.

Michael Freedland
London 1994

INTRODUCTION

'My God,' I was told by the lady who once rejoiced in the soubriquet Pussy Galore, 'he is the sexiest man I have ever seen.'

That statement was echoed by all the women working with me on this project, and the opinion it expresses is shared, I discovered, by a few million other members of their sex around the world. It is clear that Sean Connery has quite a lot going for him.

But, equally clearly, sex appeal is not everything. So this is a trek of discovery. What makes Sean exceptional? Or as the Hollywood writer Budd Schulberg might have put it: what make Sean run?

About twenty-five years ago I discussed an old-worn theory with a very different film personality. Joseph Cotten was one of those journeyman screen actors whose faces are always recognised, one who could command a more than decent fee and whose name was strong enough to look right in its position just below the title – but who could never be considered sufficiently important to guarantee a film's success.

What, I asked him, made a star? He didn't need time to think about it. There was, he said, the fat opera singer who couldn't quite reach the high notes any more but who only had to go out on stage to convince you he was still magical – a star in every sense. On the other hand, there was another singer whose voice was as sweet as honey and who looked good on all the advertising posters. But not only was he not a star – he would never be one.

Which brings us back to Sean Connery – in every definition of that same term, a star. And perhaps also in every regard the most unusual star there has ever been. But what is it that makes him both a star and so unusual?

It is not just the fact that women find him sexy. That has been the prerequisite of stars ever since someone now forgotten at a time no

I

one remembers in a place nobody can recall first dreamed up the term. When Rudolph Valentino died suddenly and mysteriously, hundreds of his admirers committed suicide like some mass immolation on a Hindu funeral pyre.

But Valentino didn't ever speak on screen. Just a handful of years later, Al Jolson shouted from Hollywood's first ever soundstage, 'Wait a minute, wait a minute ... you ain't heard nothin' yet,' and it all changed. Stars not only had to look good, they had to sound good. Better than that, they had to sound *great*, which was why Valentino would never have made it into what became known as the 'talkie' era.

The faces that had launched a million movies went with voices that gave rise to a million more catcalls. We will never know how many extraordinarily sexy girls with beautiful, soft features and the kind of breasts and hips that the film capital still allowed to be exposed – before the Hays Office morals squad got to work, that is – never got further than their screentests, simply because they had voices like Lower East Side fishwives.

So for a time, voices were more important than faces, although if there were a handy combination of the two available no one was arguing. Ronald Colman, for one, was a huge hit for that very reason – women thought he was handsome and loved the way he talked. Most Americans had never heard a British accent before and Colman's voice added a kind of quaintness to the new medium. Maurice Chevalier made a huge hit for much the same reason, although in his case quaintness overcame understanding.

On the whole, nobody ever thought of those voices of the screen belonging to anyone but Americans – which was fine in America itself but mystifying to people living in other countries who had never heard a transatlantic accent before. So unless an actor spoke like an Oxford graduate *à la* Colman or perhaps Herbert Marshall, or resembled a caricature like Chevalier, there wasn't a chance of making it in Hollywood. Cary Grant may have been born in Bristol as Archie Leach, but his accent sounded American enough, despite the fact that people liked to suggest or even believe he was typically cockney, which, of course, he never was, by adoption any more than birth.

If women thought these men sounded as sexy as they looked, they were simply defining most people's idea of what male stardom represented – an idea that remained the norm for more than thirty years until Sean Connery came on the scene in *Dr No* and said, 'My name's Bond – James Bond.' He looked superb, they said – and that voice ... What was he, Irish, Welsh ... not really American? Scottish, someone in the back of a movie theatre gallery in Duluth, Minnesota

2

dared to suggest, but nobody believed her. Didn't all Scottish men wear kilts, say 'Och aye' and drink whisky?

But here was a suave, almost Cary Grant-like figure speaking in an accent one had to study quite seriously to understand – and he became an international star. This is the first point to explain what has made Connery successful and different.

Point two is summarised by a toupee that doesn't always hide effectively a bald pate and a beard defining the ultimate chic in designer stubble. This is a star with a Scottish burr who not only doesn't look as if he has just left drama school but who very convincingly played the *fathers* of both Dustin Hoffman and Harrison Ford (to say nothing of the grandfather of Matthew Broderick).

And yet the women still find him sexy – even when he hasn't stripped to the waist revealing all that hair over his broad chest. Scottish, bald, and in his sixties – a combination that hasn't been seen before.

The third factor is that certain thing called acting ability. And that has always been an indefinable quality – in anyone who claimed it. Some twenty people among the scores I interviewed for this book tried to give some kind of explanation and came to at least twenty different conclusions, most of them contradictory: he is a man of the people to whom audiences can relate; or he is so excitingly different from anyone you are likely to meet in an English – or Scottish – pub or an American bar that you feel it's always worth the price of a ticket to see him on the screen. Or, try this one, he is so unreal that watching him is like seeing a magician. Conversely, there are those who say that everything he does is so . . . so believable.

Probably that is the explanation I like best. As believable as the gadgets handed to him by Q in the Bond films which seem to work – and really do (all, that is, except the jackpot-beating one-armed bandits in Las Vegas) although you can't imagine how. So he *is* a bit of a magician, too. The quickness of the hand deceiving the eye, although in his case it's more than his hands that move with the speed of a 007 Aston Martin in heat. Even when playing a monk in *The Name Of The Rose*, there was a speed about him. It may have been the quickness of his brain as he pondered one of the great mysteries of the medieval age, but the very time he took to work things out was accompanied by such a sharpness of intellect it seemed that this was no mere mortal working at a normal human pace.

It used to be said that actors needed to be loved by their audiences. Connery seems to have proved that in abundance – even if much of the love is centred around women's fantasies of taking him to their beds. But there is more to his phenomenal popularity than that. You don't become so well-loved and so able to command the kind of fees that amount to the entire year's budget of an average-sized banana republic by being sexy but unsympathetic.

Those who know Connery well talk of his charm, his kindness, the fun he is to be with. On the other hand, others who think they know Connery well say he is a little dull, perhaps even a trifle boring as he concentrates on his script and can't wait to get home again in the evening. There are others still who paint a portrait of a brusque figure who fails to suffer fools – or others who clearly are not foolish – gladly.

How does one explain those contradictions? Is Connery a nice man or a difficult person? Why do so many people talk of his generosity, while there are others who think he is less than free with the contents of his wallet?

Why are some people delighted to talk about him, others prepared to do so only under a cloak of anonymity, while others still fear for their bank balances? 'He will sue me if I talk,' was a sentence I heard time and time again. Sean Connery is a litigious man, but why people were afraid to be quoted saying how much they enjoyed sessions on the golf course with him surprises me. Were they afraid that under some kind of hypnotic powers I did not know I possessed, they would themselves reveal matters I never suspected? We shall never know.

Some people kindly provided me with an ever-growing, ever more fascinating tale. There were others who had clearly been warned off – a technique not strange in an industry known to attract other businesses like the law. They agreed to interviews and then mysteriously changed their minds. But those refusals merely added another dimension to the story.

Why, for instance, will Connery refuse to co-operate with anybody for a book – or even to write his own story for the millions of dollars on offer – and yet consent to magazine interviews, some for publications of very dubious respectability? That, too, is a difficult question to answer.

Since none of this gives the impression that Sean Connery is a simple man, one cannot accept at face value any one person's impression of him. He is a jigsaw, and in this book the pieces are fitted together one by one until the puzzle is revealed, complete, on the last page. What has been written so far in this introduction are mere clues, a few of the straight pieces.

It is the complicated jigsaws that are the interesting ones, and Sean Connery, the poor boy from Edinburgh who became a big star via the chorus of a West End show and classic roles at small theatres, is one of the most fascinating puzzles show business has produced in the last half century.

4

I

TIIE KID FROM

FOUNTAINBRIDGE

The name Edinburgh still has the sound of Edwardian splendour about it. Today, the image is of a cultural centre that comes to life at festival time. The skirl of the pipes, the parades of kilted soldiers in red tunics and black bearskins, the castle, the buildings constructed of local stone, all give a sense of strength. And then there's Princes Street, one of the most beautiful shopping thoroughfares in Europe, stores one side, gardens the other.

It would be nice and it would be romantic to think that this was the kind of place into which Thomas Sean Connery was born in 1930. That when his mother Euphamia – whom everyone knew as Effie – took him for rides in his pram the air was clear and there was nothing to muffle the sound of the birds singing.

But it wasn't like that. As Craigie Veitch, now an eminent Edinburgh journalist who at the time lived nearby, told me, Fountainbridge, where Tommy was born, was known as 'the street of a thousand smells'. There were breweries, McKay's 'sweetie works', and, most smelly of all, the North British Rubber Mill. To the people who called Fountainbridge home, it was also 'Auld Reekie', which, bearing in mind Mr Veitch's definition, may sound a bit like Old Smelly but really meant 'Old Smokie'. Giving it a name was another part of the campaign of the separatists.

Above all, as Veitch remembered, Fountainbridge was 'tenement-land'. Situated between the Haymarket and the Lothian Road, its streets were lined with tall, forbidding buildings made from grey-sandy stone dug from the Craigleath quarries just outside the city; buildings that the elite of Edinburgh society believed were good enough for the lower orders who had no need to keep themselves clean and, if given a bathtub, would as soon as not use it for storing coal.

Today, the tenement where the Connerys lived is the premises of the Scottish & Newcastle Brewery, but in those days it consisted of flats with shops underneath. Most of those fortresses were of the same pattern – no sanitation in the flats at all, but instead a turret-like structure at the back of the building containing a spiral staircase, and on the landings a privy, the only lavatory to serve two flats and sometimes four.

Joe Connery and the twenty-year-old Effie had moved into one of the two-room flats soon after their marriage. But even this brand of accommodation was not as bad as some of the slums nearby. There is no record of water seeping through the roof, and there was usually a fire in the grate, which also served as the cooking stove. But it was what the locals called a butt-and-ben, and people who lived in one of those were butt-and-ben folk – a stigma that those who managed to leave the tenements and felt that they had got on in the world were anxious to shake off.

Today, they have tried to smarten up the neighbourhood by refurbishing some of the Fountainbridge tenements. The gentry of Edinburgh wouldn't have gone near the place in 1930. Many of the owners of the big houses in the more exclusive suburbs of the Scottish capital even hesitated to take domestic staff from the area, as if it were a different municipality altogether – a convenient way of establishing the myth that Edinburgh was all trees and pipe bands.

When Tommy Connery was born on 25 August 1930, a dull and muggy late summer's day, he was placed in a wardrobe drawer, the first sign that the family apartment was going to be totally inadequate. The use of the drawer as a crib didn't prove anything in itself – thousands of parents would have recourse to the same receptacle for their own new-born offspring. The drawers were eminently practical – they offered warmth, were snug and ensured that the baby wouldn't roll out. And in the Connerys' case, there was just no alternative. They had no more furniture and couldn't afford to buy any. Indeed, they probably considered themselves lucky that they had a wardrobe at all. The fact that it contained a drawer was bonus.

But their home not only boasted that cupboard; it was also spotlessly clean. The mother of the establishment's housekeeping was as meticulous as her personal habits. Dust on the floor was against Effie's religion.

Joe Connery wasn't an idle man, but neither was he skilled. Getting any work at all was a considerable achievement, but his employment was always of one kind: labouring in any of the local factories which weren't laying off people by the day. This was Depression time, and Scotland and its population were rather more depressed than most. Yet Joe wasn't on the dole all that often, even if there were times when an unemployment cheque might have provided more than the stipend he received for straining his back or hauling, digging and smashing to the point of collapse.

If you lived in Fountainbridge, you were poor, a statement as obvious to the residents of Edinburgh as the fact that Parisians were French. As far as the local population was concerned, however, the Connerys were not as poor as was indicated by the few shillings brought home each week by Joe in his brown-paper pay packet. The fact that they had little Tommy, or 'Tam' as he was soon to be called (and still is) in that neighbourhood, meant there was wealth, a not uncommon attitude in areas where family values were the only kind people could depend on. It didn't make living in Fountainbridge any easier. 'It was run down,' local historian William Hopkirk told me, 'pretty run down, deprived.'

Years later, the adult Sean Connery would say: 'Sure we were poor, but I never knew *how* poor at the time.' The family were no worse off than most of their neighbours, and it is doubtful that Tommy ever met anyone from outside Fountainbridge during the first few years of his life.

The local industry did nothing to help promote the sobriety of Fountainbridge. There was the sweet factory as well as the North British Rubber Company, where Joe worked from time to time, but neither provided the staple of the area. Opposite No. 176 Fountainbridge, where the Connerys lived, was McEwan's Brewery, an institution which today likes to foster the benign image of a white-bearded, laughing little man in a bowler hat. In 1930 drinking, Scottish style, was a more serious affair.

Fountainbridge was not only home to McEwan's, but was the centre of almost the entire Edinburgh brewery business, which seems to have been prosperous enough despite the local preference (and Joe's in particular) for a drop of whisky – along with salmon the only product of Scotland allowed to call itself Scotch, rather than Scots or Scottish.

Young Tommy was Scottish all right. From the moment he could talk, he spoke with an accent that was virtually incomprehensible to anyone who came from south of the border, the sort of voice that is more often heard in the rival city of Glasgow.

Tommy's second name Sean gives a clue to his lineage. If such things could be examined under a microscope, one would see a degree of Irish blood flowing through the child's veins, stemming from his paternal grandfather, Thomas Connery, a tinker from County Wexford who had crossed the Irish Sea and settled in Scotland around 1890 before marrying an Edinburgh woman. He had brought with him his Irish Roman Catholicism, and his family remained Catholics, albeit only nominally.

Back in Ireland, his family had been known as the O'Connerys – as if it was a kind of Gaelic aristocracy. But in the slums of Fountainbridge, young Tommy knew his grandfather simply as Baldy. He knew that the old man seemed to have an inordinate interest in horses, and later, Tommy would discover that the pieces of paper Baldy was constantly folding into his pocket were called betting slips. He also knew that his father Joe had a similar interest in the nags, although whether he thought the concern was purely zoological is not now certain.

In those days, thirty years before the legalisation of off-course gambling and the opening of the first betting shops, it was something of a hazardous operation, which was probably the reason for the amount of alcohol Joe felt he required to consume. In other families, gambling and alcohol was a potent mix. It did not, however, seem to interfere with the Connery lifestyle, either physically or mentally. There was no brutality at home, no sense of neglect.

By the age of five, Tommy, like most of the youngsters in Fountainbridge, was as much a part of the scenery as the ugly buildings around him. He wore short trousers that weren't always too clean and, if not darned and patched, were rarely without holes. The shorts were always accompanied by one of those knitted shirts that button to the neck, providing, of course, that the buttons hadn't already fallen off. (There is, however, a school photograph of him wearing a suit and a clean shirt and tie, which proves what mothers are capable of when it comes to keeping up with the Campbells.)

Inevitably, he was a member of a gang, playing tag and football. He and his Fountainbridge pals used the playground at the back of the flats as their pitch. They called the ground 'the biggie' – why no one now knows, but probably for no other reason than the simple fact that that had always been its name.

He was sociable, this kid whose dark hair and deep brown eyes would have set him out in certain parts of America as one of the 'Black Irish'. At that time, across the Atlantic a youngster called Gregory Peck, the product of a similar background with very similar black hair, thick brows and eyes that gave away his ethnic origins everytime he stared, was planning his theatrical career and was soon to be hailed as the pride of the Black Irish. Neither could possibly have known of the

8

existence of the other, but who knows what part genetics play in these things?

All Effie was concerned about was keeping her child clean. At least once a week the old tin bath would be brought in from the yard where it hung and carted up the stairs of the tenement. Once in the room, it would be placed in front of the fire and Effie would heat the water in kettles over the stove, gently bringing it to just the right temperature. Tommy enjoyed his baths when his mother was in charge, but when Joe took on the chore, it was a less happy experience – his father was not quite so fussy about making sure that the water was warm.

Eventually the family decided it would be much easier if they simply used the public baths – when Joe was in work, they could just about manage the sixpence it cost. Usually, they went to the ones at Portobello, the pride of this area of the city which loved to call itself 'the Edinburgh Riviera'. As William Hopkirk told me, 'Of course, it was nothing of the kind, but it wasn't too bad an area at all, with parks and open spaces and some quite nice houses. Very much nicer than Fountainbridge.'

It was so nice by comparison that the people of Portobello weren't totally sure whether they were part of Edinburgh at all. As the historian recalled, 'It was an area that was sort of added to the city. It only became linked to Edinburgh in the last century, and the people living there really felt as though they were part of a different community.' Portobello had its tenements too, and it was home to the Brunton wire works which produced steel hawsers, but it was much better known for its promenade and the gardens behind the big apartment buildings, and its citizens were anxious to keep things that way.

The baths were themselves an exciting place to visit. They were next door to an indoor swimming pool which proudly boasted that its water came, purified, straight from the sea. The nearby open-air pool had the first wave-making machine in Scotland, which arrived on the scene at round about the same time as Tommy Connery.

Going to the pool was the biggest treat imaginable. But there were others – on virtually every occasion that he left the front door of the Fountainbridge apartment. The Connery kid found the strength to join in almost every game that was open to a child just about to start school – in his case Tollcross, an institution that attracted (although that is hardly the right word; if the school had burnt down, its entire population would have been only too delighted) most of the children from the neighbourhood.

Tollcross didn't win many prizes for academic ability; establishments catering for five-year-olds rarely do. But the range of abilities was more obvious than the mix of backgrounds, and Tommy was bright – so bright, in fact, that he worried some of his teachers. He did mental arithmetic with the speed of the bookie's runner, a skill he picked up from Joe. And before he was six he could read, although what he devoured at first were comics such as the *Dandy* and *Beano*.

With the exception of playing football, there was no more satisfying a way to spend his time than by reading his comics while eating an ice cream from the 'hokey-pokey man', who sold his wares next door to the grimy Fountainbridge tenement building. Sooner than most people would have predicted, Tommy was proving a point constantly made by defenders of the comics known as 'the penny dreadfuls': get a child into the habit of reading – no matter how lowly the literature – and he will soon move on to better books. His teachers were not terribly impressed with his reading material, to say the least – but, nevertheless, when the mood took him, reading was already an essential part of his life.

Tommy Connery pored over anything that contained the printed word, although he wasn't too concerned with the kind of nursery material considered decent for young children in the mid 1930s. There wasn't much point in showing him a book about nice tidy boys in nice tidy suits and caps, walking down tree-lined country lanes and knocking on the doors of cottages with hollyhocks growing around the front doors. Why not Martians with horns growing out of their heads? It wouldn't have seemed any stranger a phenomenon to a kid from the slums.

But does that really explain why his teachers were so worried? Could it not be that they were just a little frightened of breeding a kind of scholastic elitism so early on? After all, clever kids could get just a little too cocky for their own good. And that bred trouble for the teachers.

In 1938, when Tam was eight years old, Effie had another son whom she and Joe called Neil. The baby was named after Effie's father, just as Tommy had been given Joe's father's name. It made sense in the very family-conscious Connery household and was an example of their filial devotion – the kind that would be carried on into future generations. The relationship between Tommy and little Neil would be equally strong: for ever afterwards, Tommy would be the 'big brother', a role from which, as far as Neil was concerned, he would never deviate.

It seems Neil was proud of his elder brother from the moment he realised his presence. His Tam was always an example to be followed, especially when reports of his industry and school prowess reached him – as they always did. What Neil didn't know was that Tommy wasn't always at the top of the class. There were occasions when his scholastic achievements sank below an acceptable level and he was put with those who were somewhat indelicately called 'the thickies'.

Perhaps he was tired out by all his activity outside school, or perhaps he simply became lazy and 'switched off' in the classroom, but he was much happier catching fish swimming in the nearby Union Canal – using one of his mother's laddered-beyond-repair stockings as line and bait.

The district in which the Connerys lived seemed to be changing slightly. Newcomers were arriving. The Fountainbridge pubs now seemed to be patronised mainly by Irish immigrants and some of the English newcomers. And near them was a men's hostel – from which many of the mothers in the district tried to keep their daughters away. It didn't do much to help the tone of the area, which had not been that respectable in the first place.

Even so, it was obvious to all who knew the family that Tommy had a good home life. As far as the senior Connerys were concerned, the most serious offence the boy had committed by the time he was nine years old was smoking. He was caught by Effie who gave him a thrashing. But worse than being hit was the warning of what would happen if his father found out : 'He would beat you so badly he would break your bottom.'

Clearly, they had no knowledge of some of Tommy's other extra-curricular activities, some of them the result of dubious friendships. As a middle-aged man, Sean claimed that when he was eight years old, he became particularly friendly with a young lady of the neigh-bourhood, and that at an age when the most outrageous thing most little boys were doing was seeing who could pee the highest on the school wall, he lost his virginity to her.

One's first sexual experience is usually more strongly embedded in one's memory than even the first time behind a wheel of a car or the first trip in an aeroplane. But Sean Connery says he can't remember how it happened or precisely with whom. All he knows is that happen it did – and at the age of eight.

If the story is true, it was not only a forerunner of what was to come, but also followed something of a family tradition. At about this very time, old 'Baldy' Connery took himself along to St Patrick's Roman Catholic Church, and there Tommy's paternal grandfather and name-sake married one Jeannie McNab. The fact that he had been living with the lady for something like thirty years was not allowed to interfere with the solemnity of the occasion – or to dampen the opportunity to turn it into a celebration.

The old man was still hard at work in the betting industry. But for the best part of two years after the outbreak of the Second World War he went into voluntary retirement. Joe had had an accident at work, and had broken a hand and his nose. Now unable to undertake heavy labour, he found gainful employment back home in Fountainbridge taking over the old man's gambling round.

One day, somewhat a little too familiar with the art of pouring from a bottle of Scotland's best, Joe decided to take a rest from his commercial activities. That wasn't a course to be recommended; particularly now that he had a regular clientele who regarded his activities as a public service to the neighbourhood.

The scowls of disapproval that greeted his appearance in his favourite Fountainbridge pub that night were only to be expected. The reason for them was not. Every one of his punters was there holding out his hand, demanding his winnings.

What winnings? An innocent enough question from a man who had spent the entire day tucked up in bed. But the demands from his customers were genuine enough. Joe might not have been on the rounds himself that day, but old Thomas had come out of retirement to do a little business. When it went the wrong way, he left his son to pay up. It took Joe months to clear the debts and served as a perfect example to the younger Tommy of the necessity to take serious work ... seriously.

In later years, with the benefit of hindsight, Sean Connery reflected on how he himself had no choice. He either did things off his own bat or he didn't do them at all. There was no slough of despair for him. 'This sort of motivation,' he once said, 'is the great thing that's lacking in present-day society.' It was no more than the experience of slum dwellers all over the country and in America, too, particularly those from immigrant communities. There was nowhere to go but up, and most young people wanted to do just that.

They did not, however, necessarily want to go to Darroch Secondary School, a building as dismal as the tenements where most of its pupils lived. There was no nonsense there and young Tommy, like all his classmates, noticed the difference from Tollcross and Bruntsfield, the school he had moved to after Tollcross, immediately.

By the time Tommy went to Darroch in 1994 his dress sense had changed somewhat. Now he wore a shirt under a shabby pullover – a garment which was always sported with the tail hanging out of the short trousers – more as a consequence of fashion than of laziness.

On the whole, the girls in the class were more fastidious. They wore print dresses and the more discerning among their mothers made sure there were also bows in their hair. During the winter terms no self-respecting boy would dream of walking the Fountainbridge streets without a balaclava helmet to keep out the cold.

Craigie Veitch was at Darroch Secondary School with Tommy, although he was a year older and so in a different class. Darroch was a 'junior secondary' school, a school whose emphasis was vocational rather than academic, and whose pupils stayed on for a maximum of three years. 'It was a gaunt, grey building,' Craigie Veitch remembered. 'But it wasn't tough. By no means. People behaved themselves in those days and learned the three "Rs". If you were more commercially inclined you went to Boroughmuir. Darroch was a technical school.'

The teachers at Tollcross Primary School may not have been ministering angels, but they knew that young children could not be expected to behave like adults, that sometimes they genuinely didn't understand, that occasionally they had problems and that, just every now and again, they would welcome a shoulder to cry upon. There was none of that sympathetic nonsense at Darroch. The schoolmasters seemed to be employed there as much for the strength of their right arms as for their knowledge. One word out of place, one action defined as a breach of discipline, and the offender would be holding the seat of his pants or rubbing his ear for the rest of the day – and sometimes for the rest of the week.

A big influence in the school was a man called Pop Hendry who taught English. He was a pedagogue who always insisted that 'the well-rounded man must be accurate in his spelling', and he kept to hand a largish Chambers Dictionary which he used both as the publishers intended and as a suitable object with which to reprimand any boy stubborn enough to think that he could do without the volume's more conventional services.

The easy-going side of Tommy may have loved to read, but, as Veitch recalls: 'He was a big tough boy.' He remembers a twelve-round fight between 'Big Tam', as he was already known and a boy called Tommy Anderson. 'I remember that playground scrap. God knows what it was about. I remember the janitor coming out and interrupting the proceedings.'

By now Effie had her own job, cleaning the houses of wealthy Edinburgh folk. Her work supplemented the family income. But there were other ways of helping, too. Nearby, in Freer Street, a man called Asa Wass ran a second-hand shop that seems to have doubled as a pawnbroker's. Since the Connerys had little money with which to refresh their clothing stocks occasionally, Tommy would not infrequently be sent to sell off an unwanted garment for perhaps six-pence or sevenpence. It was young Tommy's proud boast that on more than one occasion he managed to up the price by a halfpenny.

At about this time Tommy also got himself a job – or rather two jobs, bringing in precisely three pounds a week, which he proudly handed over to his mother every Friday. In short, while still a school-boy, Tommy Connery was already earning not much less – and some-times rather more – than his father, who by now had taken a job at the Rolls Royce works in Glasgow and only came home at weekends.

Tommy found his own employment closer to home : delivering milk for the nearby St Cuthbert's co-operative dairy before going on to school (which he had already decided became duller the longer he stayed there) and working in the early evenings for a local butcher and sometimes for the coalman. All sorts of stories have surrounded his job at the dairy, suggesting that he was working there at the ages of six, seven and nine, but both Craigie Veitch and Alex Kitson (a superior of Tommy's at the dairy) say that it couldn't have been much before the age of eleven.

Tommy's daily routine would have knocked out most adults and says a good deal not just for the young boy's stamina but also for the nutrition Effie was able to give him. There was always a hotpot on the boil on the stove, constantly being refilled and almost never allowed to be emptied. Needless to say, there was also always a bottle of milk for Tommy to bring home from his morning job and a scrag end or two from his evening's employment. Sometimes Effie even produced a sweet course, although that had all the variety of a day at the dairy – invariably a bread-and-butter pudding. St Cuthbert's milk came in useful there, too.

Of the two jobs, Tommy preferred the morning work. The dairy, like most establishments of its kind, used horses to pull the wagons, some of which carried giant churns from which the roundsman would ladle out the milk into jugs brought by the waiting housewives, although sealed, pasteurised bottles were more and more becoming the norm. What *was* unusual about this particular dairy was that the horses were in better condition than those anywhere else.

William Hopkirk recalls : 'They were so good, those St Cuthbert's horses, that they were the ones borrowed by the City of Edinburgh whenever they held a civic procession. They used them to pull the carriages. There was just one problem – you had to hope that no one would be drinking a bottle of milk when they went past. If the horses heard a bottle being rattled, they tended to go a little crazy.'

In a way, Tommy went crazy, too. Sometimes, he stopped off at home on his round – occasionally just to deliver Effie's milk, often to borrow (usually without consent) one of his mother's dusters so that he could rub down the mare pulling his load.

He had always loved animals and his idea of paradise was to get behind the reins of a horse pulling a cart. There was just about enough room to sit at the front and watch the world go round. There had been a time when Joe owned such a mode of transport himself. When Joe's brother Jimmy took over the cart, Tommy had no doubt as to who his favourite uncle was.

Effie, meanwhile, knew that her boy had chosen the right job for himself when he came home after his first day complaining neither about the early morning start nor even about the difficult customers he had to serve. Instead, his conversation was restricted entirely to his horses – which went fastest, which ate the most oats, which misbehaved in the way horses are likely to misbehave, especially when they are pulling carriages in civic processions.

Tommy nurtured the horses in their stables on the first floor of the building. Actually, the horses lived on both the ground and the first floors of the dairy, with a wide ramp leading from the top 'deck' to the lower one. Each morning, the horses stabled upstairs would be led from the warmth of their overnight accommodation and the comfort of their hay and water, down the slope and onto the street.

Effie opened a bank account in Tommy's name. She was determined to teach the lad the necessity of thrift. She took from his wages what she thought the family needed and saved the rest for her elder son.

Wartime in Fountainbridge wasn't much fun. The confectionery made in the local 'sweetie' factory was rationed, there were no lights in the streets at night and there was always the fear of a bombing raid of the kind that had already brought a terror to parts of Glasgow. Even in London, the Blitz spirit was more negative than history and nostalgia have made out.

But all that was part of a national picture. Younger boys dressed up in pretend uniforms, donned tin hats bought from Woolworths and pretended to be one of the soldiers who now thronged the Edinburgh streets. But once you were eleven or twelve years old, you began to think of what it all meant. In Tommy's school, there were already boys whose fathers would never come back again.

It all came home to Tommy when the local authority decided to redistribute the classes into some of the larger private houses in the city to avoid the potential for disaster posed by congregating so many children under a single school roof in a time of air raids. All Tommy could think of was the fact that the house into which his class was temporarily evacuated was one of those to which he delivered the milk at the start of the day. It could have been a comforting thought, but it wasn't. He felt as though he was being singled out for some kind of indignity, that people would recognise him as the milk boy. For a youngster who saw his natural role as leader of the gang, it was demeaning.

But there were, even in those early war years, opportunities for getting away from the hardships of school discipline and the limitations of life in an Edinburgh flat that barely escaped the name of slum.

If anyone thought they could see a foretaste of the future Sean Connery in those war years, it would have to be in his fascination for the cinema – although cinema is perhaps a rather grandiose word for the Blue Halls, where the people of Fountainbridge would go to see not quite the latest films. Blue Halls did not show blue movies, although such things did exist, if mainly for exhibition in 'What the Butler Saw' machines at fairgrounds or in the smoking rooms of certain gentlemen's clubs that specialised in stag-nights. The industry would have described the place as a 'second-run house'; it was cheaper to show pictures which had already been seen once on general release in theatres run by one of the major circuits.

The locals had a better name for the Blue Halls : the fleapit. Someone once said that you went there wearing pullovers and came back with jumpers – the jumpers being the fleas.

Tommy, on the other hand, regarded the place as fairly close to heaven. He used to take his younger brother Neil to see the 'Flash Gordon' serials – entry twopence – and if he was feeling reasonably well off as a result of the proceeds of the milkround or of his evenings with the coalman or the butcher, he also sought out each Western that played at the Blue Halls, much like a gold prospector in so many of the pictures themselves.

He paid a high price to get into the shows – 'buying' tokens for the children's matinees (when the noise in the auditorium itself was always greater than that of the action on screen) with jam jars and beer bottles, which had become a form of currency among local youngsters.

If Flash Gordon was a kind of hero, Sean's devotion to him was second to his even greater loyalty to the Western. He liked best the ones that at the time were known as Cowboys and Indians. 'I always used to think about being an Indian,' he was to say years later. Could it be that young Connery was imbued with a sense of political correctness at a time when the heroes of the Wild West were the men in immaculately clean shirts and trousers and always wore white hats? More likely, in the eyes of the young boys who loved pretending they were horseriding, the exciting characters had to be the 'noble savages' of the Indian tribes, the ones who rode bareback. Moreover, being an Indian provided great opportunities to make wonderful noises simply by placing the palms of their hands to their mouths.

Sometimes, though, the fun was to be had away from the darkness of the cinemas and away from Fountainbridge itself. Just occasionally, Joe looked at the state of his bookmaking business or the figures on his Rolls Royce pay packet when he was back working in Glasgow, and decided he could just about afford a long-distance fare. When the sums added up correctly, there was just one place the Connery family would go – rural Dunfermline, which may have been quite near geographically but in its atmosphere could have been on the other side of the moon.

It was there that Effie's parents, Helen and Neil McLean, had set up home after retirement – which was not at all the usual sort of thing for working-class Scots to do. The fact that the McLeans did so provided wonderful opportunities for the whole family to breathe a kind of air that was as strange to the residents of Fountainbridge as was the sight of long stretches of green fields and leafy trees.

Tommy appreciated it. To some city boys, the country was so rarified that it was effeminate. To enjoy seeing trees and animals and hearing birds sing was not for the big and tough. But the Connery boys were not like that. They loved everything about it – the pond near their grandparents' cottage where they fished for tiddlers, the farm down the road from which, in a jug provided by their grand-mother, they would collect milk that was still warm and tasted a lot better than anything delivered by the co-op. They even tried to milk the cows themselves – although they showed a singular lack of talent.

They learned tricks, though, the kind that are never forgotten – like how to bore a hole in a new-laid raw egg and suck out the contents until all that was left was an empty dry shell. It was a trick that Sean would happily demonstrate to his own children in later years.

Nobody would have dared to call Big Tam Connery a 'sissy' or, as they said in that part of Scotland, a 'Jessy'. Yet Craigie Veitch insists that while Connery was tough he was certainly not rough. It is doubtful if Effie would have allowed him to be so – she may have still had the occasional job scrubbing floors in the homes of better-off Edinburgh people but she liked to be thought of as respectable. In Tommy's eyes she would always be a lady.

No one could doubt how hard Tommy worked on his rounds,

sandwiched between his school lessons. He played hard, too. Winters in Edinburgh can be tough; a bitter cold accompanied by the kind of snow that makes merely walking down the street hazardous – no snow ploughs in those days, particularly around the Fountainbridge area. And judging by the number of old people who broke limbs as they slipped on the pavement, the icy streets were almost deadly. But for energetic youngsters the excitement and potential for fun and games outweigh the danger – and Tommy was no exception.

He built himself a sledge. It was black – so black that he was sure he had the right name for it: the coffin. It said something for his imagination, and it also showed something of the recklessness with which he approached life. He may have loved reading, but he wanted activity even more.

Tommy got that all right. On a day his mother was never to forget, one of those cold, suicidal days, Tommy took his sledge out onto the nearby Meadows, a park that was ideal at night for courting couples, and in the daytime for kids playing football. In the depths of winter, it was a ski run.

This time, the run was straight ... into a tree. Tommy hit his head. It didn't prevent his walking home, but so much blood poured from the wound that Effie, virtually hysterical, rushed to a neighbour who was one of those rare people in Fountainbridge with a telephone. The neighbour called an ambulance and Tommy was taken to hospital where he had thirty-two stitches in his head, leaving scars that more than one starlet in later years might spot when his toupee slipped.

It was a time he wouldn't forget. You don't forget thirty-two stitches in your head at any time, least of all when you are twelve years old – although what appears to have been most vivid in his memory of that horrific accident was the company in which he was put. He shared a small ward with four elderly men – one of whom died in his presence. The adult Connery was to remember hearing the death rattle. He has said he had never been so frightened before in his life – and has never quite been as scared since.

Apparently, he did not have the same fear of his sledge. Either that or he was adopting the then much-publicised philosophy of the Battle of Britain pilots who, once recovered from a Spitfire or Hurricane crash, would jump right back into the nearest fighter cockpit merely to prove they were capable of doing so. Tommy rebuilt his coffin and the next time the snow was deep and crisp and even enough, he returned with it to the same hills that had been his downfall – this time, however, making sure he steered away from the trees. The scars of his thirty-two stitches were all that remained of the previous incident. Once more, like a future James Bond in his Aston Martin, Connery was fearless – and enjoyed every minute of it.

By the age of thirteen, Tommy had had enough of Darroch and it seems as if Darroch had had enough of him. Now he was going to work full-time at the dairy, starting at five o'clock in the morning, fortified by a pint of milk before walking to work. This confirmed his assertion that people needed to pull themselves up by whatever straps were available to them. Sitting at a school desk and learning from men who, even in early adolescence, he had decided knew nothing of life, was not the way to do so.

It may not have been pure socialism, a creed that has always under-scored the value of learning as well as of manual labour, but then there were few political thoughts running through his mind in those days. Indeed, it wasn't really a time for politics. Even in the House of Commons, the only party anyone really cared about was the one they would have when they beat the Nazis. As for nationalism, it was something that the Irish seemed to care a great deal about, but you didn't hear much about it on the streets of Fountainbridge.

Where you did hear political talk was in the trade unions – and that mostly focused on the need for workers to recognise when they were being taken advantage of by their employers under the guise of every-body pulling together for the war effort. Tommy joined the Scottish Horse and Motormen's Union, but mainly because he had little choice in the matter.

Living in a flat above the dairy was a driver named Alex Kitson, who in later years, as deputy general secretary of the Transport and General Workers' Union, became one of the principal leaders of the trades union movement in Britain. 'Big Tam' ('we all called him that,' Kitson now remembers, 'because he was tall and handsome') was mainly an odd-job boy at the dairy. 'Can I chum you?' he asked Kitson, who agreed that, yes, he could become his 'chum' – and work with him on the milk float.

'There was more to it than just a horse-driven cart. He had to do those odd jobs. He was interested in horses and was interested in the co-op, moving around the stables,' Kitson remembered for me in 1993. 'We were both young lads. He was a free and easy lad who saw everything that was going on and wanted to be a part of it. I never saw him as an aggressive lad at all.'

Kitson has happy memories of him. 'He was a milk lad like hundreds of others in Scotland at the time and we all liked him. When he had done his odd jobs, he'd come on the cart with us. Eventually, he became part of the scene at St Cuthbert's Court. People got to know him.'

Nothing seemed to excite him nearly as much as when he had a chance to drive the milk cart. Certainly, he was fairly indifferent to getting off a cart and going out to sell a pound of sausages to some of the better-heeled ladies of Fountainbridge.

Maybe that was why his boss at St Cuthbert's was less enthusiastic than he might have been about Tommy's prospects in the milk business. 'I'm glad he became an actor,' the man was once to say, 'because he would never have made it as a milkman.'

But then they were fussy at the co-op. In the world of dairies and particularly in the universe of the co-operative movement, St Cuthbert's had a certain cache. To milkmen, getting a job there was like working at Harrods or Fortnum & Mason, although when the Connery lad rattled his crates he didn't wear a frock coat and striped trousers – had he done so, he would surely have been laughed out of Fountainbridge. But it was an important enough place. The Queen certainly thought so in later years, and granted the dairy a Royal Warrant, the first co-operative enterprise ever to receive one.

The co-op itself in the heart of Fountainbridge was the biggest employer of labour in Edinburgh. Alex Kitson remembers it having something like 7,000 employees and the dairy was just part of it. 'They saw you into the world, that co-op, and then saw you out of it.'

I asked Kitson if he had any indication that Big Tam was going to make something for himself. 'The indication was that his ambition in those days was to get a proper job at St Cuthbert's. That was security in employment and he saw it as that.'

At this time Joe was a furniture porter working for Benns, one of the most prestigious stores in Princes Street. Sean didn't want to follow the example of his father. 'I remember Joe,' said Alex Kitson, 'a nice quiet man, from a nice quiet family.'

Half a century later St Cuthbert's finally decided to give up its equestrian associations and donate its highly-polished landaus, broughams, station brakes and pony traps to the Victorian Museum of Stables it had established. But there was nothing museum-like about Connery's work. Work it was, and hard work at that. As he once said: 'I left school at thirteen and I've been working my backside off ever since.'

Tommy's association with the horses was very much a labour of love as well as his preferred means of making a living, even if at his age there wasn't all that much choice available. 'Every youngster delivered milk or papers in those days,' said Craigie Veitch.

The appeal of the job for Tommy was the horses – and, in particular, one pony that became 'his'. Its name was Tich, and in one of those competitions in which St Cuthbert's were always entered – there was more to their public appearances than milkrounds and processions – Tich won a rosette. Tommy was so proud he would have worn it in his own ear if that wouldn't have drawn a few unwelcome laughs. Instead, he was more than content with a certificate, indicating he had been 'specially commended'. It was almost as valuable to him as his earnings, which seemed to mount up as regularly as his father's bills. There was almost seventy-five pounds in his Post Office account by the time he was sixteen – rather more than most boys of his age could count on having, even those from what might have been considered 'better-class' homes. Money was always important to him, and it wasn't for squandering.

Even so, he wasn't always the most conscientious of workers – although his love for his pony was unstinting. He nursed the animal when it was ill, feeding it a specially-prepared mixture of oats and turnips and sleeping next to it all night in the stables. He religiously burnished its brasswork and rubbed down its coat. On the other hand, when the pony's harness broke one day, he didn't seem to think it at all odd to abandon the animal and its load in the midst of the Edinburgh traffic and find his own way back to the stables.

At this time, he had no idea of a permanent career for himself, or rather of the kind of career to which he was going to devote himself. All he wanted to do was become independent – and find female company. The lad who claimed he had lost his virginity at eight was, six years later, determined not to go back on past promise. As he was once to say, 'I remember spending most of my adolescence chasing women, trying to find them. But I don't think I was successful with women at all.'

And yet one was distinctly successful with him. There are literally thousands of stories of young girls assaulted by soldiers in the Second World War. Big Tam was still a young boy when he was assaulted by a *woman* soldier. He did not complain.

It was when he was fourteen that he was quite literally picked up by the woman, a member of the ATS – the Auxiliary Territorial Service – the banner under which girls in khaki were shown to be assisting their menfolk in the war effort. This lady assisted Tommy Connery by taking him into a waterlogged air-raid shelter, removing his trousers and her own panties, in the process giving him instruction he hadn't appreciated quite so much when it was first administered six years earlier. The fact that there were two or three feet of water underfoot didn't detract from the experience. Living in a tenement he would have discovered a great deal of the facts of life simply by observing what was going on in the corridors and on the staircases of his own building – even if he had not been assaulted at the age of eight. This, though, was his own baptism of fire, and the fire in the woman who was either a nymphomaniac or was perhaps suffering the effects of some unfulfilled sexual relationship was immense. Later, he would say: 'I couldn't believe my good fortune. I remember the fantastic heat.' What registered most of all about that 'first decisive sexual experience', as he was to describe it, was the heat coming from the woman's lower body.

Both the chase and his success or lack of it were relative factors. He claims he was shy, but then so were most boys when it came to actually meeting a girl. In packs, young males then as now were full of bravado, but what Tommy was seeking was a strictly private affair, and apart from the girl soldier there were no takers for what he really had in mind for what seemed to him to be far too long.

It wasn't that the young girls in the mid-1940s with their long hair, thick platform shoes, and sweaters and blouses pointing outwards to an extent calculated to drive a healthy young male out of his mind weren't attracted to him. But a lad who thinks he is shy *becomes* shy. If he thinks he is behaving in a gauche way, he *does* behave in a gauche way.

One now late-middle-aged woman, today living in one of the better Edinburgh suburbs ('don't you dare publish my name – I wouldna want Tammy to take offence') remembers the young fellow with the thick black hair and eyebrows almost as dense as his brogue. 'He was a grand lad and I know quite a few of the girls in the area would have done anything to be with him,' she told me. 'I'm not sure that we would have given our all – nice girls didn't do that in those days. But we did what we could to attract him and we teased him a bit.'

It was the kind of tease that was as hard on the young women themselves as it was on him. They didn't want to seem forward, so they pulled back at the last minute – and regretted doing so all the time. 'We'd say,' the woman recalled for me, ' "Let's see your muscles" – you know. Nothing more daring than that, but I think that if he had rolled up his sleeves or taken off his jacket we'd have run a mile, frightened of what would come next.'

But she confessed that she and her girlfriends would go to the clubs and football games where they thought Tommy would go. 'I remember one night we all stuffed cottonwool in our brassières to make our breasts stick out, you know, nice and pointed. You should see the way Tommy's eyes popped out when he saw us.'

But if he were really going to conquer the female sex he was going to do it with money in his pocket. There was no other way as far as he was concerned. When he decided the milk business wasn't paying enough, he tried a series of other jobs. He tried his hand at bricklaying, a skilled job that wasn't easy for an inexperienced man to learn. But the girls sometimes *were* easier to pick up and he took every opportunity to do so.

Talking about being sixteen in Fountainbridge, the adult Sean Connery would note: 'Life was completely governed by economics. You didn't leave the light on when you didn't actually need it because it cost money. You had to count up tram fares. You couldn't have a bath when you felt like it – there was the price of a plunge at the public baths to think of. I wanted to do something with my life. I wanted to have pride in it, feel the joy of it. There was far too little joy about.'

2

COFFINS TO CHORUS

Young Tommy had, he was to say later in life, 'no sense of the future'. But he knew that if he were to have a future of any kind, he had to find a career that brought in a certain amount of cash – cash that served as a status symbol as much as a means of providing the family income and putting something by for whatever was to come.

In a way, his value of money in the early years was already very much like that of the film star he would later become – a film star who demanded more zeros on his cheques, not because he needed the cash but because without them he could be seen to be worth less. In his own eyes, he was worth every penny of the sweat he exerted with every lift of a milk churn, every ounce of coal he had helped shovel into one of those dirty sacks, every heave of a hod of bricks.

Money had worth to him. Even so, he didn't believe it was for anything but spending. The time came when it started to burn a hole in his bank book.

Tommy was sixteen by now and, like many boys of that age, was not immune to the urge to ride faster than was natural on two wheels. He wanted a motorcycle – and wanted it with a passion.

On the other hand, Effie and Joe were equally passionate : he was *not* going to have a motorbike. The experience a few years earlier with the sledge was enough to convince them that the life of their son, for all his apparent strength and determination, was only too fragile when put at the mercy of a monster between his legs and the heavy Edinburgh traffic all around.

For reasons that are not completely clear today and which are totally at variance with the Fountainbridge culture of the time, he accepted his parents' judgment. By all accounts, he didn't do so willingly. In fact, there are reports that he stormed out of the room, railing at his father that since he had the money he was entitled to spend it how he wished. His father retorted that he was not entitled to spend his lifeblood, and the law was laid down.

No, it was not exactly the kind of discussion that accorded with the philosophy of the group with which he hung out in the neighbourhood. He certainly wouldn't have dared tell any of his mates that his father was scared on his behalf and that he went along with the parental opposition. Either he had more sense than most sixteen-year-olds are credited with having or the passion for a motorbike was a little less . . . well, passionate than he had previously conveyed. If that was so, it was one of his first attempts at acting – and was pretty convincing.

If his pride was to remain intact, there had to be on hand a substitute in which his wealth could be invested. Tommy chose a piano. Some psychiatrist out there, knowing with the benefit of hindsight where the young Tommy Connery was going, might draw some interesting conclusions from that decision. Surely, it indicates a youngster who plainly didn't see things in blurred greys. The world may be in vivid colours – although you wouldn't have known it from looking out of the Fountainbridge windows – but like the keys on that upright piano, this was a youth who saw things in black and white, in extremes.

His mother didn't see things in those terms and would have dismissed as daft anyone who did do so. But she was pleased – and not a little amazed – by her son's choice of purchase. Perhaps like many women living in what were little better than slums, she sought a kind of refinement, and the idea of having a piano seemed to offer that. Nor could Effie have failed to notice that so many of the houses she visited 'to do' had pianos occupying the central position in their front parlours. Who knows, with a piano in the home, *they* might have a front parlour one day too.

There are countless stories of eminent musicians discovering their talents on just such occasions. Leonard Bernstein was ten years old before he was introduced to the piano brought into his parents' home by his 'Crazy' Aunt Clara. Alas, young Connery developed no such talent – nor, sad to say, any great love for the instrument. He had paid fifty six pounds ten shillings for it, but for all the good it did him he might just as well have given the money to one of the many tramps who lingered in the tenement doorways, bottles of Scotch diluted beyond recognition with methylated spirits protruding from their ragged pockets.

Joe was almost as angry as he had been at the prospect of his elder son being killed on a motorcycle. He couldn't raise the safety objections now, but there were other things to grumble about. For a man who always had one eye on the unemployment queues, spending money on such fripperies was close to being downright sinful. And then there was the effect on the household. There was hardly room in the Fountainbridge flat for an extra chair – which they would never have been able to afford to buy – and here was a hulking piano taking up space. It almost seemed as if it were denying the family a few cubic feet of air to breathe.

That argument out of the way – and lost – Joe turned to the equally practical issue of the sheer waste of money on a musical instrument no one in the family could play. Tommy conceded that he would take music lessons. But this was no more a conversion on the road to Damascus than had been the purchase of the upright in the first place.

Eventually, he just about managed to pick out 'The Bluebells Of Scotland' or 'Coming Through The Rye' – with one finger. Effie pressed him to continue taking lessons, but he was more interested in playing football.

If there was any good at all to come of the incident, it centred on the prestige of the Connerys among their neighbours. This was a family with a piano ; people of substance.

Meanwhile, Tommy had a couple of new interests in life. At times when he could have been having those lessons – if not playing football – he was dressed in a white-topped sailor's hat and the bellbottoms and ribbons of a professional seaman. It was an age when youngsters, all of them still influenced by the war, joined one of the service cadet units, almost as much as a demonstration of manliness as due to an enthusiasm for military life. Tommy had joined the Sea Cadets.

It would also, he figured not unreasonably, help with the women. He took up dancing for much the same reason.

Tollcross, into which Fountainbridge ran like a tributary into a river, was one of the busiest parts of Edinburgh. The area that had been responsible for Tommy's elementary education was now to be the site of a more advanced form of training. Despite its breweries, slaughterhouse and an LMS railway yard, it was something of a cultural and entertainment centre, with theatres and cinemas and an impressive concert hall. It was its Palais de Danse – the name in which all establishments on both sides of the border specialising in the quickstep and foxtrot gloried – that held Tommy's attention now.

Craigie Veitch used to go with him to those dances. 'He was one of the boys, one of the fellows you'd meet up with when you were seventeen or eighteen. That was what we did for fun,' he told me. The dance hall at Tollcross would later gain the reputation for being the first place in which Sean Connery practised the art of turning a step or two, to say nothing of the more subtle skill of persuading young ladies to offer him certain favours not normally included in the price of an entry ticket.

Tollcross had always been a district etched deep into his mind. In his early childhood, Tommy had never been happier than when playing on the water's edge of the nearby Glasgow–Edinburgh canal. When he was at Darroch School he enjoyed the open spaces round about, particularly the Grass Market – a large basin of land that ran under the castle rock and served as the big divide between rich and poor, with Fountainbridge and Tollcross on one side and the premises of the Bank of Scotland, the law courts and the grand St Giles's Cathedral on the other. This was Burke and Hare territory, and although the graverobbers who supplied cadavers for Edinburgh's medical students had themselves long since been consigned to permanent residences six feet under the city's sod, their memory lived on. You couldn't walk across St Cuthbert's churchyards without wondering which of the graves there had been plundered. Now the district was given a new lease of life for Tommy when, along with Craigie Veitch, he discovered the dance floor.

Round about the same time he began to take his work with the Sea Cadets really seriously. It was a life he not only enjoyed but which he decided would contribute seriously to his future – so much so, that he decided to take those bellbottoms to heart. A lot of the boys in his unit had been committed to joining the Royal Navy since first going to school. Now Tommy, aged sixteen, had himself become indoctrinated. He was going to sign on too.

There could have been a certain pragmatism about that decision. In two years he would have to do his National Service, like every other able-bodied youth in the country. Most went into the Army. A few brighter youngsters managed to get into the Royal Air Force. The Navy, however, was a different matter. Unless you were prepared to be a regular, you could never get in. Connery pondered this and decided that he, like his other Sea Cadet friends, would join now. Not only would it give him a chance to get his National Service under his belt early, it also meant an opportunity for adventure, seeing the world, making some money – and for meeting more women.

The idea of travel attracted thousands of young men every year – and caused ultimate distress for their loved ones. Anyone living near a big Navy base – to say nothing of practically any man or woman who has ever seen a movie or a television programme focusing on the

activities of men in blue – will recognise the scene : young wives, babies
on their shoulders, handkerchiefs to their eyes, watching the men sail
off, perhaps for as long as three years at a time.

There was another matter, too : he figured it would raise his prestige
among the other lads. Joining the Navy turned out to be as much an
act of rebellion as the decision to buy the piano. What it was that he
was rebelling against is not quite so clear, but he was convinced that
anyone worth his salt needed to show that he was not going to accept
the way of life of his parents. More significantly, everyone else was
doing it – at least, all the boys he admired, the ones with whom he
played football, the fellows who seemed to have all the luck on the
Tollcross Palais dance floor. Perhaps there was also the sneaking
concern that he might have lost a degree of credibility when that
motorcycle turned into a piano.

So if rebelling was the thing to do among his peers, going along to
HMS *Lochinvar* was a perfect way to demonstrate he was up to their
standards. The shore base at South Queensferry, on the other side of
the Firth of Forth from Edinburgh, was the site of his declaration of
independence.

The sea wasn't exactly in his blood, but he was convinced that
being a sailor was. That – and the ever-present hope of impressing
the girls – had been why he had joined the Sea Cadets, membership
of which he considered to be a vital ingredient in being accepted for
Naval service.

The man who wrote 'All the nice girls love a sailor' was not too far
off-beat. For Tommy, the opportunities ahead seemed immense. No
more would he hide the fact that he was going out with a girl – a stance
he had adopted ever since the time a young lady knocked on the front
door of the Fountainbridge apartment and was told unceremoniously
by Joe – and much to Tommy's embarrassment – that Tommy was 'in
his bath'.

What he hadn't quite grasped was that joining as the most junior
rating possible was as unlike a romantic cruise as anything he could
contemplate. Basic training resembled life in the Foreign Legion more
than life in foreign and exotic parts.

Most of his time was spent in training at Rosyth. He would never
have imagined as he entered the base for the first time that in his entire
naval career he would get little further than either the place itself or
his rank at the time of his arrival there.

When the training was done, he felt like the victim of some early
Victorian press gang. He was shipped out – to use a naval term,
although in fact he barely left dry land – to a gunnery school, which

he does seem to have enjoyed more. It would have been virtually impossible to have enjoyed it less.

Finally, he was moved – to Portsmouth and a hammock on HMS *Formidable*.

There were certain essentials to accomplish the moment he arrived in Portsmouth. There was no doubt which was the most important – to get himself tattooed. He chose two mottoes, designs which gave a pretty fair indication of where his loves and loyalties lay. The first said 'Mum and Dad'; the second 'Scotland Forever'.

He found other things to do which he quite enjoyed. His budding muscles didn't escape the attention of his physical-training instructor and before he could think twice about the invitation – and had he thought twice he would still have had no option but to accept – he agreed to join the base's boxing team. Something, at least, had come out of his Fountainbridge upbringing that was proving of value. And, he might have thought, wouldn't go amiss when he got back there either.

To Tommy, as to plenty of other seventeen- and eighteen-year-olds who signed on to serve His Majesty the King on one of his ships, throwing his weight around a boxing ring gave a sense of liberty, a chance to demonstrate he was not just a sailor but also a man. The tattoos fulfilled much the same purpose. They were the visible, obvious part of Navy life. In fact, he had wanted to have them since his Sea Cadet days, and at that time would perhaps have made him feel as though he were at the start of some long journey. Now they shouted out for all to hear that he had arrived at his destination.

What he had not anticipated, it seems, was the discipline of being a sailor – sleeping in those hammocks, at the closest quarters imaginable to other men of his age but not necessarily of his temperament; scrubbing decks, polishing brasswork, and always, but always, at the beck and call of a petty officer whose naval authority and air of social superiority frequently riled young Tommy and his shipmates.

So his seven years' signing-on wasn't going to turn out quite the way he expected. What was more, soon after settling in as an ordinary seaman, he was doubled up with a series of stomach pains more agonising than he could have imagined possible. Not until three years after joining up, when he could stand the pain no more, was the diagnosis made : he had developed a duodenal ulcer. There are literally millions of people who make themselves sick from drinking too much alcohol. Tommy's ulcer, the doctors decided, was a result of something seemingly much more benign – all the milk he had drunk while working for the dairy.

For eight weeks he was in a naval hospital. It gave him plenty of time to think and wonder why he had been so keen to sign on in the first place. He hadn't even gone anywhere. The ulcer only seemed to confirm the decision he had already made: he hated Navy life. He didn't even enjoy boasting about being a seaman when he went home on leave to Fountainbridge or when he visited the Palais de Danse.

Plainly, there was no future for him in the Navy, and therefore, if he stayed in it, not much of a future of any kind for him in life. He was a liability to the King as well as to himself. The Navy thought about it and decided they could do without his services.

The ulcer, therefore, came as something of a gift from heaven. The doctors may not have realised it was also a family condition – his father had certainly suffered from one, and there is also some evidence to show that his grandfather, Tom, had an ulcer as well.

He was given his papers – invalided out of the service. He went back home – with the benefit of a pension, but also with a severely dented ego. What his friends in Fountainbridge would say didn't bear thinking about. Failing to get a motorbike was one thing. Failing to be a sailor represented still greater ignominy. As for the pension, it wasn't enough to buy him a few days' breakfasts, let alone provide an income for the remainder of his life. Even in 1949 there wasn't much you could buy with six shillings and ninepence. Yet nearly half a century later, had he wanted to do so, he would still have been entitled to draw its decimal equivalent.

Now, aged nineteen and unemployed, he had to decide what he was going to do. He knew that his ties to Fountainbridge weren't exactly unbreakable – certainly, he wasn't going to stay there for ever. But it was in that area that he now looked for work – he had to start somewhere, and it was only by work that he was going to get out of those home surroundings.

He looked for jobs – hard. And he looked for entertainment – hard. Like many of his generation, he found it in a local billiard hall. Those places were part of the fabric of working-class Britain – in Scotland as much as in England. The halls were usually situated above Montague Burton menswear stores, and had been started up by the founder of the firm to take young men off the streets and give them a decent kind of recreation – in the hope that this would lead to decent jobs and the chance to buy his suits. In fact, the halls were frequently hotbeds of what were then considered to be the worst of vices – betting in particular.

They also became centres for gang warfare. One of those groups was known as the Valdor gang. One evening a Valdor member decided that the time had come to interrupt Tommy's play. It was not something he would try again. The strength of the Connery fist was enough to send him away wishing he had either joined another gang or hadn't bothered to think about the population of billiard halls.

But the gang weren't giving up. They followed Tommy to the dance hall where he had to use even greater strength to persuade them to think again. In a scene that looked very much like the inevitable moment in an early Sean Connery movie when leather-jacketed thugs slink away nursing their wounds, Big Tam really earned his nickname. He took the law into his own hands – and floored three of the intruders.

They left him alone thereafter. He took whatever work came his way, mostly using his considerable bulk in one way or another – never more successfully than at the dance hall, the management of which, as a result of the escapade, took him on as their paid bouncer.

But there was also life and other kinds of socialising outside the Palais. And since he was able to earn the kind of money few people outside what would then have been considered the managerial classes could expect, he took advantage of what life had to offer when he could. His Navy life had convinced him of at least two things : there were other people cooking stews besides his mother and there were better ways of eating than in a ship's mess hall. He had, in short, discovered the restaurant.

The one he liked best in Edinburgh was called Ritchie's. Unless he was particularly broke, a ten-shilling meal there was enough to make his stomach feel full and his lips worth smacking. Steak, mushrooms and dessert was tempting enough fare for him and his mates. It was also the kind of meal his parents had rarely, if ever, been able to afford. His father, in any case, would have felt much more comfortable in any one of the drinking establishments which he patronised, particularly the Fair Exchange or the Pontin Street Market bar.

To many of the other inhabitants of Fountainbridge, Tommy Connery was a man of wealth, which was as good a reason as any for there now being no shortage of women at the dance halls who were ready to provide him with opportunities he was still too shy to make the most of. Some Saturday nights, he had as much as ten pounds in his pockets. It enabled him to distribute his wealth fairly evenly between the Fountain pub and the Palais de Danse and the girls had begun to notice. When he did take out a young lady, however, his experiences at eight and fourteen years of age did not encourage him to take advantage of the situation – had they been filmed, most of his activities would not have needed to be censored.

That was one of the mores of the times. He may have felt frustrated, but his behaviour was no more than was expected of him by others and what, in truth, he really expected of himself. But he intended to change.

Occasionally, he did. There were moments when he had sufficient money in his pocket to take a young lady to Edinburgh's West End, which, in its limited way, had similar attractions to the district of the same name in London. Sometimes, he was more adventurous with the opposite sex and was delighted to discover that they didn't always object. But there wasn't the ease he so wished to cultivate.

It became apparent that young Tommy Connery was determined to do what seemed to him to be merely the obvious – get out of the environment in which, even at this early age, he seemed to have been misplaced. What was more, he was sure women would be better where the grass was greener.

He was conscious even now that he had good looks that made those Edinburgh girls notice him. The problem centred on not feeling able to deal with the knowing glances he got. At the root of it all was the lack of guarantee that any girl giving him the eye was also willing to give him her virginity.

But he partly understood that these young ladies were using what a future generation would call body language. His trouble was that he didn't have the confidence to interpret it – and translations weren't always available. When his friends were around to egg him on, it took more courage *not* to approach a girl than to actually ask her for a date – but when he was on his own he allowed those precious moments of introduction to pass him by. And would regret it for days afterwards.

So something had to be done. Despite his obvious strength which he demonstrated so forcefully against the Valdor gang at the dance hall, he inexplicably considered his physique to be immature and believed that if his chest and muscles felt as good to him as did his face, he wouldn't have any problems at all.

Meanwhile there was that question of work. He was going to try anything that would give him enough money to pay his way out of the slums. The ex-servicemen's organisation, the British Legion – not yet glorified with the prefix *Royal* – agreed to help.

Jack Vinestock & Company were cabinet makers, which meant that they made virtually any kind of furniture that a customer could want – a cabinet to be sure, but also a chair or a wardrobe or a table. Occasionally, too, there were coffins – so beautifully polished that people outside the business wondered about the sense of burnishing a casket to mirror-like perfection only to submerge it six feet deep into the dank ground.

The Legion got to hear that there was a vacancy at Vinestock's and suggested that Connery might like to take up the job of assistant to the firm's french polisher. He grabbed the opportunity. He didn't intend the job to last long, but he was not going to be one of those lazy youngsters who were prepared to live off unemployment benefit. So he did it all – not just polishing the coffins, but also learning how to size up a potential client – large caskets for six-footers plus, medium and small according to their statistics. He might have been happier learning more about the rest of the business, possibly even getting an apprenticeship, but it has been the coffin polishing that people now most like to remember.

Even if in his own mind he had no ambition to polish coffins the rest of his life, the actual decision to leave was taken from him – by his employer. Sean said the work of polishing the wood gave him severe backache, so he sat down. The man said that he was being lazy – and fired him.

But the job had had its advantages. He became friends, for instance, with a colleague called John Hogg who had a part time job at the nearby King's Theatre. He suggested that Tommy might like to join him. Like to join him? It was an invitation that made him jump for joy. There was only an opportunity for the occasional stint of odd jobs, but something about the theatrical life stuck. He knew nothing about the stage, but this was a new existence with a new kind of crowd and, in its way, he knew it was something to savour.

But it didn't bring him enough money. Especially not enough to do what he yearned to do most of all – join a local weightlifting class.

He paid the fifteen shillings membership fee, and for a further one shilling and sixpence a week became a fully paid-up member of the Dunedin Weightlifting Club. He went every Monday, Wednesday and Friday, which might be considered devotion beyond the call of duty. But he was in it for serious reasons – as he was to admit later, 'It was not so much to be fitter but to look good for girls.'

Tommy had bought a new tracksuit – an item of clothing not every youngster in Edinburgh owned in the early 1950s – and a chest expander. It did the trick, and after about a year he achieved his goal. His shoulders were broader, his chest was what at the time was described as 'manly' and his legs were as firm as the trunks of the trees in one of the local parks.

For some time now, Tommy had been playing with a football team that had been granted – at least in the eyes of most local people who knew about such things – the status of semi-professional. The Fet-Lors – a team established by Fettes College and Loretto School, institutions that believed they had a duty to help boys less fortunate than their own students mainly by establishing boys' clubs – were so good that they felt they could match any professional group on the pitch. He himself was as able as the best in the team when at the top of their form. But they were not the only team he played with. When he turned out for the Bonnyrigg Rose side, he was actually paid for the privilege. That was what he considered a profession.

His football activities were so enjoyable, and seemed to result in such satisfactory scores, that he allowed his imagination to turn to the idea of actually playing the game for a living. Professional footballers earned twenty pounds a week in those days, which seemed very big money to a kid from the tenements. One had to take into consideration the fact that the prospects were limited, and that a playing career was extraordinarily short, but even so the idea was seriously tempting.

Especially as he actually had an offer to play for the leading Scottish club, East Fife. He was even offered a twenty-five pound signing-on fee. It was more money in one lump sum than he had ever seen before. But when he considered it seriously, the magic of chasing a ball around a pitch and the smelly, sweaty dressing-room sessions afterwards went quite suddenly. Soccer was a game to play, not to work at.

He had other ideas of how to earn money. When he heard that a local art school were looking for male models, he volunteered to supply their needs. One of the artists in the class was a young lady who had been one of his silent admirers before he had joined the Navy.

She told me : 'He posed in the briefest of slips covering the essentials, but really it served to make him all the more exciting to us. I remember one girl daring me to go over and touch him – nowhere indecent, just touch his muscles – but none of us would. But sexy ! I had never seen anything that ... well, I suppose the expression is 'turned me on' as he did. My, I wanted to touch him, but I wouldna dare. I think if he had spoken to me, let alone asked me out, I'd have been ready for anything. But I think he was even more shy than I was.' Connery himself would admit that he found it all rather embarrassing. He agreed that sometimes he even blushed.

His busiest time sitting with just that pouch to maintain his modesty was in the spring of 1952. Thirty years later, the artist Martin Mackeown was to write that he had felt 'sorry for the well-built young man with a dead-end job and no future while I was busy working to become a great artist.'

There was other modelling work, too. He posed for some body-building magazines, once again revealing enough of himself to make him tempting to those who bought the publications for reasons other than developing their own muscles.

Then he moved on to yet another type of work. He got a job in the machine-room of the Edinburgh *Evening News*, but if he had had any ambitions within the newspaper business it would have been upstairs with the reporters. The dirty, oily, noisy room where he worked, and which left its equally dirty, oily mark on his hands and face and the noise of the printing machines buzzing in his ears for hours after he left it, was not for him. So he looked for more pleasant ways of earning his crust.

For a brief time, watching Tommy Connery at work was rather like seeing a scene from one of those beach movies so popular among American teenagers in the 1950s and early 1960s. He was once more going to those baths at Portobello, but not to the public tubs. Instead, he was working at that remarkable outdoor pool next door – as a lifeguard.

An essential qualification for the job was to know how to swim. But, incredibly, Tommy was taken on as a lifeguard before he could do a serious stroke. So he took lessons from a friend. As Craigie Veitch told me: 'He couldn't swim down fifteen feet and retrieve someone from the bottom of the pool. You've got to be very, very confident to be a lifeguard. But his friend taught him and brought him into membership of the elite guard, as it were.'

It was work he enjoyed – not least of all – once again – because of the girls who might not pretend to be in trouble but were likely to show an inordinate interest in what would happen should they choose to do so.

But there was at least one occasion when he dived into the water to save a swimmer in more trouble than he at first thought. The woman was drowning and if he had not gone to her rescue at that moment she would never have survived.

It was satisfying work, but not satisfying enough. He was still a part-time bouncer at the Palais de Danse, and liked to think he was the best bouncer in Scotland. It was a reputation that had even greater effect on the customers of the establishment than on its proprietors. More often than not, the mere sight of the young, splendidly-built Mr Connery approaching was warning enough for a potential problem to disappear. That was the kind of tough guy the halls wanted, one who presented more of a threat than a promise.

Playing at the dance hall for two weeks a year was the bandleader Ray Ellington. The two became friends and used to work out together at the gym where Ellington was a welcome visitor. It was the first friendship for Connery that didn't have Fountainbridge stamped all over it, the first time Tommy got to know a celebrity, and he enjoyed it like a small boy given a new toy.

There was another job that gives a more prophetic view of what was going to happen in Tommy Connery's life. He heard that young men were needed to 'play' – the word is somewhat grandiose since all they were expected to do was walk on and off – soldiers in an Edinburgh production of Anna Neagle's latest spectacular, *The Glorious Days*. Anna Neagle had been Britain's top film star in the 1930s, starring most notably as Queen Victoria in a movie of the same name, but had hit hard times when her film producer husband Herbert Wilcox went broke. Taking her show to Edinburgh was not going to be one of her most notable triumphs. Nor would it be Connery's, even though he got closer to real stage work than he had ever managed in the odd moments he was employed at the King's Theatre.

He liked the work but in truth thought it no more a career move than delivering milk had been. And a good deal less fun – and less rewarding – than being a lifeguard. When he appeared in the show at the Empire Theatre, he didn't have any grandiose dreams of future stardom or of success being just around the corner. It was merely a step beyond coffin polishing. But it was a job, and anything that paid money was worthy of his attention. Besides which, he was discovering the joys of clothes. What in London had been known as the 'Spiv' look had reached Edinburgh and 'Big Tam' sported the longest jackets with the most detailed draped shoulders he could find. The quality was terrible but the image seemed readily created for him and he had the money to pay for it. The girls were suitably impressed.

It was about this time that someone suggested he ought to think about entering the Mr Universe contest, which received much more public attention in the United States than in Britain, but figured quite prominently in the body-building magazines for which he had posed, particularly those which were genuinely aimed at the sort of readers who might one day hope to appear in their pages themselves.

The London heats for Mr Universe 1953 were held at the Scala Theatre, a building sufficiently far away from the West End to actually need events of the kind. In fact, the only time it was ever used otherwise was for its annual performances of the children's play *Peter Pan*.

Tommy decided that this was the time when he could really show what he was made of. He now had his own motorcycle – there was nothing his parents could reasonably do to prevent it; indeed, it would have seemed rather strange if a Mr Universe contestant did have to take parental advice, let alone bow to parental demands.

It took him nine hours to travel down from Edinburgh. When he got to the theatre, he was entered as Number 24 in the contest – wearing white briefs that revealed more than they covered. He was introduced as Mr Scotland.

He says he looked around him at that contest and knew he wasn't going to win. 'When I stood next to some of them at Mr Universe, I looked like a girl.' Sure enough, he didn't become Mr Universe, getting no further than the British heats.

However, girls who were brave enough to attend the function – in the 1950s, a woman went to Mr Universe contests rather as men in mackintoshes went to strip clubs, looking left and right before daring to walk into the building – could be heard to catch their breath as Tommy went to the front of the platform, flexed his muscles and, again, seemed to burst out of those briefs. The message got around.

Tommy was declared runner-up and was given a medal. But there was more to come. There were people at the contest who knew their way around such things. People of influence. In fact, it got as far as the casting director for the show currently running at the Theatre Royal, Drury Lane.

Drury Lane, as the theatre itself was known, had always been regarded as London's most prestigious theatre. But it now had a new reputation as the British home of Rodgers and Hammerstein, America's most successful ever creators of stage musicals.

The theatre had been chosen as the British venue for *Oklahoma!*, the show that changed everything – a serious musical play which in one swoop killed the idea of gormless young things running into a room and asking, 'Anyone for tennis?' When *Oklahoma!* was coming to its natural end, Rodgers and Hammerstein had no doubt where they wanted their next musical to play – Drury Lane.

The show was *South Pacific*, about a Navy nurse on an island – in the South Pacific, of course – falling in love with a French planter. The story was strong and so was the music. The planter, Emile, sang 'Some Enchanted Evening' to the nurse, Nancy, who replied by alternately declaring she was in love with 'A Wonderful Guy' and then stating she was going to 'Wash That Man Right Out Of My Hair'.

The music and the leading players, Mary Martin and Wilbur Evans, were superb. But there was another side to the show that made it as important for theatrical history as it was entertaining. More than any previous musical and possibly more than any musical to come, this was the show that *needed* a chorus. At a time when costs were not as prohibitive as they would be forty years later, there was a gaggle of nurses on the island – curvy girls looking wonderful in tight white uniforms, each with a soprano voice as high as her heels. Even more vital to the show were the sailors on the island. For them, there was the unforgettably wistful 'There Is Nothing Like A Dame'.

A crucial factor for the male chorus was simply to look good. He attended an audition, said he had done a great deal of repertory work in Scotland and added that, of course, he could sing and dance. But the producers wanted him for his physique, not what he could do with it.

As Dennis Selinger, a man later to play a vital part in the Connery career, told me, 'He was great for that chorus. After all, he only had to stand there and look good. Nobody could tell who was singing and who was not. He didn't have a great voice.'

Certainly his voice was not good enough for a West End show, but, as Dennis Selinger said, that wasn't important. The voices were at the back. The front row of the chorus had to be of Mr Universe calibre and no one doubted that even if Connery was not title material, he was certainly up there with all the contenders.

Once more, he had his admirers. Admirers? That was an under-statement. There seems to be ample evidence that women went to the show to see the front row of the male chorus as much as to enjoy the music and listen to the stars. In the 1890s, there had been the 'stage-door Johnnies', men who hung around the artists' entrance in the hope of getting chorus girls to go out with them. Connery had the pleasure of being mobbed by what could have been called 'stage-door Jennies'.

Dennis Selinger saw it all. 'The girls thought he was wonderful,' he told me. So wonderful that he was the subject of a certain amount of competition. 'He and I were going out with the same girl,' Selinger remembers, 'and he nicked her from me.' The girl's name was Carol Sopel.

Part of his success was simply that he enjoyed the chase as much as the women appreciated being the subject of his interest. As he once said: 'I've always loved women. Blonde, brunette, but preferably foreign. They're more attractive than Britons.' Whether any of the girls lining up outside Drury Lane were anything but British is doubtful. In 1953, the age of mass travel was at least a decade away. The world had not yet discovered the au pair girl, and young foreign women didn't travel to Britain any more than British women, who had probably saved up for weeks for their gallery seats at Drury Lane, could go abroad.

Tommy's stint in *South Pacific* was plainly an interesting time for him. Nobody could then be sure that it was also going to be an important one for his career. But he thought about that a great deal now. What was at first going to be merely another one of those jobs that had studded his young life like the metal pieces on the soles of his football boots suddenly turned into something more.

He found he enjoyed going out on stage – and not just because of what happened afterwards. He didn't see anything 'Jessyish' in putting on makeup to do it. He was fired by the surge of adrenalin when he went on. When audiences cheered ecstatically every new line of 'There Is Nothing Like A Dame', he felt as though they were paying homage to him himself – never mind the fact that not much sound came from his lips when he sang and that, even if they had heard him, his Scots accent was so strong few would have understood anything he was saying.

He couldn't have forecast how much he would enjoy it. Now young Connery was in the public eye and he realised for the first time just how much he revelled in it. The attraction he obviously had for the opposite sex convinced him there was no cause for a lack of self-confidence. So completely assured was he of this that he seemed to have lost his shyness. He had no more girl-fright than he had stage-fright. And he was earning fabulous money. Every Friday he picked up a pay packet containing more than anything his father had ever earned or even approached. The theatre and Actors' Equity agreed that the gentlemen of the chorus were each worth twelve pounds a week.

Now Connery decided he was going to make the theatre his career. He had no doubt about that. But he wasn't going to make a habit of working in the chorus if he could help it. In truth, there weren't many choruses like that of *South Pacific*. Most line-ups consisted of beautiful girls who could kick high enough to show their panties, and effete young men who couldn't quite make it into the ballet. When this show was over, there were few opportunities for young men who could neither sing nor dance, but who simply looked good baring their chests.

He had wondered about his name. Connery was okay, he decided – but Tom or Tommy? It didn't sound quite right for the tough guy he felt all those years at Fountainbridge had surely marked him out to play. For a time, he had been known among his friends as Shane. It seemed to go with his physique and since every one of them had gone to see the Alan Ladd film of that name – none of them realising that Ladd was so short and puny he had to stand on a box during scenes with actresses who more often than not were taller than he was – it seemed appropriate. It was an image he enjoyed fostering.

So why not call himself Shane Connery? Somehow it didn't work.

He contemplated all the other male names that were suggested by well-meaning friends and decided, after all, to keep what he had been christened with – his own second name, that is. The programme listing the members of the *South Pacific* chorus recorded one of its members as Sean Connery.

3

SOUTH PACIFIC

South Pacific marked the beginning of a new era for Sean, and a complete change in the Connery lifestyle.

There were other members of that Drury Lane line-up who were happy to make the chorus their lives. They knew there was no chance of stardom for them, but turning up at the theatre for five evening performances and two matinées a week was a whole lot better than standing in a dole queue or working in a factory or office. Sean, however, made it clear right from the start that this was one more step on the road to his eventual success. Not just another job but part of a process.

A generation later, he would say: 'It all seemed like a giggle. It only became difficult when I really decided to take acting seriously.'

Sean had remained a keen reader ever since those first introductions to the world of books when he was at Tollcross Primary School. He had decided that not only did he like reading, but he appreciated its value. He didn't want people to think of him as a Scottish lout – his accent gave that impression all too easily. He wanted what he thought of as the kind of learning that brought culture.

With that aim in mind, he had been engaged for months now in a course of learning he had mapped out for himself. It was going to take a year and a half, he estimated, to get through the books he not only wanted to read, but knew he should read. Every week he cycled to Chelsea Public Library and took out one of the set texts on his self-imposed curriculum: Dickens one week, Thackeray the next, with a Shakespeare anthology in between.

As he said himself, 'I was like a mole, digging my way through the world's literature.'

He read *Finnegans Wake* and then *Ulysses* in those far-away self-conscious days, with the books' jackets covered in brown paper and, if he possibly could do so, sitting behind a screen. But what really counted was the opportunity simply to read them and to know them.

'It was terrific for my ego and confidence to be able to converse, like overcoming a major hurdle.'

Sean was beginning to fancy the idea of becoming what he would later call a 'serious actor'. So he went to the home of 'serious actors', the Old Vic.

He applied for an audition with Robert Helpmann, the actor-manager ballet dancer who ran the operation. He chose the drunk scene from *Macbeth*, which most people would think was a decidedly optimistic choice in that particular building. He, on the other hand, took the attitude that the 'Scottish play' was especially suited to a man with his accent – and the intoxication theme wasn't all that unsuitable either.

It didn't impress Helpmann, however, who still would have preferred an Englishman playing a Scot. And that would have been difficult for Sean. As Sean reflected generations later, 'The thing was that I could not even *understand* English. I could only follow it as a tune. You know, 'Now then my Lord Buckingham, now by heaven, methinks . . .' and so on. That sounded to me like music but not speech. And then I heard Richard Burton. He always sounded Welsh to me, however he spoke – and I could understand what he said very clearly.'

That was the point at which Sean Connery decided to leave his Scottish accent alone. Clearly, he couldn't have done anything else.

South Pacific went on tour. Inevitably, Sean had to give up his routine at the public library. Now he was being invited to join a group of people who, for the most part, had never read a book in their lives.

When the tour reached Manchester, the offer of a completely different life came up. As often happened on these occasions, the cast was asked to field a scratch football team, and played against a junior United side.

Matt Busby, manager of Manchester United Football Club, was the Mayer and Goldwyn and the Warner of the English football business. A Scot like Connery himself, he ran Manchester United like a fiefdom and the results of his training and tactical skills as they were practised on the Old Trafford ground justified the glory by which he was surrounded. Not for nothing were the team players known as the 'Busby Babes' and not for nothing either was the aircraft disaster in which his team was decimated a few years later regarded as one of the great calamities in the game's history. And now that same Busby wanted Sean Connery to be one of his players.

Busby, ever on the lookout for new talent – which partly explains his success – was at the *South Pacific* match and made copious notes of the way young Sean Connery played. Afterwards, he invited the youngster to meet him. The upshot of the session was that the older man offered the young 23-year-old, a kid whom he assessed as having great talent, a contract with United. He would earn twenty-five pounds a week – twice as much as his weekly salary in *South Pacific*, which he regarded as riches beyond measure.

Connery was flattered – and tempted – by Busby's offer. But his former reservations about professional soccer resurfaced and he was subjected to one of the most sleepless nights of his young life. A career with United would be very different from his life up to then as yet another chorus boy night after night in *South Pacific*. A change in his life as proposed by Matt Busby seemed very attractive. But was that where he wanted to go?

He really did want to be an actor now – a real one, not just someone looking for a job between being a Portobello pool lifeguard and polishing coffins. Certainly it was better than being in the *Evening News* machine-room, but he saw it as much more. It was going to be his career. So he talked to an older actor in the cast, an American named Robert Henderson, before discussing it again with Busby.

Henderson put it on the line. He asked him seriously: 'Don't you want to be an actor?'

'What would I do as an actor?' Sean later remembered asking.

Henderson stated the case: 'If you go play soccer now,' he said, 'it'll take you a year or two to get on to the team and if you don't make it, that's it. In acting you can go on for ever.' Henderson couldn't have possibly known how prophetic those words were. As a much older Sean Connery noted: 'Robert Henderson takes a lot of the credit for putting me where I am today. And I'll bet there's a long list of people who'd like to ring his neck.'

Sean himself didn't ring Henderson's neck, and told Busby he wouldn't be taking up his offer. It was not something that had happened very often to the manager before, but he probably could not help feeling a sense of admiration for his countryman. Sean also possibly saved his life by the decision. Had he accepted, he could have been one of the victims of the Manchester United air disaster on 6 February 1958.

Sean wanted to be an actor with every breath in his body, but he didn't

43

really know what *kind* of actor. Despite his ambition to move on, he enjoyed *South Pacific*. It was not just an exciting show, the most talked-about theatrical production for years, but it was fun being part of its cast. There was a certain camaraderie in being one of the gang, it satisfied that ego, and was undemanding enough to represent the easiest twelve pounds he had earned in what we now know as not exactly an inactive or lazy life.

But it wasn't exactly wealth. Yet even though he had no real money, there were, nevertheless, still all the desires of those with cash. Some-times, instead of sitting at home worrying about his poverty, he would take off for Harrods and there, in the huge spaces of the white-tiled food hall, buy himself jars of caviare. 'The guilt I felt just going up to the counter – that was terrible.'

And he continued his reading programme. This time, he talked his ideas on literature into a tape recorder, which was not at all a con-ventional household instrument at the time. He noted the books he still wanted to read, and read onto the light-brown shiny tape lines from the volumes he thought were not only worth remembering, but which he enjoyed trying to interpret. If nothing else convinced him of the need for elocution lessons, this exercise certainly did.

In every town in which *South Pacific* played Sean found a library, and there he always picked up a couple of books. He also found other theatres if they existed, discovered the time of the matinées and soaked up what they had on offer – straight drama, other musicals, comedies. He went to see everything that was on the stage, and loved what he saw.

Something he would learn later was that not everything he saw was brilliant or even good. But at that stage he was like a young writer who would pick up a book or a newspaper or magazine and be convinced that everything he read was amazing, for the simple reason that it had been published in the first place. Sean was sure that every actor he met had the greatest of talents, the kind that he could only aspire to – even those in repertory who had never got near even a West End chorus line. 'As time went on, I came to realise that this was absolute nonsense. I had imbued them with talents they didn't have.'

Sean was now moving up the ladder. A second tour of the show was scheduled and when the company came back to Manchester, there was someone new in the part of Lieutenant Buzz Adams, the role introduced in London by a certain Larry Hagman, son of the star Mary Martin and later in life to earn his own stardom as the villainous J.R. Ewing in the television soap *Dallas*. The role was now played by Sean Connery.

It was during the show's second visit to Manchester that a newcomer joined the cast. Victor Spinetti, a bright-eyed young Welshman of Italian descent, who was to go on to play character roles, feature as the archetypal major-general in the 1990 British production of *Pirates Of Penzance* and star in his own one-man show, was, like Sean, at the beginning of his career.

Spinetti had just been cast in the role of one of the more important members of the Navy team, Stewpot, and was appointed understudy to the actor playing what was, in effect, the third lead in the show, Luther Billis, the loud-mouthed, soft-hearted sailor with a ship tattooed on his stomach who nightly brought the house down singing 'Honey Bun'.

The newcomer and Sean shared a dressing-room first in Coventry and then at the Manchester Opera House. On the first night at Manchester, one of the dream situations in show business folklore came true. Eddie Leslie, the actor who played Luther Billis, took the traditional good-luck expression of 'break a leg' a little too literally. He had just performed the 'Honey Bun' number, had brought the house down as usual and was walking into the wings, when he tripped over and crashed onto the stage – and actually *did* break a leg. Spinetti had had only two rehearsals and was standing in the wings. Behind him was Sean – who pushed him on to the front of the stage.

'He was wonderfully supportive,' the actor recalled for me. 'I was standing there quivering. I was still dressed in the outfit I had worn as Stewpot, but Sean said, "You're on," and whoosh ... I was on.'

He stayed on – and the part became his. That it did, he says, was in no small way due to Sean. It was the beginning of a long friendship. They shared digs together in Moss Side, Manchester. Now that Spinetti had a new part to play, he had to learn it to perfection. Sean sat up with him all night that summer, going over his lines and songs with him, drinking black coffee to keep alert.

As Spinetti said: 'It was an extraordinarily innocent era. None of us had pills or anything to keep us awake.'

Connery told him what he didn't really need to know: 'You got through this on nerves. Tomorrow night, you've got to give a performance.' On that first night, he had gone from scene to scene doing just what he could remember. That wouldn't be acceptable a second time, although the Manchester *Daily Express* had given him a good review.

In between the learning sessions, they played one tune over and over again on their portable record player – 'Cherry Blossom Pink And Apple Blossom White'. 'I can never hear that tune today without

45

thinking of Sean Connery and that night, with him pushing me to get it right. He literally pushed me into the lead in the show. Unknown to me, the producer of the show had flown up from London and was sitting in the front watching me, and decided I could have the part for the run of the show.'

Sean and Victor always shared digs after that, wherever the show went. Spinetti rode with Connery on his motorcycle as they went from town to town.

That December, both Sean and Victor were in London and together they went to Spinetti's home in Wales for Christmas – Edinburgh was too far away for the brief holiday break they had, and it was also a very expensive fare home for him. Sean liked Wales. 'He was struck by how similar it all was to Scotland,' Victor said.

Sean became a sort of confidant and role model for his fellow performer. One night, Spinetti told him of his objections to another member of the cast, a South African who constantly made disparaging remarks about 'niggers'. 'I'd punch him if he said that again,' said Connery. 'Right,' said Victor, and next time the man offended him he administered a sharp left hook to his jaw. The man fell to the floor and Spinetti walked away. He had never had a fight in his life before. Sean practically fell down laughing when Victor told him. 'I didn't mean *that*,' he said.

Now, though, Sean had to look to the future, when there would be no *South Pacific* on the boards anywhere and when he would want something more. That he even realised there could be something more was due once more to Henderson.

Henderson played the part of Captain Brackett in the show. He was now in his late forties but had a reputation in the business that attracted a great deal of respect. He had not only been a successful Broadway actor in his time but was also a director of note. For him, being in a touring show now was close to 'resting'. He was still taking young Sean Connery under his wing, and they talked theatre together. He was indeed as much an influence as any of the drinking–footballing pals Sean had had in Fountainbridge.

Henderson recited names that were no more familiar to Sean than the team players of, say, the Moscow Dynamos. He passed him books to read, the kind that his teachers at school would possibly have disapproved of in the same way they did his fondness for the *Dandy* or *Beano*, although this time because the subject matter was beyond the ken of most people living in or near the Edinburgh slums.

Sean read Stanislavsky's seminal works on what would be adopted in America as 'The Method'. He read Thomas Wolfe's *Look Homeward*

Angel. He pored over and devoured – just as he had those comics – *War And Peace.* Suddenly, a new world was opening for him and he wanted to be part of it. He assessed his own potential and came to a not unreasonable conclusion: he needed, he said, to look like a truck driver and talk like Dostoevsky.

Speech was one of his troubles. Strangely – possibly because he himself spoke with an American accent and accepted Sean's brogue as no more than any other 'foreign' tongue – Henderson doesn't appear to have suggested elocution lessons. Connery could have done with them. He had mastered his one or two lines in *South Pacific* – mainly warning of the approach of the Japanese to the island – but in real life he might easily have been considered as foreign as a Japanese spy himself.

There were moments when he had to pick up whatever extra work he could get. Over the years, the story has got out that, back in London, he earned some pin-money as a babysitter – for the film journalist Peter Noble and his wife. Today Noble insists Sean only did it for him once and says that Connery himself hates recalling it. But it was extra cash – with an additional ten shillings thrown in should an emergency require him to change the baby's nappy.

Sean was beginning to appreciate what the classical theatre might offer him. He hadn't seen much of it, but he *had* read *The Wild Duck* and *Hedda Gabler* and in his more reflective moments considered how he would have coped with the lead roles, as different from that of Lieutenant Adams as they were from life in Edinburgh.

He wanted to know more about the technique of acting and took lessons from a movement teacher – because, Sean said, he was concerned with what he called the 'physical side of acting'.

His teacher was Yat Malmgeren, who had come from his native Sweden to dance with the Kurt Jooss Ballet Company before setting up in business as a teacher. Sean was told that the Swede based his teaching on the work of a Hungarian dancer called Rudolf von Laban. It was known as 'time and motion'; motion was connected to the timing of a dramatic operation, the way a hand works in conjunction with the recital of a line.

Three times a week Sean took lessons in theory, and four times a week the theories were put into practice. He wasn't quite a Method actor and he never planned to be one. But he was going to be an actor who knew what he was doing.

As he said in the late 1960s, 'What used to pass for reality in acting is a joke now. When the Stanislavsky theory first came over, people were knocked out to witness this "happening" before their eyes. Partly it was the idea of just taking away the fourth wall of a room as you looked at the scene on the stage of a theatre, but mainly it was the completeness of all the actors concerned.'

Sean Connery was going to be an actor who was concerned about his audiences, a group of people who, if they were intelligent enough, were always asking, 'What's it all about?' He learned a lesson or two. 'If a stage production is done correctly, you should be able to understand fifty per cent of what is happening, even if it's going on behind a glass screen.' That was to be something of a *credo*, particularly with his work on a different kind of screen.

In a good play, the words were almost superfluous – not a message to delight a writer. 'Good as the words are, I believe you'd understand eighty per cent of the play just from the movement. Which is a very good test of acting.'

There was a confidence about Sean now that was easy to spot. It was most evident in the relationships he now had with women. They were easy if not uncomplicated and he went into each of them with the same confidence he showed on stage.

The problem was that not all of the girls appreciated that he came from a culture in which the theatre never figured at all. When the *South Pacific* tour reached Edinburgh, he thought it was only right to go drinking with his mates. The young lady with whom he was involved at the time couldn't understand why she was being excluded from this tradition. He tried to assure her that it was nothing personal, but in the 1950s drinking at the Fountain was a male preserve. Her answer: he had to choose – it was either her or a night knocking back the pints with the boys. He thought about it – and went drinking. There was nothing that was going to make him change the habits of a lifetime.

If he had changed, his father might have had ideas on the subject. Joe Connery was an old practitioner of the ancient art of showing how he could hold his liquor – or not, as the case may be. Rose Street, running parallel to Princes Street, was a place of fame in Edinburgh, mainly because it could boast more pubs per square yard than any other thoroughfare in Britain. There were so many in Rose Street that the 'Rose Street Run' was not a sport for boys. To make the run from one pub to the next took all the ingenuity and strength that came to a man who had spent years looking deeply into a glass. You started at one end of the street and if you were still on your feet by the time you reached the end – or if you reached the end in any condition at all – you could claim to be a man of some ability.

Joe Connery decided it was his solemn duty to take the run. By so doing, he was paying tribute not only to his own capabilities but also to the various breweries which had set up business in the area. Not least of these was the firm of Campbell, Hope & King.

The night Joe went on the run he ended up between the tramlines in Princes Street. He was immediately placed in the care of the local constabulary and the following morning appeared in the dock at the sheriff's court.

The sheriff looked at the character in front of him. 'Mr Connery,' said the sheriff, 'what happened to you?'

'Well,' said Joe, 'there were three big men who knocked me doon in Princes Street.'

'You don't happen to know who they were, do you?' asked the kindly sheriff.

'Oh, I do ken,' said Connery senior. 'They were three big men by the names of Campbell, Hope and King.'

The magistrate took it in good part, smiled and fined him five shillings.

There were other matters that Joe took much more to heart – like his son's career. Joe gave Sean all the support that a devoted father might have been expected to offer. His very presence with Effie at the theatre when the show came to their city proved that. They were given the best seats in the house and cheered their son as loudly as if by doing so they were paying for their tickets. But there was also sage parental advice on offer which Sean had the sense to accept. His father might have liked his drink and never have reached any great pinnacles in his own work – as we have seen, his greatest achievement was simply to be in a position to pick up a weekly pay packet – but he was blessed with common sense that his son probably appreciated more in middle age than he had in his youth.

One such piece of advice he never forgot: 'There is always a price to be paid for success,' said the man who had never had that success himself. Years later, with the experience behind him of arguments with top Hollywood producers and of fans thrusting autograph albums in his face, Sean said: 'As a kid I could never understand that. But now I do.'

In his *South Pacific* days, the price was mainly the one many men crave – the adoration by young women of the kind of physique and appearance that had got him the chorus job in the first place and had earlier landed him the modelling work.

However, there were problems that would not have come to less attractive young men. One of the most difficult of these concerned the same Carol Sopel whose attentions he had won over when he first joined *South Pacific*.

It is almost inevitable that some men and women working together day after day in a show, eating and drinking with each other after a performance, do get romantically attached. That was certainly the case with Sean and Carol. They were so close that fellow members of the cast thought that a wedding was in the offing.

For a time, Carol and Sean thought so too. But there were problems. Carol's parents quite simply didn't think a young man in the chorus was good enough for their daughter.

Carol accepted her parents' wishes less than happily and so did Sean – at the time there was nothing either of them thought they could do about it. As Spinetti noted, it was an altogether more innocent age.

'Carol was absolutely beautiful,' he told me, 'and her parents were determined she could do much better. Sean was devastated. He was very much in love, absolutely heartbroken.'

Sean's mother had taken a shine to Carol. At the Fountainbridge flat, she had greeted her as if she were already a daughter-in-law. 'They seemed a pair, and as far as Effie was concerned it was a lovely match.'

It took Sean a long time to get over Carol. 'We walked through the snow in Dublin all night when that happened,' Spinetti told me. 'That was my contribution – to try to help him through that trauma. After all, he had done the same for me by giving me my career. It was really a torment for him. But then it was over.'

Not long afterwards, Victor Spinetti by chance met Effie in London. She asked him not to say anything to Sean, but she had made the long journey from Edinburgh, sitting up all night on the train, because Carol was in hospital and had asked to see her. That night, Effie slept in Victor's flat – and until this day Sean has never known that she was there. 'He would be furious.'

Later Carol made an unhappy marriage and then divorced, still saying she loved Sean.

In truth, Sean himself was still enjoying his role as a sought-after male and there were plenty of other women waiting for the opportunity of being Sean's girl. At the front of the queue was Julie Hamilton, a young news photographer with the kind of pedigree that was totally new to Connery. Her mother was Jill Craigie, eminent scriptwriter and documentary director. But Ms Craigie's husband, Julie's step-father, was even more well known: he was the former editor of the London *Evening Standard* and one of the best-known left-wing Labour

MPs, Michael Foot, who thirty years later would be Leader of the Opposition.

Julie has since said it was a case of love at first sight, although she later admitted her memories of their first meetings are anything but pleasant. 'God, what a yob,' was what she first thought of Sean Connery. He was 'big and boring'. And she could no more understand his accent than she could his tattoos.

He and Julie had been introduced by the film actor Ronald Fraser. It was not an auspicious moment. If sparks didn't exactly fly between them, there was a degree of abrasion which didn't bode well for the future.

Fraser had been in a play at the Lyric Theatre, Hammersmith. Julie had gone to see the play and met her friend at a nearby pub afterwards.

Fraser then introduced her to his chum. He didn't make a great first impression: all Julie noticed was a pair of old jeans – long before the days when it was fashionable to tear holes in brand new jeans before putting them on for the first time. And his 'silly smile' – a smile that revealed all too frequently teeth with gold fillings.

She didn't want anything to do with him. Yet they kept bumping into each other – and because they did, she got to see more attractive attributes in him. It all became clear at Ronald Fraser's wedding to his girlfriend Elizabeth at Hampstead Parish Church in 1956. She felt sufficiently confident in her bridesmaid's dress to think that all eyes in the church that weren't actually looking at the bride were focused on her. Until, that is, she realised they were looking at Sean in all his finery. He was an usher, dressed in Highland gear, complete with kilt. He was 'incredibly' good looking, she conceded.

She was, in fact, quite overcome 'by the beauty of the man'. They said polite things to each other, offered toasts with Fraser's champagne and seemed to click as satisfactorily as their glasses clinked.

Fraser remembered their rapprochement at the wedding: 'We had all become great chums. He was very keen and that sort of stuff. And, of course, he looked so good. I was newly out of RADA at the time and he was also just beginning.'

Sean and Julie were just beginning as a couple, too. No one at the time could know how far – if at all – they would go together.

By most accounts, Michael Foot and his wife were no more thrilled by Julie's association with a penniless actor than she had been herself just a few days earlier.

That was not to say that they disliked Sean as a man. On the contrary, he and Foot found plenty to talk about. The younger man would ask the now already veteran politician and journalist questions about the world, the answers to which he could never have picked up through the saloon bar wisdom of Fountainbridge. Julie said that seeing the two men wrapped up in detailed and apparently intellectual conversation only made her love him more.

But that wasn't enough for the Foots. They had other ideas for Julie. They wanted to see her settled with someone who was already better established and who had a more assured future ahead of him.

After all, these were hard times for young Connery, and Julie was finding success more easily than he was now that *South Pacific* had closed. It was, he has said, his 'Too Period'. He went to auditions, hoping to come home with the promise of an Uncle Vanya under his belt, only to be told he was too big. Or he was too young. Or too Irish – a suggestion that raised an eyebrow for someone who was so proudly Scottish. He was told he was too Scottish, too.

What work he could get hardly paid the rent for the damp, one-room basement flat where he lived in Shalcomb Street, Chelsea, near the King's Road – an area which within the decade would be one of the fashion centres of swinging London but which showed no signs of such glory at the time of Sean's tenancy.

He seems to have been reasonably content with his lot, except when he was out of work and signed up at the local labour exchange for a weekly dole of six pounds. His outgoings, he reckoned, were ten pounds, but Julie and their friends helped out when they could and his needs were minimal. Apart from Sunday lunch, which Julie prepared for him at her own expense, Sean cooked for himself – using Effie's old recipe. Like his mother in the old tenement, he had a pot constantly bubbling away on the stove in that flat. Ask him what it contained and the answer was either stew or porridge, depending upon his mood. In truth it was more likely to be a combination of the two, a fact that didn't exactly fill the visitors to Shalcomb Street with confidence.

Among those visitors was Victor Spinetti. 'All he had apart from his dole were the few shillings he had in this Navy discharge pay. And all I had was the fifteen shillings I had got from the Army. So we used to buy a bag of bones from the butcher's and make those huge pots of stew which we used to go back to Shalcomb Street to eat. They were great meals, and Julie was always around at that time.'

Despite the difficulties, Sean and Julie were determined that their futures were going to be intertwined. Soon they were sharing a flat – not an altogether usual circumstance in the 1950s, even in the world of theatre. They were breaking certain conventions, not least in failing to get married.

'Julie was very pretty,' Ronald Fraser remembered for me, 'very pretty and very bossy.' She encouraged Sean in his career and he on his part watched with pride when pictures by Julie Hamilton were published in her newspaper, the *Daily Mail*. The feelings the couple had for each other were loving and tender, but Julie, says Victor Spinetti, 'was madly in love with Sean – and very jealous of him.' In fact, she hated having visitors : 'She didn't want to share Sean.'

Victor went with Sean back to Fountainbridge. 'Effie was a marvellous lady. She kept that flat absolutely spotless then as she had when Sean was young, I imagine. The washing was hanging, clean and fresh, around the coal fire in the living room.'

There was still no toilet inside the flat and the tin bath was still hanging on the wall outside. 'But you really could eat off the floor, it was so spotless, although I know that's a tired phrase. But the way she kept the place made it anything but the slum it might have looked from the outside. We both recognised that Sean and I had similar backgrounds. My home in Wales was very much like that.'

There was also the similarity of family affection. 'Effie thought Sean was wonderful and he absolutely adored her.'

Now he tried for stage roles in London, but the auditions amounted to nothing – or rather nothing more than being told to do what Robert Henderson had failed to suggest: take those elocution lessons. He tried for movie roles, too. But the part he thought he could get in the British film *High Tide At Noon* slipped out of his grasp simply because he was too – that word again – dark. Then he thought the American studio Twentieth Century–Fox were ready to give him a chance in their forthcoming feature, *Boy On A Dolphin*. Except that the dolphin swam away out of the reach of an actor who was suddenly too tall. Only the thought that every actor on the threshold of a new career met just that sort of problem prevented disappointment turning into depression.

Much of the encouragement he now needed came from his and Julie's landlord in Kilburn, a Communist journalist who had been one of the few stars of the party's newspaper, the *Daily Worker*. Llew Gardner would go on to be a television current-affairs presenter as well as a columnist on the Tory *Sunday Express*. He and Sean found they could talk together, an essential requirement when it came to establishing a friendship. Being able to talk led to being able to trust.

When Gardner suggested that Sean really ought to consider seriously the idea of elocution lessons, he took the advice to heart and began a course of instruction. 'He did well at them,' Gardner told me shortly before his death. 'There was no resemblance at all between the way he talked after taking the lessons and his accent before.'

However, that he never lost his burr is evident. That a difficult accent didn't disappear immediately is clearly on the record. It seemed to many that his tones were as impenetrable as a fog on the Firth of Forth.

Round about that time, he went for an audition with the producer–director team of Peter Rogers and Gerald Thomas. Later the pair would be best known for the 'Carry On' movies, which they brought out with the regularity of new saucy seaside postcards. At this time, they were casting a film called *Time Lock*.

The introduction came from one of the most respected names in the world of casting directors, Maude Spector, who now proudly says: 'Sean Connery? I discovered him – although great actors are never really discovered. They are always there. Their talent will out.'

As she told me, 'I saw Sean on the stage in a couple of plays and I knew he had something going for him; something that would make him very much in demand as a film actor. He had tremendous presence.'

She brought him to Rogers and Thomas who confessed they were delighted with the introduction.

'He didn't have to do very much,' Peter Rogers told me. 'It was a small part. He came to us through normal casting procedures: a casting director saw him; we saw him and liked him.' But it was a small part.

'It had to be,' his partner rejoined. 'It was very difficult to understand a word that he said, he was so broad. To make things worse, the actor playing a labourer working with him in the picture was an Irishman – I can't remember his name now – and we couldn't understand what he said either. Between the Scotsman and the Irishman, we might have been making a foreign film. But it didn't matter.'

Indeed it did not. Sean played the welder brought in to help free a child caught in the time lock of a bank. 'He looked wonderful with his sleeves rolled up,' said Gerald Thomas. 'He was burly. He had the right muscles. His face, dark, strong and very handsome, was ideal for the part. You could *believe* him. He wasn't one of those limp-wristed actors, who wouldn't have looked right lifting a hammer.'

The fact that Connery looked tough and had the right physique for a man who worked with sweat pouring off his body might have been enough to give him the job. But he also was allowed the luxury of actually acting and saying a few lines – his Scots burr notwithstanding – that made an impact of sorts. He thought he had an impossible job, making a hole in the safe that would enable him to reach the trapped boy. It was so impossible that he had to shout and argue his frustrations.

'And he did it very well,' said Thomas. 'He was very convincing. There were no problems with him. He got into the scene very well, particularly when he had to lose his temper. I imagine he is very good at losing his temper in real life.'

Sean made the most of working at the Rogers–Thomas stable. 'He was a grafter,' said the director. 'We liked him very much. Even at that stage, he was a very ambitious character. He was watching, studying every one of the actors on the set to see if he could learn anything. As soon as I turned round, there was Sean Connery watching someone else at work.'

'We thought he was very suitable,' said Rogers. 'But I have to say we didn't think there was anything particularly outstanding about him.'

Except for one thing – as Gerald Thomas put it. 'He was a great physical specimen. He looked very good.' But, like Rogers, Thomas said, 'I didn't mark him down as a particularly good actor. He didn't make an outstanding impression. There was something about him, nevertheless, which you remembered – unlike the Irishman whom I have now completely forgotten.' But there was a confession to make, too : 'Had he not turned into James Bond, we might not have remembered Sean Connery either.'

But they had no idea what the name Sean Connery was going to mean. In fact, they were about to cast their next movie with John Mills and someone suggested Connery for a small part. 'We thought about it,' Thomas told me, 'and we decided that no, he wasn't really what we were looking for.' Today, Rogers and Thomas tend to talk about that in the same way that anglers spread out their arms and remember the one that got away. Like the time they also thought that paying £500 for the Beatles to record some title music for another picture was much too much. 'We weren't prepared to pay more than £150. Just think of the residuals that we missed !'

It wasn't, certainly, that Sean Connery would have been too expensive for them. For *Time Lock*, a 75-minute picture based on an Arthur 'Hotel' Hayley book, they paid him £100. It represented four days work. 'It was what his agent asked for and was about what we would have paid anybody at that time, £25 a day. It wasn't a union minimum or anything like that.'

'And,' said Peter Rogers, 'he seemed very satisfied with it. He was a traditional small-time player. There were no parties or invitations to dinner in a £23,000 picture.'

His partner, remembering the film being made in 1955 at the Beaconsfield studios, added: 'And we thought he was being overpaid at the time. After all, he was a very minor actor. About tenth in the pecking order on that picture. Very minor. Even so, he was a very arresting personality. You wouldn't walk past him in an identity parade.'

The yarn about having overpaid his journeyman actor was one of those jokes which, with the benefit of that old twenty-twenty hindsight, seems appropriate, a compensation for the self-denigration of admitting what the partnership had missed. But at the time, the pair looked at their books and seriously had to wonder if he was really worth the sort of cash they paid. They also probably knew that to the average citizen of Fountainbridge, £100 was very big money.

As for Sean himself, he was satisfied with a great deal of what he was doing. Except that satisfied is a relative term. He was satisfied with it as he had been satisfied polishing coffins, or satisfied minding machines at the Edinburgh *Evening News*. It was a temporary satisfaction and he didn't want it to become anything else.

As Peter Rogers told me: 'He was just one of those ships that passed in the night. But I like to think that he might have thought he benefited from *Time Lock*. Every actor benefits from repertory, which is what this was.'

Gerald Thomas is always glad that when he and Connery meet at film functions or at Pinewood, Sean remembers *Time Lock* and its producer and director affectionately. 'And he always says he wants to be remembered any time we have a comedy in his line.'

Sean's mother had never been very happy with all the jobs her son was doing. But he always told her not to worry; he wouldn't leave one before he had another. Now he felt much the same. He had a job that he enjoyed and this time it was going to be a career. Sean knew all the stories about actors scratching around for work, but he was hoping with all his heart that he wasn't going to be one of them.

But he wasn't changing. When he went back to Edinburgh, his mates were the same young men with whom he had gone to school and played by the canal as a boy, and couldn't understand at all the way 'Big Tam's' mind was working.

One man called Willy Hamilton tried to entice him back to his old job at the dairy. 'Why go buggering about in the theatre?' he wanted to know. Sean told Hamilton that 'buggering about in the theatre' was precisely what he intended to do.

To Effie, the game of musical chairs was just going through another one of its phases, even if now it was more *musicals* chairs.

She never expected very much and her son was plainly a hard worker – and in their family and circle the work ethic was the most important factor of all.

To her, his prospects of success were so remote that it would have taken Alfred Hitchcock himself knocking on her door saying that Sean was a star in the making for her to have believed it. Certainly, she didn't put much faith in the Sikh salesman who came to sell her a bedspread. The turbanned Indian gentleman was a salesman-cum-fortune-teller.

His first object when he knocked on the door of the Fountainbridge apartment was to sell the bedspread. Mrs Connery's primary intention was to resist, or at least that was what she conveyed. Whether it was normal housewifery or simply that she didn't really want the piece of haberdashery in the first place, we can't be sure. But, as her son Neil told it, she succumbed to the bedspread only after she had beaten the man down to what she thought was a reasonable price – three pounds and ten shillings.

The deal done, the man turned fortune-teller. 'You have two handsome sons,' he told her. She smiled in agreement. 'One day, lady, one of your sons will be famous. Very famous.'

Her reaction was simple, down to earth and just what a good mother from Fountainbridge would be expected to say. 'That'll be the day,' she replied. Neither she nor Sean knew that the day would come relatively quickly.

However, they would have certainly been right in guessing that fame would not come from *Time Lock*. Neither would it hail from *No Road Back*, another picture that would have escaped your attention should you have been looking for a movie starring Sean Connery made in 1956. He was lost in a plot which featured the Canadian actor Paul Carpenter and merely *included* Sean playing a crook – who not only spoke with a thick Scottish accent but stuttered, too.

It would be kind to describe *No Road Back* as a 'second feature'. Had it been a fourth feature it would have been thrown back at the distributors RKO, who handled it only to satisfy the now unofficial British quota system which required cinemas – at one time by law – to show a certain number of home-produced products. As it was, theatre managers couldn't get the reels of film into the vans and back to the Wardour Street offices of the company quickly enough.

Hell Drivers wasn't much better, and if it were an improvement at all, it was only because the previous film had been so terrible. The stars this time were Stanley Baker and Patrick McGoohan, playing two truck drivers competing with each other for a bonus that came for transporting the most rock from a nearby quarry. Sean was one of the team working with the men.

He looked tall and spare, with the bushiest eyebrows and darkest mop of hair seen on the screen since the Lassie films. But most of the time you missed him if you blinked, and you lost what he said should you have been unfortunate enough to blow your nose. He seemed to have most to say in the dance hall scene – which could have been set in the Tollcross Palais where he had been the bouncer. You might just have caught him saying something like, 'Would you like to dance?' to the female lead Peggy Cummins. You also would quite possibly have noticed him actually doing a quickstep or two while Stanley Baker watched, not altogether approvingly. Herbert Lom, uncharacteristically, was the good guy in the movie.

Needless to say, *Hell Drivers* seemed no more likely to enhance Sean's career than anything that had gone before it. That did not prevent some ambitious distributor a generation later bringing it back – 'starring Sean Connery'. It was an old trick and like many old tricks it brought in the customers.

Later, Sean would say that one of his most affectionate memories of the movie was its director Cy Endfield doing magic tricks. Endfield was a member of the Magic Circle. 'He used to throw all the cards in the air, and be left holding four aces.'

There was more luck for him on the stage in the mid fifties. For a time, Sean was in repertory theatre. As Gerald Thomas said, rep was important – it was the nursery of the British stage. Some of its greatest actors had started out in small – some of them quite beautiful – local theatres which changed plays on Monday evenings the way that cinemas changed movies.

At Oxford, he appeared alongside the then young Jill Bennett – who would become Mrs John Osborne and later commit suicide. He was in the play *Point Of Departure* at Kew. He did reasonably well, growing more confident with each production.

Also at Kew, he played in *Witness For The Prosecution* and in *A Witch In Time*. A new play each week; while working in one, learning the lines for the next. Hard, hard work but as good a training ground as any for an actor who wanted to really take his acting seriously.

Then he made what promised to be the film that would turn him into more than that everyday actor who flexed his muscles and twitched his eyebrows, mouthed a few words nobody could understand and then disappeared from view without anyone really knowing who he was.

Action Of The Tiger was about a French girl (always good for the sex interest it seemed to promise, if not deliver) played by Martine Carol, who was trying to rescue her brother who is locked up for political reasons in a jail in Albania. Sean's role involved the not particularly unpleasant task of trying to ravish Martine Carol, a great and beautiful star in the early 1950s, who bared her breasts on screen at a time when that was something which only the French ever did.

The lead was played by Van Johnson. When Martine revealed that she thought Sean would have done it better, Connery was not the only one to agree. The director, Terence Young, made a mental note.

Sean asked him if he were going to be a success in the picture. Young really knew what he was talking about. 'No,' he said without trying, it seemed, to make the young man feel better, 'but just keep on swimming and one day I'll make it up to you.' Neither of them could know just how much he was going to make it up in years to come.

Meanwhile, Sean was making his way, slowly and not particularly auspiciously, in television. Early on, he played a crook in an episode of *Dixon Of Dock Green*, which was to develop two reputations. The first was to demonstrate what every foreigner knew – that the British policeman was wonderful. Former comedy actor Jack Warner giving a one-finger salute as a copper who looked as though he were about to draw his old-age pension for the second time round was a part of the staple diet for British black-and-white television audiences on Saturday nights. The second thing for which it was to be famous was its unofficial role as a training ground for actors who would one day make reputations of their own.

Paul Eddington of *Yes Prime Minister* fame had one of his earliest breaks on the show. A regular in early days was a youngster who would achieve a certain amount of fame under the name Michael Caine. Sean appeared in the show as ... you guessed it ... a crook. But how good he was or how bad his work had been is now a matter of conjecture, only to be determined by a mere chance discovery in some old BBC vault. No one seems to have seen the episode for years or know if it still exists.

Nor does anyone remember much about the episode of *The Jack Benny Show* in which Sean appeared. Benny was probably second only to Bob Hope as America's favourite comedian. His television show began in the late 1940s (it had been a popular radio programme for years) and continued until shortly before his death in 1973. He once told me that it didn't matter if the best laughs went to his guests, such as Laurence Olivier or even Henry Kissinger. People remembered that the funny lines came on *The Jack Benny Show* and that was all that concerned him. But Sean Connery? 'Sorry, I can't remember him,' Alice Faye, formerly one of Hollywood's most popular female stars who appeared on the show regularly with her husband Phil Harris, told me.

No one who saw Sean on another BBC programme in that same busy year, 1957, would, however, have forgotten him quite so easily. In *Requiem For A Heavyweight* he for the first time made people think that he was a real actor. They didn't even mind the fact that sometimes his accent was still so strong you had to sit with your head bent close to the set to try to understand it.

Those wide shoulders and that hairy chest covered half-pages of Britain's newspapers as they told the story of how the unknown Sean had been selected for the part of the boxer – after Jack Palance had turned it down.

This was going to be the BBC's first chance to shine internationally in the world of television drama. The BBC thought they had landed Palance, he of the smooth, whispering voice that was all the more menacing because of its low decibel output. That voice was equally effective when playing the part of a victim as he would have done in this play. Anthony Quinn was also considered for the part, but filming would have to be delayed. The BBC didn't want to wait, and decided to go for an unknown. An unknown named Sean Connery.

The Canadian director Alvin Rakoff knew he was taking a risk, both because of Sean's lack of experience and because, once again, of that accent. Not that he was afraid no one would understand him, but simply because this was very much an American story about a very American boxer, which was of course why Palance had seemed such good casting in the first place. But Rakoff decided that if Sean could trim the brogue enough, it could be relied upon to so confuse the audience that he might just get away with it. As events would prove, get away with it he did.

Fortunately for Sean, nobody seemed to notice another phenom-enon of the play. A tiny part in the last scene was played by Michael Caine.

Just how novel the idea of an unknown playing the part was can be judged by the amount of space given to the play in the London *Sunday Pictorial*. It actually did have a picture of those Connery shoulders and chest over most of its entertainment page. Writing in the paper, Paul Boylif said – and this is a sentence that deserves to be immortalised in some Hollywood hall of fame recording the first jobs of the super-stars – that Connery had a great deal to offer. 'Physically Sean (pronounced Shawn) has the pleasant strength of a Marlon Brando type.'

As he said, Sean (pronounced Shawn) 'looks like a boxer and is as well-stacked with biceps as any beefcake boy. For proof, see picture. And kindly leave the room, the girl who whistled.'

Boylif was impressed by the now 26-year-old. But not too impressed to avoid the conventional questions of the day. He wanted to know how Sean liked to spend his time. He was told he still enjoyed riding the bicycle he had bought for thirty shillings. As for as his ambition, it was simply to have a cottage in the country and to own a horse and trap. And his career? 'I don't fit in anywhere as a juvenile . . . I like old clothes.'

Alvin Rakoff wasn't particularly interested in his old clothes, or clothes of any kind. Rightly, he decided that Connery's strength lay in his bare chest and most of the viewers, particularly the women, seemed to agree. But what he discovered was that there was more to this young man than a set of biceps and the kind of chest that looked like an offensive weapon. He found out what Sean dreamed of someone discovering – that he could really act. It helped him realise the fact for himself.

Nobody watched the show with more enthusiasm than the Connery clan in Fountainbridge. They had just bought their first television – a momentous event in any family in the 1950s, a time when an aerial sprouting out of a house chimney was just about the best status symbol you could have. Joe and Effie had just introduced a set with a seventeen-inch screen into the apartment and invited Mrs Pearson, their neighbour from along the corridor, to come and watch with them. They sat, glued to the set, holding on tight to the side of their chairs, occasionally wiping the sweat from their foreheads, as though they themselves were in the ring, bracing themselves for the next bout. When it was all over, they were heard to sigh with relief – and considerable pride.

'My heavens, that was smashing,' said Joe in a phrase that instantly entered the Connery family annals.

What they knew nothing about, as they watched the drama, was the other drama going on behind the cameras. Electricians were in dispute with the BBC and were threatening to pull the plugs mid emission. Fortunately for the career of Sean Connery, it didn't happen. Seventy-five minutes of live television was an ordeal not for the squeamish, but he managed it more than well enough.

Incredibly, Connery only made twenty-five pounds from his role in the live television play. Of course, Jack Palance would have got more, but even he would not have made any fortune. Ten times the Connery fee would have looked astronomical in the early 1950s.

The Times decided that Sean was 'physically miscast' – a strange thing to say about a man who looked so perfect a specimen, unless they thought ugliness was a requirement for the ring. In truth, Cassius Clay (later to be known as Mohammad Ali) hadn't yet shown it was possible to box without having your nose and ears flattened. The paper did, however, give him an opportunity to redeem himself. He was, they said, 'shambling and inarticulate', but that he had a charm that made his love affair with Jacqueline Hill work.

The *Sunday Pictorial* writer liked *Requiem For A Heavyweight* as much as did the people in show business. They now marked Sean Connery out for the future. There would be more work to follow and it looked as though the quality was only going to get better

In a way, it was the real making of Sean Connery the actor. The following morning, the telephone didn't stop ringing – almost literally. It was a cliché not too far removed from the world in which Lana Turner could be discovered sitting at the soda fountain of Schwabs drug store, which would itself have its Connery repercussions before long. But there were agents on the phone : agents wanting to speak to Sean Connery and agents wanting to know if he had agents. There were also film companies who didn't bother with such niceties. Suddenly, the young man with the big chest and the big voice was in demand for more than twenty-five pounds a show, for more even than a hundred pounds a week.

Sean's career was taking on an importance even he had never imagined before. But there was still a private life for him. He and Julie were still living together, now in a small mews house near Llew Gardner's Kilburn flat; he watching her sort out her contact prints ready for publication, she going over his lines with him. She had already decided that in career terms he was on his way to something quite remarkable.

There was, however, no such guarantee about their future together. She still hoped against hope that he might regularise their relationship.

Sean took Julie to meet his parents. Or rather Julie took him. She could drive and he couldn't, which gives some idea of how things were going to change for him. The days of the Aston Martin were, after all, not that far away.

Julie thought that was going to be the prelude to their getting married. In the 1950s, few young men took their girlfriends home to mother – and father – without certain facts clearly delineated. Sean, however, seems to have decided that it was no more than an opportunity to go home to Fountainbridge, spend an evening at one of the local palais de danses he had patronised in his single days and, of course, go drinking. In that respect, Julie was luckier than most of her predecessors. He took her to the Edinburgh pubs with him – and she took her camera.

That in itself was something of a triumph. Going into Foys or one of the other Fountainbridge hostelries was a ritual as important to Sean as giving his mother a kiss on his arrival. On reaching Edinburgh Sean showed distinct signs of a tetchiness that was only going to be assuaged by fulfilling this requirement.

After the niceties of the introductions had been completed, Sean looked at the other male members of the family, indicating with the kind of mime that did not really require very much dramatic experience that he would welcome the opportunity for a drink. Julie thought that was a very good idea. What was not a good idea was Sean's reaction. The pub was not, he pointed out, a place for women. A drink in a pub was men's work.

It was, she would later say, one of the first indications that her affair with Sean was not going to last – even though the photographs she took later on of the male Connerys, drinks in hand, smiles on lips, with appreciative neighbours, show that for the moment it was a battle she won.

Despite the culture shock – which was much bigger than she would have imagined – she liked his parents and would have been happy to be their daughter-in-law. Certainly a lot happier, it turned out, than the way her own mother would have been about any marriage between the two. Jill Craigie still opposed any such notion. Julie only had to mention the fact that she might be *thinking* of marrying Sean for her mother to explode like some newly-detonated bomb. Michael Foot, apparently, was less concerned and adopted the role of peacemaker between the two women. It didn't stop Julie bursting into tears and seemingly leaving every meeting with her mother with red eyes.

They were, however, going to get a lot redder. Sean was now working on a television play with a beautiful, blonde actress named Diane Cilento.

4

The Time and

the Place

Diane Cilento fulfilled most of the requirements of the early 1960s tabloid writers. To call her a starlet was less than kind because she was an established actress, yet it was an accurate description: she was acting in leading roles but was not yet a star. As for her appearance, she would have looked wonderful in any of the poses starlets were expected to make. She had the face, she had the pout, she had the flowing, natural blonde hair, and she had the figure that curved in all the right places.

But there was more to her than to almost any of the other young women the papers appreciated so much. She had been born in Rabaul in New Guinea, but was taken to Australia as a baby and grew up in Queensland with her parents, both eminent doctors. Later, she lived in New York when her father, Sir Raphael West Cilento – of Italian ancestry – was seconded to the United Nations.

She and Sean had been on stage together at the Oxford Playhouse in Eugene O'Neill's *Anna Christie*. And now, in August 1957, Britain's current leading independent television company ATV were featuring it for their showplace *ATV Playhouse*, reuniting the Oxford company in the process.

Diane was married to the Italian writer André Volpe at the time, but it didn't stop her inviting Sean to her home to rehearse, away from the pressures of the studio.

Quite suddenly and very obviously to people around them, Sean was smitten by this woman who was now building up an impressive curriculum vitae, having played the lead role of Helen of Troy opposite Michael Redgrave in Giraudoux's comedy *Tiger At The Gates* and being featured opposite Kenneth More, the number-one matinée idol

64

of the 1950s, in the movie, *The Admirable Crichton*. She had also played the leading role in a touring production of a musical about Zuleika Dobson, which, actual mileage covered on the road apart, didn't get very far.

Diane, however, does not seem to have regarded the fascination as in any way mutual. She was to say: 'My first impression of him was that he had a terrific chip on his shoulder. He'd come to my place and stretch out on the floor. I felt he was trying to see if he could make me angry, so I purposely didn't react.'

Neither picked up what the other was trying to convey. 'Later,' Diane recalled, 'I realised he had no ulterior motives, that he was just being himself.'

Before long, she accepted that she liked the 'himself' he was being. He, for his part, liked a great deal about her.

In fact, he was now more taken with Diane than he was with Julie. And, with rather less discretion than his experience in the arts should have dictated, he told her so.

In that famous confession to Julie he happened to mention, almost casually, that Diane had 'incredible eyes'. He also told Julie that he no longer loved her the way he used to. It was not exactly tactful, certainly not a recipe for total happiness.

Nor was the fact that Connery had quite clearly fallen for Diane at first sight, just as Julie always said that she and Sean had found romance themselves. But now it was over, and she knew then that they had to part. She scribbled a couple of rude words in lipstick onto a mirror and left the house for good. Julie later revealed that it was years before she could bear to watch Sean on television or go to one of his movies.

They didn't meet again for three years. By then, Julie was married and had a baby son. Sean asked his name. 'Jason,' she replied. He told her that if he ever had a little boy, he'd call him Jason, too.

But in 1957, Sean wasn't looking that far ahead. Diane seemed right for him if only because she understood the way his career was going. She read with him, reintroduced him to the techniques of the Method – she herself had been dubbed the 'High IQ sex kitten', which she might or might not have appreciated – and together they read Stanislavsky's advice to young actors.

Not that he seemed to need much advice now. He was in steady work, with a whole succession of telephone calls – almost as many as had followed *Requiem For A Heavyweight* – showing he was in demand. Some people considered him an overnight sensation, but the night had been quite long and only now were his dreams coming true. He certainly wasn't rich yet, but hopefully the strain of trying to make do on six pounds a week dole money could now be relegated to memory, never to be resurrected.

But there were nightmares among the dreams. Sean and Diane were in love and resembled more and more that handsome couple of popular mythology. But quite suddenly in 1959, Diane was struck down by tuberculosis. It was a disease that had all but been eradicated by modern drugs, but people still did catch TB, and because of the success of those drugs, the strains that still survived tended to be the serious ones. For weeks she was desperately ill, and during those weeks Sean realised that he was equally desperately in love with her.

He turned down the chance of a big part in the Charlton Heston–Sophia Loren epic *El Cid* to be with her. When she started to recover, he made plans to work on stage with her again, just for a chance to be together. Today, Heston himself says he was sorry not to have the opportunity to work with him.

The man still dubbed 'Britain's Brando' seemed to be going very far indeed. The newspapers carried feature articles about him, always using the nickname whenever the opportunity presented itself.

When writers spotted him in restaurants, it was an excuse for a piece about the newly-discovered heart-throb. Patricia Lewis noted in the London *News Chronicle*, then the most sober of Britain's popular daily papers, that he dressed the part: 'Like a stockbroker's bowler and brolly, so jeans and a suede jacket identify the young actor. (When you've arrived, there's no longer the urge to advertise; success wears a sober suit.)' Which also demonstrates how long ago 1957 was.

So does the mode of transport that Sean used to arrive at the restaurant in question. 'With a squeal and a flourish' Sean came on a scooter. That worried Patricia Lewis because 'the beautifully pro-portioned bigness' (every woman had to note that; to fail to do so might call into question her own femininity) 'of Mr Connery was never meant to balance on a small sea-green scooter.'

She could have been right. But more importantly, she knew that he was going to be, even if he wasn't yet, an important enough person to write such twaddle about.

'He is,' she went on, 'the contemporary hero ... designed on Amer-ican lines. Tall, broad, with features more rugged than regular, he looks earthy, unschooled and basic.' There was an element of rough trade about her description, as though this writer saw herself in a kind of Lady Chatterley role. 'In addition, he has the fatal formula for a toughie: eyes that are brown, expressive, a hint questioning; a forehead crunched up with frequent puzzlement; a nose that's not very neat; and a mouth inclined to pout.'

Patricia Lewis, however, plainly knew what she was talking about. After going into inconsequential detail about his wardrobe, she concluded: 'The future, Mr Connery, is all yours.'

Sean was beginning to give evidence of how he was looking to that future. He was more confident, more willing to accept the plaudits. He was also earning more money.

Not that this was a man who had yet developed expensive tastes – Harrods caviare apart, that is. True, he had taken up golf, but he played it much the way he had played his football – on links owned by the local authority. He had started doing so in Edinburgh, where golf is anything but effete pastime, more a way of life.

One of his closest friends for some time had been the exquisitely beautiful redhead actress Adrienne Corri. Friends say they were actually in love with each other. Now he was also friendly with her husband, the actor Daniel Massey. It was the kind of friendship that also bred deadly rivalry. Adrienne discovered this the moment she suggested that Dan needed a hobby.

'I claim responsibility for turning Sean into a golf bore,' she told me. 'As any woman married to an actor will tell you the biggest problem is that they are always in the house, always under your feet, making cups of coffee, always answering the telephone. Well, I hit on the idea of suggesting that Dan should take up golf. I didn't realise how serious he would become about it.'

One day, he was going out to play golf when Sean came to the house. What happened on this occasion was almost epoch-making bearing in mind what has happened since. 'Ah, golf,' said Sean, 'I think I've got some clubs somewhere.' He found his clubs and immediately arranged to play with Daniel.

'Soon they were both secretly taking lessons from the same pro and there was a deadly rivalry between them,' says Adrienne Corri. 'Before long, they *both* became golf bores.'

But perhaps Sean wouldn't have devoted so much time to the game if he had not already become much more confident in something far more important to him: his career. Certainly, work looked as though it were not only coming, but beginning to mean something very big indeed.

Then came the chance that every young actor craves – the opportunity to go to America. Twentieth Century–Fox offered him a two-year contract, which he accepted with the enthusiasm of a greyhound chasing a hare. It would be the first and last time he agreed to be connected exclusively with a major studio. Over the years, the word 'contract' has come to have a dirty meaning to actors. But to those in Sean's position, it seemed to be a nine-letter word spelled H-o-l-l-y-w-o-o-d. He signed, and the studio said they wanted him to work in a new film called *Another Time, Another Place*. Opposite Lana Turner.

Lana Turner was coming towards the end of her meteoric Hollywood career that indeed had begun with the soda fountain at Schwabs, which was where she – or probably more accurately, her curvaceous figure – was discovered. The agent who spotted her decided that the bust was worth employing and since the girl went along with the package, so be it.

Not for nothing was she known as the Sweater Girl. Every movie Lana Turner made featured her wearing a tight sweater. There was no need for the cleavage of Jane Russell. Turner's breasts encased in the finest cone-shaped brassières that the costume department could rustle up had delighted American GIs as much as had Betty Grable's legs.

Another Time, Another Place was a series of disappointments, the biggest of all for Sean being the fact that it was not shot in Hollywood. Twentieth Century–Fox decided the story was the perfect vehicle for another one of those quota-fillers they were going to make in Britain. Miss Turner would partly satisfy the studio's home office and Sean playing opposite her would be a matter of local interest in England – and Scotland. No one was allowed to dwell too much on the fact that Lana Turner making the picture in England was in itself a demonstration that the star wasn't quite as great as she used to be.

But at first, to both Twentieth Century–Fox and Sean himself, *Another Time, Another Place* appeared to be a near-perfect first film under their new contract. It also offered Lana Turner a chance for a big comeback. She was still only forty, an age when to be called a has-been not only hurts but seems irredeemable.

She had gone through some unhappy experiences recently, although losing her looks was not one of them – her face was still beautiful and her bosom still a credit to her sweaters. But she was trapped in a horrific love affair and her career seemed on the dustheap with the arrival of a single letter from MGM : after all the years she had brought money to that studio, she was being released from her contract and there was nothing she could do about it. For as long as there had been a Hollywood, stars and other actors had been put on suspension for breaking the terms of their agreements with the studios. There was no way an actor could suspend a studio.

Lana had recently starred in the television series *Peyton Place*, which only just escaped being called a 'soap opera' by virtue of the fact that soap operas were shown every day and this series was on the air only a couple of times a week. Also, it had to be admitted that more effort was put into it and the acting was, on the whole, a lot better than that of the average soap. If *Peyton Place* seemed to be a springboard to more important things for other cast members such as Mia Farrow and Ryan O'Neal, it was thought to signify the end of Lana's career.

Despite all the doubts about where Lana was going, Sean was, nevertheless, flattered to be chosen to star opposite one of the legends of Hollywood. He was also glad of the opportunity to show he could do something with the role.

It was a time for research. Since he was playing a wartime radio correspondent, he set about listening to the men who had been the real thing. He put his tape recorder to work and played a series of something like 130 recordings of famous radio war reporters on the air – like Richard Dimbleby and Wynford Vaughan Thomas of Britain and America's Quentin Reynolds, and the dean of them all, Ed Murrow. He listened to their words and felt he was picking up some of the emotions that went into making their work so memorable.

The fact that he didn't have all that much chance to demonstrate just how much research he had done was not allowed to affect the way he played the part of the reporter. He couldn't have worked harder had there been an Oscar in it for him, which he knew there wasn't – in earlier days, the picture would have had trouble fighting for more than a B-movie status.

Nevertheless, the producers were putting a certain stock on their male star. The billing for the picture inevitably had Lana Turner in the lead and then added, 'Introducing Sean Connery'. It was a fairly traditional choice of words – but what about everything he had done up to then? It was a fundamental act of faith in Sean and what lay ahead for him that Twentieth Century–Fox thought the other chapters deserved to be put back into the vault and that he was worth 'introducing' all over again.

Leslie Halliwell, the film historian whose opinions on movies now relegated to the archives are always fairly incisive, said of *Another Time, Another Place*: 'Drippy romance, unsympathetically played and artificially set in a Cornish village ... Lana Turner unsympathetically played an American newspaperwoman who has an affair with a British war correspondent.' (Unsympathetically played by Sean Connery.)

Lana was dreadfully disappointed by the picture, what she had to do in it and what was said about it, but Sean was still at the stage when he could afford to be glad that someone was spelling his name correctly.

In Fountainbridge, Effie and Joe couldn't have been happier. As far as they were concerned, he had been a star since *South Pacific*. They had felt much the same pride they glowed with now whenever they had seen him in any one of his previous low-budget pictures in which he had low-down-in-the-list billing. But now he was with a *real* star. Sean saw the situation for what it really was: a bigger than usual opportunity. And there *was* a lot to be said for working with Lana Turner.

'Who can forget Lana?' he said in 1992. 'A lovely lady.' It was she, he maintains, who asked for him to join her in the picture.

That affection for the Sweater Girl was to last through the years. When he heard that Lana was stricken with throat cancer, he was genuinely sad and wrote to tell her so. When he was twenty-eight, however, he could only think how kind she had been to him.

'I adored her,' was how he put it.

The newspapers couldn't quite understand why. And he, unfamiliar with the ways of the press, couldn't understand why they couldn't understand it. 'How does it feel to be thrown in with an old woman?' one man asked him. He said that he didn't think about it – and probably wished later he had done the gallant thing and slugged the reporter.

'They really worked at it, those people, asking me questions about her age, and everything.'

The age difference certainly didn't affect the film. In fact, he was convinced she looked younger than he did. However, if age wasn't a problem, other things were. And although the press were guilty yet again, this time most of the blame could be pinned on the Twentieth Century–Fox publicity department.

As always, the scribes in the Fox PR outfit were looking for angles. When it appeared that Sean and Lana were getting on as well as they were, they played the usual Hollywood trick – dropping enough hints to be arrested for causing litter.

The hints were of a nature as old as the business itself – that it could just be that the two stars of this new movie were more than just good friends. As far as anyone could tell, Turner and Connery had got no further than enjoying a dinner together. But the newspapers in America thought that they could arrange for two and two to make five, and a certain gentleman of somewhat unprincipled nature made it six.

Lana Turner's lover was the gangster Johnny Stompanato, who fancied becoming a film producer – making Lana's films in general and this one in particular. He heard that Lana and Connery were getting on too well for what was supposed to be a professional relationship and took the first plane to London, intent on altering the shape of Sean's nose and, in the process, the shape of his career.

Stompanato decided that this was just the time and the place to rid himself of this dangerous rival, found Connery and took out a gun – which he cocked and then pointed at the actor's chest.

It could have been a scene from a James Bond movie, except that none had been made at that time. Before the gangster had a chance to squeeze the trigger, Sean punched him in the jaw and Stompanato went reeling the way a hundred of his own victims had done in the past.

Possibly out of fear of what one of the New York 'families' might contemplate doing, Sean has kept remarkably quiet about the event ever since.

What he was not allowed to ignore was a series of letters that Lana had written to her lover from London – in which she happened to mention that Sean had taken her (and her daughter Cheryl) to the theatre. It was a very red rag to a very ugly bull.

The letters only made the mobster all the more furious. Stompanato wasn't used to being bettered, and took it out on his mistress, beating her up at the house she rented in London as often as he slept with her. In the end, the police were called and he was ordered to leave the country.

A few months later, Stompanato was himself the victim of one of the most celebrated Hollywood slayings in history. He was stabbed with a butcher's knife – by Lana's daughter, Cheryl, while her mother looked on. A few minutes earlier, Cheryl had heard the couple quarrelling and leapt to her mother's defence when he threatened to disfigure her: 'I'll carve you up. I'll cut you good, baby,' he told Lana.

The case went to trial in the most celebrated Hollywood real-life court action since the Fatty Arbuckle scandal of the 1920s. Lana was a witness for the defence. The jury took only twenty minutes to dismiss the murder charge. It was, they decided, justifiable homicide.

Sean was in Hollywood, too, at the time, working on his next film. If thieves stick together, so do hoodlums and murderers. One of those who remained loyal to Stompanato's memory was the current monarch of Murder Incorporated, Mickey Cohen. He sent word to Connery, warning him that the town was not big enough for both of them.

It was again like a scene from one of the low budget movies which Sean had been doing his best to get out of – but with an American accent thrown in. A man phoned him in his room and said: 'You Sean Connery?'

'Yeah,' he replied.

'You get your ass out of town,' the caller told him and hung up.

The implication was quite clear to Sean: there was a contract out for his life. He didn't wait to find out how serious it was, and instead moved out of the Hollywood Roosevelt Hotel. (Sean's accommodation was a good demonstration of his status at the time. The Hollywood Roosevelt Hotel had once been the film town's leading hostelry and was on Hollywood Boulevard itself. But, like the boulevard, the hotel was becoming run down and 'real' stars were now being accommodated a few miles away in Beverly Hills.)

Sean had a movie to make with Disney – *Darby O'Gill And The Little People* – and not even death-threats were going to stop him taking advantage of his first opportunity to work in Hollywood. He now moved to the San Fernando Valley, and stayed in a lodging house close to the Disney studios. His preference for downmarket accommodation took some explaining to the Disney people, he said afterwards, as, knowing the vanity of film actors, it was the unlikeliest place to find a young man who thought he was on the threshold of stardom.

Even though it was made in the movie capital, *Darby O'Gill And The Little People* was set in Ireland, but was as typical of Disney as any definition in a studio manual. It was full of as much whimsy as could skirt the blarney stone – all about the capture by leprechauns of a caretaker who falls down a well.

The movie gave him one unexpected opportunity to broaden his experience: he made a record. In the picture he danced and sang. He did well enough, it was thought, with 'Pretty Irish Girl', which he performed in the movie with the female lead Janet Munro, for it to be released on disc.

It was a time when every bit of film music was being sold in record shops in an attempt to satisfy what seemed to be an insatiable appetite for movie soundtracks sold as twelve-inch LPs. Everything except the music accompanying the ice-cream sellers immediately went on to vinyl. *Darby O'Gill And The Little People* didn't become an album but the Connery-Munro duet was a single that perhaps sold a single copy but not much more.

By then, *Another Time, Another Place* had opened in America – long before the originally-planned dates. Twentieth Century–Fox had planned a long publicity campaign that was way over the original budget. But the Stompanato affair had changed everybody's thinking – the killing and the Turner–Connery connection were two vital assets that could not be wasted. So the picture opened while people were still talking. Unfortunately for all concerned, what they started saying now was not worth hearing – or reading.

The only good thing that the critic of the *New York Post*, Robert Rice, could say about Sean Connery was that he was a Scot 'who is making his American movie debut, has impressive black eyebrows and the engaging trace of a burr, which are probably better reasons than most for Miss Turner to fall in love with him.'

As for Lana herself, Mr Rice noted: 'Miss Turner is a performer, if that's the word, who needs a good deal of help from screenwriters, directors, photographers, costumiers and anyone else around.' The only acting in the picture, he decided, came from Glynis Johns, who played the reporter's widow. 'Miss Johns ... manages to behave like a real live person from time to time.'

Of course, in *Darby O'Gill And The Little People*, nobody was expected to play any real-live persons, at least not so that you would notice. But the Disney organisation had a lot of hopes for both *Darby* and for Sean Connery.

Maude Spector, who introduced him to the studio for the picture, said they talked about putting Sean under contract. His arrangement with Fox wasn't really working out and it seemed only a matter of time before he would be released. Disney believed they had more sensible plans for his services. 'But then they thought better of it,' Spector told me. 'They had a hunch he was going to be such an outstanding actor that it wouldn't have worked. Before long, he would have wanted to break away to do other things and make more money, and they knew it. They told me they didn't think it would be worth it for them.'

But the studio pondered the idea for some time. Disney wined and dined him. When he came to New York, they gave him two seats for one of the top plays in town. The other ticket, publicity men had decided, would go to a starlet they were planning to groom. But Sean arrived at the theatre alone – the starlet didn't turn up.

So, remembers Victor Spinetti, Connery took the spare ticket to the box office and tried to return it. 'Always the perfect Scotsman,' as he put it.

The theatre management, however, weren't in the mood to help. They insisted there were no returns. For Sean now there was nothing to do but take matters into his own hands. He strolled alongside the queue outside the theatre and offered it to a man eager to see the show.

When he sat down waiting for the performance to begin, the man slid into the place next to him. Unfortunately for Connery, he instantly recognised him as the star of the film he had only just seen, *Another Time, Another Place.*

He was more than just a little excited at his discovery. 'My name is Mark,' he said. He kept repeating it: 'Mark.' He couldn't get over his good luck. 'I'm Mark.'

People had to hush him; his enthusiasm was such that he was disturbing the play. 'I'm sitting next to a movie star,' he kept telling them.

In the interval, Sean left to get a drink at the bar – in those days on Broadway, you couldn't get anything stronger than an orange juice, which is what he ordered. He was surrounded by dinner-jacketed men from the Disney front office and their elegantly-dressed wives. Sean was the centre of their attention and of the conversation – until the man to whom he had given that spare ticket arrived on the scene and greeted Sean – much to his embarrassment, as he had never met him before. 'Hello, Sean,' he said, in a familiar manner.

There had been no opportunity for Connery to tell the Disney people that their starlet hadn't shown up. Without that information to hand, they began to look somewhat concerned – and glanced anxiously in the direction of the stranger.

Sean saw the way things were going. But he still felt impelled to be polite, and tried to introduce the man. 'I'm sorry,' he said to him, 'what's your name?'

'Mark, Sean,' said the fellow. 'Mark, you remember.'

The studio men and their wives said polite goodbyes and beat a gentle retreat. So did all the talk of a long-term contract.

Says Spinetti today: 'Of course, it was the best thing that ever happened to him. Otherwise, he would never have moved on to James Bond. I once said to him, "Did you ever send that fellow a cake or a thank-you note?" He changed Sean's career for him.'

After his experiences with Disney, Sean did his best to show that he was at heart a classicist – which was why he was featured in 1959 in a Greek drama at the Oxford Playhouse. In *The Bacchae*, he starred opposite Yvonne Mitchell and Michael David.

But that was not to say that he totally ignored the world of commercialism. Later that year, Sean got himself involved in a Tarzan movie – *Tarzan's Greatest Adventure*. It wasn't the greatest adventure in the world for him, playing his now familiar role of a villain whom no one wants to see come to any good; in this case as a diamond hunter. The picture was shot on location in Africa, and thereby earned an entry in the list of Connery Significant Steps.

Later in 1959 he played the moving character of John Proctor in Arthur Miller's *The Crucible* (set in seventeenth-century Salem, Massachusetts but clearly a powerful swipe against more contemporary witch-hunts headed by Senator Joseph McCarthy) on BBC television. Another television play that satisfied all his cravings for culture and great literature came his way. Sean saw playing Count Vronsky in *Anna Karenina* as the Great Vindication. He seemed to be protesting all the time that he was a serious actor while finding few opportunities to prove it, and now here was the perfect opportunity in the perfect medium to show what he could do.

Perhaps even more significantly, the fact that he was playing opposite Claire Bloom in the BBC play demonstrated what he had always claimed – that he was as good as any of them and better than most. It wasn't every actor who was invited to co-star with one of the most beautiful and most talented actresses on either stage or screen on either side of the Atlantic. Not only was she just about the hottest property the Old Vic could get hold of – the highest accolade available to a classical actress – she had first achieved international fame when Charlie Chaplin discovered her and made her his female lead as the dancer in *Limelight*. That was a qualification to be taken seriously as far as Sean was concerned, and, almost as if her achievements rubbed off on him, he regarded this as one of the greatest opportunities of his career.

It was an opportunity he grabbed and of which he took the utmost advantage. *The Times* said that of all the actors in the play, 'the most successful was Mr Sean Connery, a headstrong, passionate Vronsky.'

Sean looked set to make a name for himself as a classical actor. Quite obviously to those who knew him, that was indeed the sort of reputation he wanted. But it was not one encouraged by either his bank manager or his landlord.

Then in November 1960, a remarkably middle-aged-looking Sean once more played together with Diane at the theatre for which they had both developed a lasting affection, the Oxford Playhouse – this time in Pirandello's *Naked*. Cilento looked enticing. Sean had a greying beard that made him look like a cross between a professor and a rabbi.

Diane had the lion's share of the review in the *Daily Telegraph*. She played Ersilia 'with pathetic and complete conviction'. Sean wasn't even mentioned, although his photograph appeared above the piece.

The fact that Sean was thought worth photographing, however, perhaps said more than anything that might have been written.

Later, *Naked* moved to the Royal Court in London, the 'art house' which had introduced John Osborne's kitchen-sink dramas, and Sean appeared in one performance, mainly to be with Diane.

Sean was proud of her. He was overcome by her beauty but he also revered her for her intelligence. Nobody he met was left unaware of the fact that Diane herself had translated *Naked* from the Italian, which was very much her second language.

Sean also admired her acting, and when she received her Academy Award nomination for her part as a wench in *Tom Jones* (it has gone down in history as the shortest role ever to receive an Oscar nomination, if not the award itself – she was on screen for no more than a few minutes in the opening scenes) he couldn't have been happier had he received the plaudits himself.

As for his own work, his sights were elsewhere. When the opportunity arose to go to Canada to play Macbeth, he jumped at the chance. 'You shouldn't wait until you're forty-five to play Macbeth,' he said and proceeded to demonstrate the fact.

It was not his only venture into Shakespeare around this time. In 1960 the BBC, still reeling under the impact of the arrival of commercial television five years earlier was about to embark on the first of its massive drama endeavours. *An Age Of Kings* was a massive dose of the Bard – a fifteen-hour distillation of Shakespeare's historical output with an emphasis on his dramatic biographies of Britain's monarchs.

The first four episodes, aired on Thursday evenings, was a serialisation of *Henry IV: Part One*. In effect, this was *Henry IV: Part One* Part One and Part Two and so on. It was a novel idea in an era when the very notion of such a series was novel, too. The series was filmed at a time when most things went out live – with all the agonising risks of scenery falling down and actors forgetting their lines in a nervous sweat.

There were no such problems for Sean Connery playing Hotspur in the episodes (Robert Hardy played the King). The problems he did have were the now familiar ones that centred around his accent. The critics didn't like it, but then this was the time when Shakespeare had to be performed only by people who spoke with Oxford accents. In putting their faith in Sean Connery, the BBC were showing that the world was moving on. And by doing as well as he did, Sean Connery was demonstrating he was an actor who cared enough to add a new dimension all of his own.

Reviews criticising Sean were certainly not strong enough to influence the BBC – who had set their minds on producing the best television drama in the world – to look elsewhere when they had a good part in mind for him. Despite his contract with Twentieth Century–Fox, most of his work did now seem to be for the small screen.

An Age Of Kings was followed by *Without The Grail,* also for television, in which he performed with the eminent actor Michael Hordern and the Chinese actress Jacqui Chan.

Another television play, Terence Rattigan's *Adventure Story* in which he played Alexander the Great, was more important. He even made the cover of the *Radio Times.* All of this proves something that most people have long forgotten: in 1960, two years before he was to become an international star, Sean Connery was already an important actor. Nobody was 'introducing' him any more.

Clearly things were improving for him. It didn't look as though he were going to have to repeat the experience to which he was constantly referring now that life was so much better: 'I've been down to my last quid many more times than I care to remember.'

But nothing was absolutely perfect. Opportunities for better things occasionally cropped up, only to be dashed at the last moment. For one ecstatically marvellous moment, it seemed he was going to be picked to play opposite Ingrid Bergman, a prospect not to be treated lightly.

Without question, Miss Bergman was one of the great stars of all time. In *Casablanca,* in particular, but also in *Notorious, Spellbound* and the earlier *For Whom The Bell Tolls* and *Gaslight,* she had been both beautiful and powerful. She was older now, but Twentieth Century–Fox had a role for her that promised to be excitingly different – playing Gladys Aylward, the missionary working in China, in *The Inn Of The Sixth Happiness.*

She was going to – and was intended to – dominate the picture, but there was also the part of the Chinese warlord. Word got out that Sean was being considered for it. There was plainly something about those eyes that could make him a not incredible Chinese, even one with a Scots accent. But before long, the studio chose the German actor Kurt Jurgens for the part – an even more incredible Chinaman, but an actor with a bigger name.

Sean had to be content with something much more conventional. In 1960 he was yet again involved in London gangland in the kind of movie – complete with contemporary furniture, young actresses with dirndl skirts and bouffant hair, and a nightclub resembling the sort of coffee bar most people would want to avoid – you might still be unlucky enough to see if the video is accidentally left on in the middle of the night. *The Frightened City* was not a great moment in Connery's career, to say the least.

The one thing that can be said in favour of the film was that Sean made an impression on the other members of the cast – particularly the young Welsh character actor who played his fellow burglar, Kenneth Griffith. 'I think I knew then that he was going to be a star,' Griffith told me. 'He was as straight as a die, a very nice man. Most important of all, I saw the quality of his acting.'

And conscious of the importance of good acting, too. 'He was always trying to get away to the Oxford Playhouse and do a classical role if he could.'

More significant still for Griffith is that the memory of those days remains with Sean. 'He still treats me as a peer, which I find absolutely astounding. He remains as nice as he was in those days, and as nice as when he was a coffin polisher.'

On The Fiddle, in which Sean played an RAF airman, had rather more to commend it. Once more it was a case of Sean benefiting from the company he was keeping. Just as he had in *Time Lock*, he searched for examples of other people's acting to follow. There were plenty of performers around for Sean to watch as minutely as did the director Cyril Frankel. Cecil Parker, Wilfrid Hyde White, Kathleen Harrison, John Le Mesurier, and Harry Locke – all part of the best repertory company in British cinema history – were studied by the now maturing Sean. So was Alfred Lynch. That habit of watching the way other actors worked was proving to be a hard one to break. Especially since no one yet had decided to do the same with him.

Or so he thought. What was not generally known at this time was that people were deciding that the young Sean Connery had more than a modicum of talent.

Whereas previously the press seemed to be interested only in his appearance, articles were now appearing in both newspapers and magazines dealing with his work – and not just the work in hand but with the work to come in the future. That didn't happen to actors who passed like extras in the night.

He was sufficiently notable for some writers even to ask why he was not yet at the top of anyone's casting schedules. One such writer was Freda Bruce Lockhart, who put it quite bluntly: 'It is a real mystery to me,' she told readers of *Woman* magazine, at the time the best medium of all to reach the female market, 'why no film company has built Sean into a great international star.'

Other writers were noting it, too, although not many of them went as far as Freda Bruce Lockhart, who said that Connery reminded her of Clark Gable 'with the same rare mixture of handsome virility, sweetness and warmth'. Either she knew Sean better than anyone else or she had been swayed by her own emotions. Even when he became a superstar, no one would say that about him. The handsomeness and virility were not in question, but sweetness? Warmth?

Sean ventured back into the West End early in 1962. Dressed up this time in Roman costume, he played the role of the Roman Conqueror Holofernes in Jean Giraudoux's play *Judith*, which had been translated from the original French by the eminent Christopher Fry. But the audiences stayed away from Her Majesty's Theatre.

The plot revolved around the Roman Holofernes who takes the Jewish girl Judith as one of the spoils of his job, only to fall in love with her just before she murders him. As Philip Hope-Wallace noted in the *Manchester Guardian*: 'Holofernes, as played by Sean Connery in a gold bikini, suggested an Irish wrestler at the Metropolitan: flights of fancy as when he urges Judith to be a cheerful pagan girl, sat very wryly on him.'

The effect of it all? People wondered. Even Twentieth Century-Fox thought the time had come to cash in on their investment in Sean. They offered him a role in what for months had been billed as their big spectacular of 1962 – bigger than anything since their massive calamity, *Cleopatra*. *The Longest Day* was a different package altogether from *Cleopatra* – a reflective look at D-Day 1944, the events of which were sufficiently recent to be within living memory and far enough away for audiences to be able to be dispassionate about its failings.

The film was an example of the star-fever from which Hollywood studios were suffering at the time, which along with the wide, wide screens was considered to be the only way to beat television at the start of a new decade which had not yet started swinging. John Wayne, Robert Mitchum, Henry Fonda, Robert Ryan, Rod Steiger ... the list went on. It included Sean Connery, appearing for no more than a couple of minutes together with Kenneth More and Norman Rossington. He was featured as a young clean-shaven Tommy in a tin hat.

Soon afterwards, Fox decided they could do without him. Weighing up the facts that they were sending Sean a regular cheque for doing almost nothing and that nobody had any better ideas, they decided to release him from his contract. It was to turn out to be one of those legends of film history, another case of the one that got away. The studio had no idea how short-sighted they were being. If *Cleopatra* had been a disaster, saying goodbye to Sean Connery was close to a tragedy for them.

They had no notion that an idea was afoot elsewhere. The only problem was who was going to make that idea work. It all seemed to come together with a question that appeared as fantastic as it was tempting. Sean Connery, the man with the muscles and the voice strangled by his accent, the fellow who looked his best sitting in the cab of a lorry perched at the end of a quarry, was being offered the most unlikely part that had come his way since he pretended to sing in the chorus of *South Pacific*.

'How,' he was asked, 'would you like to play James Bond?'

5

INTO BONDAGE

James Bond was everything that Sean Connery was not. Just about the only thing they had in common was Fettes College: Bond was a pupil there; Connery had delivered its milk. Sean once said that he didn't have the problems at his own school that Bond had with his. Bond was expelled.

Sean, for all his lack of star billing, was also real. James Bond was a figment of Ian Fleming's imagination. But his appeal in the decade after World War Two had been immense. To an admittedly comparatively small reading public, the derring-do of Secret Service Operative No. 007 had a remarkable fascination in an age not far removed from the time when uniforms on the streets of London were as familiar as red buses.

Bond, of course, was a man more often seen in a crisp white dinner jacket than an officer's tunic. But he was nevertheless a commander in the Royal Navy, a rank to which an ordinary seaman – particularly one with the words 'Mum and Dad' and 'Scotland Forever' tattooed on his arm – could never have aspired.

Above all, there was that sophistication of Bond, which had not only been drooled over by the readers of a whole shelf-length of Fleming books, but which, in comic-strip form, was one of the most popular features in the *Daily Express*, in those pre-tabloid days the most influential, best-selling middle-ground newspaper in Britain. People on Bond's side of the Atlantic didn't know too much about dry martinis at that time and the demand that his drinks be shaken and not stirred was an affectation that remained unfathomable.

The idea of an undercover agent who not only possessed a strange licence to kill, but was also a sophisticate who knew his women as well as he knew his drink was plainly a good idea for a film. Before long, making the Bond pictures became nothing less than an obsession for a pair of producers who squabbled their way to a fortune on the back of 007.

Investing in James Bond made millions for Canadian Harry Saltzman and New Yorker Albert R. Broccoli (a descendant of the Italian farmer who gave his name to the green vegetable, 'Cubby' Broccoli, as he was known in the business, was to become almost as famous and almost as much of a household name).

It had been Saltzman's idea originally. Indeed, he had had the idea since first reading a Bond book in 1959. He saw it as more than just an adventure story, more than just a detective yarn (as several American critics who had plainly never read a word of one of the Bond stories had dubbed them) and more than just another knock-'em-dead wine-women-and-song tale. Fleming had given Bond a suave approach that might have owed a little to the Bulldog Drummond–Saint school, but the character had a dimension which his predecessors had never had: the mystery and the mystique of the secret service.

Others from time to time had shared Saltzman's view. There had been a television version of *Casino Royale* in the United States a few years before that was as wooden as the scenery and made no impact on anybody who wasn't in the mood for a good laugh at the producers' expense.

Earlier even than that, there had been talk about making a full-length Bond movie. Sir Alexander Korda, at the tail end of a career that had produced epics ranging from *The Private Life Of Henry VIII* to *The Four Feathers*, with *Rembrandt* thrown in for good measure, rang up Ian Fleming and suggested a film version of *Live And Let Die*, the second novel to feature James Bond. But before a third was published, Korda had lost interest. Or rather, his bank manager had: the Hungarian-born mogul was broke.

Then the Rank Organisation entered the picture. Rank, too, had been losing a lot of the lustre – and much of the money – it had picked up in the war and early post-war days, when only Ealing could rival the company in its claim to actually *be* the British film industry. The studio thought that *Moonraker* would fit their bill. But they only entertained the idea for six months and then let go their option.

So Saltzman had it to himself – or so he thought. He wanted an option to film every one of the books, and Fleming would have been happy for him to do so – except that he had already sold the rights to *Casino Royale*. They had been bought for something like £5,000 and were by then languishing in an office somewhere in Hollywood. So was a series of scripts for a television show called *Commander Jamaica*, also written by Ian Fleming. When that didn't see the light of the California day, Fleming turned the project into *Dr No*, another James Bond book.

Fleming was an unhappy man. His marriage was on the rocks, he had a severe alcohol problem and he had suffered a heart attack. He wanted to see Bond on the screen. He needed the ego boost. He was also not averse to the money it would bring him.

The fact that it all came together was due to the writer Wolf Mankowitz, whose reputation had been made with a series of films, novels and plays mainly about London, like the show *Expresso Bongo* and films such as *A Kid For Two Farthings*. Mankowitz knew Saltzman and was also one of a group of friends that included Peter Sellers and Diane Cilento. It was through Diane that he first met Sean. He decided on the strength of that first meeting that Connery was his idea of the perfect Bond. He introduced Sean to Saltzman at precisely the moment Saltzman had made up his mind he was finally ready to make a Bond movie. Even so, the producer needed some convincing. The decision to have Sean starring in it would take a little longer.

For $50,000 – which even in those days was not a particularly large outlay, although certainly a respectable one – he bought an option for the entire Bond library, with the exception of the no-longer-available *Casino Royale*.

That was the point at which Cubby Broccoli arrived on the scene. He, too, thought that Bond would make a good film. When he heard that Saltzman owned the option, he reasoned the time had come to think in terms of a deal.

Both had been in the film business for some time. Saltzman specialised in kitchen-sink dramas like *Look Back In Anger* and *Saturday Night And Sunday Morning* and, his addiction to the Bond stories apart, was anxious to come out of the kitchen. Broccoli had been a tough, hard-bitten agent, the kind who sent producers quaking to their lawyers. It had been his stewardship that kept Lana Turner so active for so long. When he ceased to represent her, he founded Warwick Films. His movies included *The Red Beret* (called *Paratrooper* in America), *Cockle-shell Heroes*, which was another wartime story and, most notably, Rita Hayworth's *Fire Down Below.*

Now Saltzman and Broccoli were going into partnership under the banner of Eon Productions. It was a sound move on their part. The money they needed to make their films would be more easily available to a team of two men with a decent track record than it would be to just one. 'I think they were made for each other,' Wolf Mankowitz told me. 'They were both very easy to get on with. Saltzman is very intense, an extrovert, post-Mike Todd producer type. Cubby was very quiet with a solid, money background.'

Their partnership established, the duo had to work out who their bankers would be. They decided to go direct to a top studio, one which not only had distribution facilities, but all the soundstage backup, too. And if the film flopped, it would be the studio that footed the bill – muttering something like 'That's show business' at the next stock-holders' meeting.

They approached Columbia, who were taken with the idea and entered into negotiations. Columbia was a big studio. It liked spec-tacular colour movies and its present directors were anxious to show that they had their fingers on the pulse of the business every bit as much as had their founder Harry Cohn, who had made the studio's name with such pictures as *It Happened One Night* and the other Frank Capra films and, later in the 1940s, *The Jolson Story*, which in many ways had been just the same sort of gamble that Bond represented. And, they might have thought, had turned into just the success they hoped Bond would be.

But then they had second thoughts. Any Bond picture they made would have to come in at under one million dollars and that was beginning to seem unlikely. The accountants at Columbia's New York office decided that this was just, as one put it, 'a rather silly British thriller' and cancelled their thoughts on the project.

United Artists stepped into their place and a deal was struck – but only after thinking about it very carefully indeed. 'There just wasn't much enthusiasm to make it at that time,' the director Michael Winner recalled. 'Everyone thought it was going to cost more than it was worth.'

Winner himself hadn't been invited to direct the picture, but by then almost every other director had. 'Even I was asked to do it,' Peter Rogers told me, 'and I wasn't even a director.' Rogers thought about it and decided he would rather produce 'Carry On' films.

At about this point the second problem in the scenario arose – concerning a Bond title that would before long become one of the best known – *Thunderball*. Ian Fleming had commissioned a film treatment of the book by Jack Whittingham and Kevin McClory. But Ivar Bryce, a businessman who had agreed to finance the project, decided that movies were not his business after all, and withdrew his support.

It now had to be decided whether *Thunderball*, which Fleming wanted to be the first book to be filmed, could be part of the option for which Saltzman had paid. Before long, the High Court in London

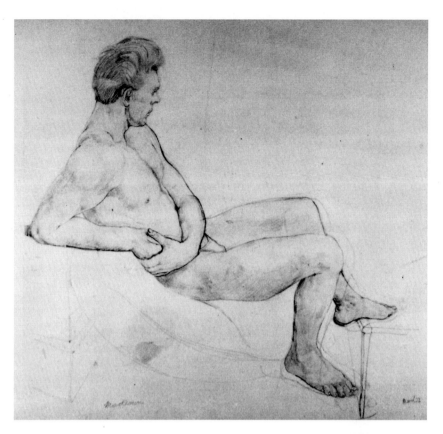

Sean the artists' model – as drawn
by Martin McKeown.

The scene that had the girls
drooling: Sean's attempt at being
Mr Universe in 1953.

Connery the footballer, third from right, second row; star of the Fet-Lors of Edinburgh.

Sean relaxing in an Edinburgh pub on a visit home during his early years as an actor.

Above Sean during rehearsals for *South Pacific* (1953). His role as a chorus boy marked the beginning of his acting career.

Above right Sean as 'Mountain' McClintock in the television play *Requiem For A Heavyweight* (1957).

The classical Connery as Holofernes in *Judith* at Her Majesty's Theatre, London (1962). With Ruth Meyers.

With Lana Turner in *Another Time, Another Place* (1958), one of her last films and one of his first more important roles.

The rough and ready look in *Action Of The Tiger* (1957).

A little whimsy in *Darby O'Gill And The Little People* with Janet Munro (1959).

Left With first wife Diane: a quiet
moment with the *Goldfinger* cameras
turned off.

Above That special relationship with
baby Jason.

Sean directing Diane and Robert
Harding in *I've Seen You Cut Lemons*
(1969).

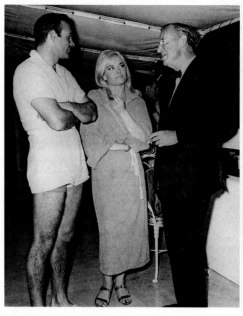

Above With Shirley Eaton and Ian Fleming on the set of *Goldfinger* (1964).

Left The archetype Bond as everybody remembers him in *Dr No* (1962).

Sean and Ursula Andress in *Dr No*.

st good friends: Sean and Claudine Auger
_ the *Thunderball* set in the Bahamas.

ght Bond and the Bond Girls in *You Only*
ve Twice (1967).

Connery the stuntman in *You Only Live Twice*.

Sean's first Western, and his first and only film with Brigitte Bardot: *Shalako* (1968).

Bond is back. The mature Sean promises he will never say never again (1983).

ruled that, like *Casino Royale* it had to be regarded as apart from the main deal – which is why it could be remade twenty years later as *Never Say Never Again* – but even before that decree was reached, Eon decided that the first picture now had to be *Dr No*. There was nothing to stop them coming to an arrangement with *Thunderball* later, but as we have seen, no one had got that far yet. They had to think of the first, and still possibly the only, Bond picture.

Not even Ian Fleming himself could have imagined what this fellow Bond was going to become. The first Bond book, *Casino Royale*, had appeared in 1953 and had been succeeded annually by sequels ever since, all of them selling extraordinarily well. But the book-buying public (even in countries speaking the eleven languages into which they had been translated) was still small compared with the impact of the cinema and the then burgeoning television audience.

Nor could Broccoli or Saltzman, even in their most optimistic moments, have realised what they were about to foist onto the world. There had been huge successes that had made a lot of money in the picture business before; they were the dream of every producer. There had been sequels of successful films before and there would be plenty in the years to come – particularly those with numbers added to the original title – but very few ever made as much money or impact as the first of the genre. To contemplate a seemingly never-ending series that would go on for at least thirty years, almost every film making more money than the one before, was almost beyond decency.

Before long, what the pair would have in their hands and on their minds was a cinematic goldmine. What they also had was a 31-year-old actor who would not only measure up to the character of James Bond but would set the pattern for everything that would follow. What that actor himself had was the passport to a future that suddenly looked as golden as Bond's cigarette case.

It would all turn out to be as different from Sean Connery's own plans for his career as anything that could be imagined. The serious actor who had played Macbeth and Hotspur was about to go swanning around Jamaica and find himself mixing in the most secret of secret-service circles.

How the casting of Sean Connery as Bond came about owes more to public appeal than almost any film since *Gone With The Wind*. His name as put forward by Wolf Mankowitz had registered with the producers, but they weren't prepared simply to take the writer's recommendation at face value or even, for that matter, to follow their own hunches.

Deliberately, word of their plans was allowed to get out. With the connivance of Saltzman and Broccoli, the London *Daily Express*, which had been running its James Bond picture-strip for years, organised a poll to choose the man its readers most wanted to make the cartoon character come alive.

Of 250 nominated actors, Sean came out on top – which refutes to a large extent the legend that until Bond, he was a complete unknown. Sean couldn't possibly have imagined how important that dose of whimsy would be to him.

The producers were delighted, particularly Broccoli who had marked out Connery as an actor to watch the moment he saw *Darby O'Gill And The Little People*. They invited Sean to a meeting at their South Audley Street office, a location some distance from the heart of the British film business in Wardour Street but on the edge of Grosvenor Square, site of the US Embassy and some of the most prestigious Anglo–American operations in the country. It created just the right impression with people who were going to deal with them.

Connery made the same sort of impression on the producers. They saw the way he looked, the way he moved his body – Sean taking advantage of all he had learned from Yat Malmgeren – and offered him the part. Without a screen test.

Wolf Mankowitz was delighted: 'I thought he was right because of his low-key type of performance. To put it mildly, he always underacted, which seemed to be right for that kind of part. He seemed to be the obvious choice. Saltzman and Broccoli followed it up.'

Mankowitz took no particular credit for the choice. 'There was nothing very complicated to it. People talk about casting, and somebody says, "What about So-and-so?" It wasn't based on performance. Just seemed like a good bet.'

The meeting at the South Audley Street office put the bet on the table. As Broccoli was to report: 'In thirty minutes he sold us both. It was the sheer self-confidence he exuded. Every time he made a point, he hit the desk with that great fist of his or slapped his thigh. It wasn't just an act either.'

Saltzman said: 'We'd never seen a surer guy. Nor a more arrogant sonofabitch. We spoke to him and saw that he had the masculinity the part needed. When he left, we watched him from the window as he walked down the street and we all said, "He's got it." '

What he got was the biggest cult job in film history. But other actors had been considered. James Mason, for one, had thought the part was his, complete with a fee that Saltzman and Broccoli had decided was outrageous and a guarantee that he would not be required to star in more than two Bond pictures. It was this second condition that the producers said was unacceptable, although in truth they were more worried about the fees demanded. No one really thought there would be more than two pictures in any case.

If not Mason, it could have been David Niven, who quite clearly most resembled the Fleming Bond image – except for his failings in the muscle department. Other names mentioned included Trevor Howard and Richard Burton, both of whom could have satisfied most requirements. Another suggestion was Rex Harrison, but there was always the risk he would turn Bond into a Professor Higgins look-alike, and the idea of 007 wearing a tweed hat and muttering things about the rain in Spain may not have done the trick.

There was talk for a time of making Bond an American, but after the *Casino Royale* television fiasco, that wasn't pursued too avidly. And there was also another handsome young actor whose name cropped up – a man who had already played a second-division Bond type in a popular British television series, *The Saint*. His name was Roger Moore. Ian Fleming had casting approval, and Moore fulfilled one of his principal requirements: that the part should go to a relatively unknown actor. But Saltzman and Broccoli were equally insistent that Connery was the man they wanted – and, they decided, he was *almost* unknown. They said it tongue-in-cheek: had they been told to look for an easily recognisable face, they could have justified that, too.

Connery was told he had the job – despite the fact that he was not a little different from the Fleming ideal. Ian Fleming's main problem was that he didn't see Connery as the star; he wanted Niven. But he came round to the idea of Connery. His later description of the attributes that got Sean into Bond's shoes explains a lot. 'His height and bearing, graceful panther-like walk, the warm voice still retaining its Scots burr and his faintly rebellious air were impressive.'

Even so, he was eventually asked to do a screen test after all, – having already been told the job was his. The test wasn't for him, he was assured, but to help with the selection of his leading lady. What he didn't know was that United Artists were unhappy with Sean as James and that about twenty other actors were being auditioned.

The test merely confirmed the belief of both producers that they were on to a good thing. None of the other actors measured up to Sean Connery. The only problem was that United Artists still didn't agree. A telegram from the company's New York office said tersely: 'SEE IF YOU CAN DO BETTER.'

It was a devastating response. Charles (Jerry) Juroe, who was to become chief European publicist for the Bond films, thought differently from the United Artists executives. 'I remember seeing that screen test and thinking: this is a very ballsy guy. Among British actors it wasn't a quality many seemed to have. They had a much more gentlemanly approach.'

Saltzman and Broccoli knew the answer to the United Artists telegram: they couldn't do better. Nor were they going to try. There comes a stage, once all the other considerations have been made, when one has to go by instincts and gut reactions. The new picture was going to be *Dr No*. The star would be Sean Connery.

Wolf Mankowitz was pleased with the choice as he set about writing the script. (In the end, the writers credited would be Richard Maibaum, who wrote many of the later Bond movies, Johanna Harwood and Berkeley Mather.) 'I thought Connery was a likeable enough chap, but not someone you could get very close to. He was a very cold character who kept his business to himself. It wasn't necessary to throw one's personality around in those days. And I think he was right. It was good for his mystique.'

Broccoli agreed with Juroe's recollection about Sean being 'a ballsy guy,' and long before that phrase became common usage, he expected Sean to prove it on screen. But before doing so, Sean was going to prove it to the media.

He started giving detailed interviews about himself and about Bond. Some of them caused quite a stir. He discussed with the American-born writer Susan Barnes – later to marry the future Labour Foreign Secretary Anthony Crosland – his notions about hitting women. The interview, published in the London *Sunday Express*, would haunt him for years. But then Bond was part sadist and anyone who knew anything about Ian Fleming's character would know he wasn't one to shrink at the idea of striking a pretty girl.

It didn't matter, Sean said, if he hit a woman who annoyed him. 'An open-handed slap is justified. So is putting your hand over her mouth.'

He was, he told Barnes, a man of passion and, despite Bond's reputation, not a sadist who calculated how much he could hurt a woman.

In her article Susan Barnes gave the impression of a slight frisson between them.

She quoted his saying: 'When thinking is removed, the result is passion so pure that it becomes a matter of life and death. That's why a little mouse of a wife is able to put the breadknife in her husband's chest.'

He demonstrated to her how hard a man could punch. ' "A right to

the solar plexus" – one great fist smashed through the air – "a left to
the jaw that sends her halfway across the room!" – a left fist was driven
so close to my own jaw that I scrunched a little lower onto my couch.'

Soon, he was asking her: 'Are you in love at the moment?'

She reported: 'I concentrated on finishing my notes on the knife in
the husband's chest and then, monosyllabically, answered the question.

' "You see," said Mr Connery, the vertical grooves in his face deep-
ening into a grin, "you used your defence mechanisms just then. You
didn't bat an eyelash and you carefully finished writing down your
sentence before you answered me. I think you are very mobile." '

Then came the moment of truth in Sean's St John's Wood mews
house. 'I was wondering just now,' he put to her, 'what you would do
if I walked across the room and kissed you.'

She remembered: 'I asked Mr Connery if he would mind very
much testing his feminine mobility theories on somebody else. He
shrugged, took a swallow of vodka and continued.'

He told her that one of the first reactions of what he considered a
mobile person was to cross their legs. 'I glanced down and to my
chagrin I observed I was sitting with my legs crossed.

' "That is a binding movement," Mr Connery went on, looking
enormously pleased with himself and taking another hefty swallow of
vodka. "If you are attracted to someone you sit like *this*," Mr Connery
leaned forward, his knees apart, his hands outspread.'

She went on: 'It is possible I had begun to look a little tense. In any
case, Mr Connery reseated himself on his couch and reverted to the
subject of mobility in women. "Mobility," he said, "leads to adap-
tability, mobile women can be serene, too." '

Looking back on that confrontation some thirty-two years later, I
asked the writer for her reactions to that 1961 interview. Was she as
intimidated by him as she appeared?

'I think it was just that I often took the mickey out of myself and
gave the impression that I was a little bit alarmed about him,' she told
me. 'But I liked him and found him quite affable. I didn't really feel
intimidated by him. I think actually he was teasing me in a macho way
which in the 1960s didn't seem all that unusual to a young woman. It
was just par for the course. All I can remember all those years back
was having amiable feelings for Sean Connery after that interview.

'He certainly kept one on one's toes, and he had a striking, distinctly
macho presence.'

He told her he liked her because she was feminine, 'and all feminine
women are adaptable'. She laughs at the memory now.

Sean wasn't quite as convinced as to the wisdom of becoming James

Bond as he made out. He worried he would become typecast by the part, to say nothing of his desire to show he was a 'serious' actor.

He talked it over with Diane and she had no doubt about the answer: he had to take the part. 'If it were not for me,' she went on record as saying, 'Sean might never have become James Bond.'

But the fact that he did so had more than a little to do with his attitude to the project. What Sean had to realise was that the spoof character he was about to play wasn't just something to do for a laugh. Almost like John Wayne in a Western, the only way it would work would be to take it very seriously indeed – as seriously as the United Artists bankers took the opportunity to invest their million dollars.

Broccoli and Saltzman chose Terence Young to direct *Dr No*. Young was a reliable enough director with some interesting credits to his name but very little, if anything, that was spectacular.

He had started out in the film business in 1939 as a screenplay writer and his first directing job was *Corridor Of Mirrors* in 1948. Three years later, he directed the Parachute Regiment's favourite movie *The Red Beret* for Broccoli and two years after that co-directed *Storm Over The Nile*, a not too successful remake of the classic story *The Four Feathers*. He seemed happiest with pictures that had a theme of war – any war. *They Were Not Divided* about the advance on Berlin was another of his pictures that connoisseurs will recall without flinching.

Sean might also have remembered *Action Of The Tiger* and Young's promise to make it up to him. Now was his chance.

Saltzman and Broccoli chose Young to direct the picture because he came fairly cheap as far as front-line directors were concerned. But there turned out to be another, more important reason. He was a smartly-dressed Englishman (nothing too showy but with an under-stated elegance, even when working in casual clothes on the set) who could get away with playing Bond himself.

Indeed, Young decided to make James Bond in his own image. He saw Connery's potential immediately. Sean was going to get £7,000 for his role: he was going to be a star on a featured player's salary. People earning that sort of money weren't usually going to cause trouble when given instructions by a director.

Once Young was convinced Sean Connery had both the physical presence and the acting ability, he started playing Pygmalion. He prescribed a short haircut; Sean's eyebrows were trimmed; his voice was given a dose of elocution training – the accent was still there but you could no longer cut it with a knife.

When Sean had worn a dinner jacket in one of his earlier black-and-white films, he had looked at best like a trainee cinema manager, at worst like the dancehall bouncer he really had once been. Now the silk lapels and braided trousers seemed to belong to a man who wore them every evening of his life.

The director made it clear from the outset what he expected of Bond, which was why he took Sean to his own Savile Row tailor. Only there and at his shirtmaker's in St James's could he be satisfactorily kitted out for the role. If clothes make any man, they were certainly making this one. The clothes set the tone and the pattern for Bond's whole character.

Ken Adam was the production designer on *Dr No*. Today, with his slight German accent, his closely-cropped grey hair and tanned appearance, he could play a Bond villain himself any time he wanted to move to the other side of the camera. He sits behind a big desk, chomping on a huge cigar, sipping a glass of whisky. All that is missing is the purring white cat.

Like others working on the movie, Adam saw Terence Young as having the strongest influence of all on Sean. 'It became a big challenge to mould this rather simple Scotsman into this sophisticated character,' he recalled for me. 'It was really a part in which he had to be coached on *Dr No*. But it was obvious he was taking to it like a fish to water.' It wasn't just the visits to the tailors and shirtmakers that Young took it upon himself to organise. Like a girl at some fashionable finishing school, Sean Connery had to be given lessons on the finer things of life. Young schooled the ex-milkman in the correct table manners to use when he went out to dinner, not merely to pass the port to the left but which knife to use for what and how to talk across a table without disturbing the other dinner guests. It was as basic as that.

'Terence,' said Adam, 'who always had a certain panache – he had been in the Guards in the Second World War – took to him so that, in a way, Sean became his baby. It was like a father–son relationship.'

Sean took to it, too – not like some everyday fish to water, but more like a salmon to the North Atlantic. It was a giant move and he plunged in with all his senses and nerve endings working. As Ken Adam told me, he seemed to enjoy every moment of it. The rough diamond liked becoming a sophisticate.

Not that Sean had dressed like a labourer before being given the Young treatment. 'In his own way, he was quite well dressed,' Ken Adam's wife Letizia remembered. 'But Terence Young changed his image completely.' When you saw him drive the famous Bond Aston Martin, no one for one moment would have imagined that this was a man who had once travelled to London on a beaten-up motorbike and who had gone to the local library on his bicycle.

Sean not only looked right sipping those Martinis; he gave the impression of having done so since attaining the legal age for drinking. Similarly, there was that ease with women. As he had told Susan Barnes, he didn't mind hitting them. Now, on screen, they existed in distinctly expendable quantities; he no more had any compunction in shooting a woman than he had in taking her to his bed. But he did so with impeccable manners. The man with the Beretta handgun could indeed sometimes look like a sadist, but only one who said 'please' and 'thank you'.

As for the gab, this was a man with the gift for it. Those tones that had been so refined were ideally suited for the soothing words extended to the office secretary, Miss Moneypenny. They were never better than when he introduced himself to the lovely Honey Ryder, played by Ursula Andress.

Terence Young realised very early on that in Sean Connery he had found his perfect James Bond. But what nobody else could have understood at that stage was that Sean was not just finding a new role for himself, he was creating a whole new phenomenon and with it a new kind of mystique. 'My name's Bond ... James Bond,' he said as he lit a cigarette.

The pattern for all the other Bond movies to follow was established from the start: the throbbing title music and the white dots running across the screen in the credits sequence; the gun sight in which Bond appears, fires ... and as the title is revealed, the screen turns red.

There were to be other rules for the James Bond film. Firstly, despite all his, shall we say, unsporting behaviour, Bond had to be seen to be the representative of the good guys. The British maintained a stiff upper lip and were always a force for good. If Sean Connery couldn't demonstrate that fact, he was no James Bond. He made it abundantly clear from the opening frame of *Dr No* – the story of the disappearance of an agent in Jamaica which Bond is sent to investigate – that he was, in the end, on *your* side.

Another rule set down by Terence Young – a keen James Bond reader and fan of practically everything Fleming ever wrote – was to be more readily discarded in future.

He wanted the film of *Dr No* to follow the novel closely, and it did. Characters like Sylvia Trench (played by the beautiful Eunice Gayson) and Felix Liter (Jack Lord) were regarded as essential ingredients because Fleming had laid down that they were, but they and others became more easily expendable as the series progressed.

The talk around Pinewood studios was that this was a picture on which a great deal had been lavished, such as exciting gadgets, impressive-looking sets and the odd trip to Jamaica. But nobody was going to be allowed to go beyond that one million pound budget.

Nor was anybody willing to forecast how good it was all going to be or how much money it was going to make. Sean Connery was seen around the studio, walking across the car park, eating with other members of the company in the commissary. But nobody thought he was going to be a big star. They heard he was making £7,000 and that was thought to be about right. But consider him a strong commodity? Few did.

There were, however, the odd people in the business who thought otherwise. One of them was Michael Winner, then at the beginning of his burgeoning career as a maverick director.

It was 1962, long, before the successful *Death Wish* movies that were to make Winner's own name and fortune. He was making a never-to-be-remembered film called *West Eleven*, about the offer of £10,000 to a 'drifter' to commit a murder by contract. The director, who still thinks that the picture written by Keith Waterhouse and Willis Hall was a very good one, decided that the young Sean would be ideal as the hired gunman.

His producer Daniel M. Angel, however, thought otherwise. 'No,' said Angel, 'he's just a B-picture actor. You can't use him.'

It was one of the producer's less prescient decisions. 'He also said,' Winner told me, 'that Julie Christie was a B-picture actress and I couldn't use her, and that James Mason was a has-been actor and I couldn't use him.' That was one of the reasons why Winner decided before long to go it alone and become a producer himself. *West Eleven* had to content itself with the same Alfred Lynch whom Sean had studied so carefully just a picture earlier. The female lead was played by Kathleen Breck 'who hasn't been heard of since' and Eric Portman played the part Winner had in mind for James Mason.

Why did he think of Connery for the part? Winner still sees in Connery today the unique qualities that attracted his attention in 1962: 'You feel there is a great combination of sophistication and danger, roughness and integrity. It shines through all the time.'

It didn't shine through for Daniel M. Angel, however. He had only read about James Bond in the trade papers. He was too clever to believe all the hype coming out of Pinewood. Every time someone mentioned Sean Connery, out came that same dismissive phrase about him being a B-actor.

In his more contemplative moments, Sean himself wondered why he got the Bond part.

'Nobody is more surprised than I am,' he said, 'although I suppose it had to happen sooner or later.' That, in a statement to the *Saturday Evening Post* magazine, was a monumental piece of immodesty from a man whose reputation, such as it was, was of someone who seemed content to take life as it came and never blew his own trumpet.

Asked to assess his views of the role, Sean could get serious – providing he wasn't talking to a pretty girl like Susan Barnes, who would divert him onto the subject of woman-bashing. 'I see Bond as a complete sensualist,' he told one interviewer. 'His senses are tightly tuned and he's awake to everything . . . I particularly like him because he thrives on conflict – a quality lacking in present-day society.'

The *Daily Express* asked him about being 'tagged' as Bond. They obviously knew what had been worrying Connery. Sean feigned not to be worried. 'I suppose I would have been if I hadn't done a lot of other things,' he said. Alas for him, they were words to be wrapped up, put away and then eaten.

Playing Bond, he had to synthesise this man who was both irresistibly sexy to women and able to adopt without compunction a fiendish brutality that wasn't always quite as British as his motives – which were never in question.

His relationship with Miss Andress was equally certain. Playing the daughter of a marine biologist killed by the villain, Dr No (Joseph Wiseman), she has to be rescued before she is bedded.

The scene where she appears from out of the surf, the water clinging revealingly to her white bikini, will never be forgotten by the Bond *aficionado*. With a dagger at her hip, and pouting her lips in readiness to sing 'Underneath The Mango Tree', she looked possibly even more alluring than she would have done naked. It is one of the all-time great moments in the kind of cinema that doesn't take itself too seriously. She was Venus in a role that Botticelli himself could never have contemplated.

Sean liked Ursula Andress. In fact, he was to say that she would remain forever his favourite Bond Girl.

But Sean liked to say he was more interested in his work. He was the one who seemed to be calling the shots. Even when in a short-sleeved shirt he wrapped his muscular arms (allowed to suggest rather than show in detail the tattoos) around Miss Andress's stunning figure barely covered by a wet blouse as they stood waist-high in the water, it was clear that Bond was intended to be the sexiest person in the movie.

There were stories among those working on the set of *Dr No* that an affair was going on between the two stars. It was the talk of the studio – particularly in the 'fringe' departments like the hairdressing and makeup rooms where gossip always thrived. The rumours became even more credible in their view when the actor John Derek, then Ursula's husband, made a surprise visit to the set in Jamaica.

Not everyone knew about his life with Diane Cilento. 'He kept his private life very much to himself,' recalled Wolf Mankowitz. 'It always seemed to me to be a kind of *sub rosa* relationship.'

The backdrop for *Dr No* was perfect, especially the part made in Jamaica which Sean enjoyed thoroughly. It was Fleming's turf, and Terence Young, via Connery and Andress, made it Bond's, too.

It appears they got on well enough, this Bond and his creator. Sean, for his part, thought the writer was a 'terrible snob', but he liked the stories which Fleming was weaving about himself. Was it true that Fleming had actually got into the Kremlin and met Stalin? He claimed that he had. The mere telling of a story like that had much to commend it.

Certainly Fleming got on better with Sean than he did with the film's director. He was convinced that Terence Young was going to 'fuck up' his story. But since Young was so like Bond himself he replied in kind, saying something like 'nothing Fleming wrote was exactly immortal'.

The one thing Sean couldn't get out of his mind was the way his life had changed. One minute he was wondering if he would ever get away from those small, unimportant roles, the next he was being invited to lunch by Fleming himself – a wonderful chance to observe the table manners the writer had quite assuredly given Bond. 'It's funny about heads and tails,' he said. From that moment on, the coin was quite definitely spinning to land on heads.

That it did so was also the triumph of Terence Young. Recalled Ken Adam for me : 'He was never loutish. In my opinion, he is an extremely sensitive person, which is why he is such a good actor.'

Offscreen at Kingston, Sean broadened his social life to an extent none of the regulars at any of the Fountainbridge pubs would have thought possible. Not only did he dine with Ian Fleming, he was being invited to dinner by Fleming's best friend and neighbour in Jamaica, Noël Coward, wearing his velvet dinner jacket and smoking a cigarette through a holder – a pose that tickled Connery's fancy more than he liked to admit.

There had at one time been talk of Coward taking the role of Dr

No himself, but he decided against it. Sean always thought it was a decision 'the Master' later regretted.

Coward and Connery analysed the Bond character – Coward said he was a snob, which fitted in perfectly with Sean's conclusion about Bond's creator.

They liked each other, and struck up an improbable friendship : the son of a working-class couple from Edinburgh and the sophisticate who didn't always like to remember that he was born in Teddington, Middlesex. Sean was invited to dinner at Coward's house more than once – but the dinner he remembers most was the night he and Chris Blackwell, head of Island Records, went there after filming in the nearby bauxite mines. They arrived at the house covered in red dust. Coward was playing his grand piano. He called out to them, 'Come in, dear boys,' and continued with his piano playing – accompanying his own LP of the Coward 'live' act at Las Vegas.

When the two visitors had washed and brushed themselves up, they returned to the great presence – still accompanying himself. Later, they would meet in London ; Sean visiting Coward at his suite at the Savoy and then being taken by him to see the latest Danny La Rue show.

One thing about Sean becoming James Bond worried him more than it concerned the producers. He was losing so much hair that he now appeared to be more balding than just thin on top – a family affliction that had affected both his father and, of course, his grandfather, 'Baldy'. Sean was already spending more money than he could afford on so-called 'special' treatments, but they were having no more effect on him than any doctor would have predicted.

What concerned him was the scar on his pate caused by the accident with the 'coffin'. The producers decided that Bond would simply have to wear a toupee. He accepted his new 'rug' as he accepted the suits he had to wear in the picture.

But it didn't make him like the situation any more. As he later said, 'It was a nightmare. I thought : How can I live like this ?' In part, he couldn't – and didn't. The toupee might have been *de rigueur* on the set, but it wasn't at home. Nothing was going to persuade him to adopt the hairpiece in his private life.

It worried him a great deal, Letizia Adam recalled. It was one 'weakness' in Sean that was open for all to see.

Just the same, the people working with him on the *Dr No* set had plenty of time to assess the kind of person this Sean Connery really was. Some of them, like Ken Adam, had known him before. Adam, the designer whose mind's eye saw not just the exotic locations that were going to be used, but the internal sets – from the swish offices and super-super luxury hotel suites to the vast underground and underwater laboratories and bomb factories – that were to be as much a trade mark of the Bond film as the girls and the guns, decided that Connery, a man of whom he was very fond, was 'a black-and-white character'. As he explained, 'That was what appealed to me about Sean. Black *was* black and white *was* white. There were no greys. In a way, there was no sophistication. He was very straight in his viewpoints and very honest in what he had to say about anything – or anyone. There was nothing superficial about him. Incredibly good looking and very much a man's man. He was obviously very successful with women but I think he felt more at home in a man's environment.'

Connery was not, despite the opportunites he had available to him, a flirtatious person. Nevertheless, he loved kidding around. 'There was always an atmosphere of teasing, of practical jokes.'

Women had discovered that about him before. Now it was put to the test and, the stories about Ursula Andress apart, Diane would have been pleased to know that on this picture he was keeping his reputation. He wasn't openly flirting with the girls. In the evenings after the day's shooting was done, he seemed content enough to go drinking with the cameramen and other technicians.

In doing so, Sean was immediately fitting in with what was a very British institution. In Hollywood big stars – and those who thought they were going to be big, even if they weren't so already – tended to stick together to the exclusion of 'lower' people in the business. But in Britain there was still the hangover of the Buxton Club mentality.

The Buxton Club was the name given to a 1950s gathering of promising young men in the film industry, men who would meet over a drink to discuss their progress and lack of money. In that era of the British motion picture industry, there was much to talk about, most of it optimistic.

Adam had been a member of that set as had other set designers and technicians. So had people like Richard Attenborough, Stanley Baker, Peter O'Toole, Michael Caine, Terence Stamp and Bryan Forbes. 'Everyone who was involved in the making of black-and-white films was there.'

All that set, recalled Adam, welcomed the arrival of Sean Connery in their midst. As he had said, he was a man's man and this was a male-dominated group. 'They liked the fact that there were no frills about him. He never played studio politics either.' That meant that in those early Bond days he was not continually fighting the system.

Things would change. But it also meant that he wasn't automatically thrust into a particular camp. While he was not being denied the fascination of bitching about producers and their appendages, there was no danger in having him around either. The lowest 'best boy' or 'gaffer' could depend on Sean Connery being on his side – if justice was, too.

The remnant of the Buxton group were used to 'hanging out' together, and now Sean was not only agreeing to join them, he was revelling in it. 'We became great friends because we really all grew up together.'

There was no question that he *was* a man's man, but women appreciated him even without a sexual connotation. Letizia Adam told me about him: 'We liked him because he was always so straight and so masculine, but also because he was very vulnerable.'

That could have been why Diane took to him so easily.

Ken Adam was convinced there was another reason for Sean's getting on so well with Ms Cilento. He was the sort of man attracted to likes, not opposites. 'She is also a very black-and-white person. They could communicate with each other. Also, she didn't want anything from Sean.'

'I really loved him,' Letizia explained. There were no complications. 'I am not sure how he would have reacted to me if I had not been a mate, you know, if I had not been Ken's wife. He treated me as a chum. I was very much pro him. I would tell him if his hair wasn't right – I won't mention the other word – and he appreciated it.'

Diane certainly didn't seem to mind. She was, nevertheless, keeping to herself – and to Sean – just how close their relationship was. She had obtained a divorce and now she and Sean had decided to get married. Even if they hadn't been totally in love with each other – which they were – the mores of the day would have indicated that they should do so. Diane was pregnant. But she wasn't telling anyone about it or about their plans.

The only other people who did know were the two sets of parents – the aristocratic Cilentos in New York and the Connerys in Edinburgh. Sean took her to the Fountainbridge apartment amid fears that she and the family would not go together at all well. The concern was unfounded. Diane, having decided that she was marrying Sean and not Joe or Effie – who she seems to have liked enormously – and was going to live in London, not in an Edinburgh near-slum, was delighted with the welcome she received in her fiancé's home environment.

For the moment, nothing was going to be said to anyone else. There were more pressing matters with which they had to deal.

Bond's already considerable cult status was helped in no small way by word getting out from the White House that one of 007's most devoted fans was President John F. Kennedy. That was not a recommendation to be taken lightly and the studio made the most of it.

Even while *Dr No* was still in production, the sales operation for the film, to say nothing of the promotion of James Bond and of Sean himself, was getting into full swing. Connery was pressed into performing all the celebrity PR stunts that had previously seemed to be of little importance.

Stories were circulated about his past successes (why else cast him as James Bond?). He had, Weston Taylor reported in the *News of the World*, turned down opportunities to play the television title roles in both *Wyatt Earp* and *Maverick*. He rejected them, said Mr Taylor, because he was the kind of actor who preferred to work indoors. It must have escaped the writer's notice that he was also the kind of actor who preferred to act – doing almost anything apart from polishing coffins or posing virtually nude for female art students.

Because of the paper's strip-cartoon serialisation, the readers of the *Daily Express* who considered they had a proprietorial interest in everything that appeared in *their* paper (such was the power of the *Express* in those days) watched the progress of filming very closely. What they read about Sean Connery they liked.

The success of the Bond film was particularly important for the Express group. If the picture was a success, it boded well for the circulation of their papers and the Bond strip which would then be worth considerably more than they had contracted to pay for it.

In the *Sunday Express* Sean gave his own idea of what the part of Bond represented. 'Like some other people in the northern countries, James Bond is very much for breaking the rules,' he declared. 'He enjoys freedoms that the normal person doesn't get. He likes to eat. He likes to drink. He likes his girls. He is rather cruel, sadistic. He takes in a big percentage of the fantasies of lots of people – although it's difficult to get many of them to admit they'd like to be Bond. I have no compunction at all about admitting that I like to eat, I like to drink, I like girls.'

And he couldn't avoid getting back to that business about hitting women: 'I don't think there's anything very wrong about hitting a woman. I don't, though, recommend hitting a woman the way you hit a man.' He did not elaborate.

There was no evidence of that attitude on the set of *Dr No*. 'There was that great charm,' recalled Ken Adam. 'We all saw it.'

What they also all saw, thirty years before he was to make what was almost a professional political stand, was his intense commitment to Scottish nationalism. It was not yet a serious political movement, but had it been so, he gave every impression of being ready to stand for Parliament.

'It was so obvious,' said Adam, 'that he was first and foremost a Scotsman.'

Sean was soon mouthing all the ungrateful things big stars are supposed to say. Press agents? They were 'manipulating parasites' who created monstrous images. That is not how *his* (or rather Eon's) European press agent at the time remembers it.

Charles (Jerry) Juroe was the official publicist for the Bond films – indeed, he has only just retired from the job and is still retained by the Broccoli organisation as a consultant.

Juroe was engaged to make Sean Connery seem as much James Bond as Bond was Connery – at least, that is the way the producers wanted people to see it. Broccoli and Saltzman knew they had a product that needed to be sold. Once the novelty of talking to people like Susan Barnes and the other more attractive columnists had worn off, this was one part of the selling operation that stuck in Sean's throat. He did not want to be a salesman and didn't enjoy the salesmen's pitches of which he had to be the central attraction.

Jerry Juroe saw it all. 'At the beginning it was all the kind of thing you would do for almost any picture. At that stage, we didn't know what was going to happen later on and it was just another film.'

But Saltzman and Broccoli had other ideas and, as a result, Sean was subjected to the press conferences, the publicity stunts – many of which he refused to do – and the phoney picture sessions, of which there would be many more in the years to come. But already they wanted him photographed playing games he didn't want to play and had never played in real life, and photographed in 'homes' in which he never lived.

'Despite the assumption that this was just another film, everyone in Europe thought that *Dr No* was something rather special,' said Jerry Juroe.

The excitement generated within United Artists was so great that another $100,000 was added to the $900,000 budget – principally to be spent on jazzing up the ending with what has now become the Bond tradition: the violent explosion that seemed to indicate the dropping of a nuclear bomb. When that sort of financial investment is made, still more money has to be spent on publicity in an attempt to recoup the enormous outlay.

The problem was that Sean let them know how unhappy he was

with it all. He was a private person and intended to remain so. 'But he certainly went along with everything I asked him to do in the first film,' said Juroe.

And yet, despite the publicity, despite the finesse, United Artists were not impressed with the final print. The story got around that they hated the picture. Even Saltzman and Broccoli weren't all that sure. After seeing a preview, Broccoli is reputed to have said that the best thing about the film was that no one was going to lose more than one million dollars – perhaps less.

The studio delayed its release for months. At length, they agreed to a sneak preview of *Dr No* in California, one of those masochistic occasions during which studio executives who are not already suffering from ulcers spend a whole evening taking pills to avoid developing them.

They shuffled in their seats at the preview theatre outside Pasadena in California, watching the public's reaction. (Jack Warner, the most famous of the Warner Brothers, used to judge a film's success or failure by the number of times members of the audience left their seats to go to the lavatory. 'It's no good,' he said once. 'This is a two-piss picture.')

Eventually, the time came to read the cards which had been so assiduously completed by the people who had been the first to see *Dr No* in America.

One by one, the cards piled up and one by one the cards showed that the audience enjoyed every moment of the movie. The one word that seems to have cropped up more than any other was 'wonderful'.

When the film did eventually open at the London Pavilion, the critics were enchanted. 'Sean Connery,' wrote the same *News of the World* which had firmly believed he had rejected international television stardom, 'fits Fleming's hero like a Savile Row suit.' And the most important statement of all was left for the last line. 'This new screen hero will be around a long time.' Rarely have words in a popular newspaper been more prescient.

The film itself was 'great stuff, magnificent mayhem'.

The audiences clearly thought so. Now, all over the world, in virtually all the places on which James Bond himself would call as easily as a commercial traveller covering his sales territory, people were saying the same thing.

As a result, the publicity budget was increased still further and Sean Connery, *aka* James Bond, was brought in to do more of the work that the 'parasites' were demanding. Jerry Juroe insists Sean gave no trouble. In fact, he told me, 'On *Dr No* he couldn't have been more co-operative.'

He voiced no complaints about the problem which even then was raising its head in a lot of people's minds, once it was realised that there would be another James Bond picture after *Dr No* – the problem that James Mason said had bothered him so much: type casting. 'You never heard anything derogatory either in private or in public from him then,' said the publicist.

They went to Italy on what was perhaps Connery's first ever publicity junket out of the United Kingdom. This was old-fashioned bang-the-drum stuff: Sean, the publicity man and three girls – a blonde, a brunette and a redhead. 'The suggestion was that James Bond never travelled without a complete set.'

It turned into one of the most amazingly successful stunts of all time, the kind of campaign that, had such things existed, would have figured in the curriculum of an army-type staff college of budding publicists. And like the best campaigns, it was very, very simple.

Sean, looking for all the world like James Bond with his three women, all dressed (or almost undressed) to look like Bond Girls, went to a casino, played the tables and, as he stood by the roulette wheel, his Bond hairpiece in place, his dinner jacket immaculately pressed, he won. Won so much, in fact, that he virtually broke the bank.

Now, that in itself, was impressive. But it was *how* he won that money that monopolised the headlines in virtually every newspaper in every country where *Dr No* was either playing or about to do so. He used, he said, the same system as Bond used in *Dr No*. Ian Fleming backed him up. It was a plan he had developed for himself years before and one he still used every time he went into a casino, rarely coming out the loser. But there had never been a win of this size before.

A couple of papers smelled rats, and said that it couldn't be proved that the win was genuine, but the casino seemed to think that it was. They were happy to leave things like that. Today Jerry Juroe admits, 'It was a complete phoney. We had bruising types hanging all over the place, so that it looked real. But it was great publicity for the film. It was great publicity for Sean and it was great publicity for the casino.'

Once the cameramen had snapped and gone home, the money went back whence it came.

Jerry Juroe found Sean an entertaining travelling companion. 'But it was the sheer fun of having this much excitement created merely by the presence of the actor that made it not just an ordinary publicity tour.'

They travelled by train and car down the length of the boot of Italy, visiting Turin, Rome, Milan and Bologna. 'It was very nice. We'd have sing-alongs on the way.'

There were no restrictions on the trip placed by Sean himself. They got up early and went to bed late. 'I found it very hard keeping up with him. We ate and drank very well.'

They also went to several football matches. 'He loved soccer,' said Jerry Juroe, perhaps not knowing about the Busby connection. 'I think the high point of our trip was when we went to a match between AC Milan and the other Milan team – he just loved that. We sat in the box of the owner.'

And there were moments of down-to-earth reality. 'You could talk to him in a very businesslike manner. You didn't have to explain it in a way that showed you were concerned about his ego being crushed. You could be extremely frank with him – something you couldn't do with all actors.'

Forewarned about certain journalists, Sean was prepared for difficult or stupid questions and reacted, for the most part, without any petulance.

Back in London, there was another part of the game which he accepted willingly. He went to restaurants with the publicist and when people approached him for autographs he gave them. 'I don't think he got a particular kick out of it, but he responded graciously because he thought it came with the territory.'

Before long it seemed people considered any interruption of his 'private' life a territorial demand, and he would be less willing to respond.

The most important review as far as the cinema trade was concerned appeared in what was still called the showbiz 'Bible', *Variety*. If *Variety* liked a product, the business would go out of its way to sell it.

Variety was ecstatic. '*Dr No* is a high-powered melodrama that crackles with intrigue and suspense and sizzles with romance. There is even some humour of a respectable level to lighten the mixture. The movie has no high-powered names [which shows the effect Sean Connery himself had had up to then on the box office] but this won't matter. *Dr No* is a perfect picture of its special kind and exactly fits that often cited but generally misunderstood catagory, "pure entertainment".'

In *Esquire* magazine, the political analyst and academic Arthur M. Schlesinger wrote an adulatory piece about the film's significance and confirmed John F. Kennedy's fondness for it. Since Schlesinger was part of the Kennedy set, his words were seen as coming with the authority of the White House. Quite clearly, going to see the movie was now as sociably acceptable as it was for women to wear copies of Jackie's pillbox hats.

It was said that because of that sort of social cachet, Allen Dulles, head of the CIA, consulted Ian Fleming on the agency's next moves on Cuba. How would James Bond have tackled the job of getting Fidel Castro out of the way?

Writing in the *New York World Telegram*, Bernard O'Hanlon said that Connery fitted the Bond part like a glove. 'He is more than sufficiently handsome and virile. He wears his clothes elegantly. He talks with a suave mid-Atlantic accent.'

Unless Mr O'Hanlon had seen a specially-dubbed version of the film, this review shows just how effective Sean's performance had been. That accent still had very definite Scottish nuances, but they could have been said to have fitted very well into his Fettes College background. But the fact that this was not obvious says a very great deal about the strength of his performance.

The effect that Bond had on both the male and female members of his audiences was overwhelming. They jumped into falling-apart second- and third-hand roadsters and pretended they were driving Bond's Aston Martin. Boys took girls into their arms and imagined that the twinkle in their eyes resembled Bond's. In Edinburgh and other parts of Britain, they were ordering their usual pints of beer and joking to the barmaids that they wanted them shaken and not stirred.

As for the women, they *were* both shaken *and* stirred. Sean Connery was the hero of the hour, the sexiest thing they had seen on screen to date and they didn't need a newspaper columnist to tell them so.

It was like the early 1940s when the young Frank Sinatra had girls lining up for his performances, sitting in their seats all day, beside themselves with excitement. Now their daughters were doing the same for Sean Connery.

Albert Broccoli now knew why Connery had been the right choice. 'The difference with this guy is the difference between a still photograph and film. When he starts to move, he comes alive.'

Broccoli was doing all he could to make Connery both move and come alive. But Sean still couldn't quite understand why it took all that time to happen. 'If America had been discovered as many times as I have, no one would remember Columbus.'

His life was changing. But the Connery family made it clear that they weren't going to allow it to change that much. When *Dr No* had its Scottish première in Edinburgh, Sean called in at the Fountainbridge tenement as soon as he arrived in the city. He was greeted by his father. 'Hello, Tam,' said Joe, 'Have you been away?'

The comment was designed to bring Sean down to earth with a thud. It could well have helped him as he took stock of what the future held for him. What was he looking for? Certainly success in the film business. That did not mean, however, that he wanted to be, as certain writers were now suggesting, the new Cary Grant or even the next Clark Gable.

'I suppose more than anything else,' the now 32-year-old actor said at this time, 'I'd like to be an old man with a good face. Like Hitchcock or Picasso. They've worked hard all their lives, but there's nothing weary about them. They never wasted a day with the sort of nonsense that clutters up a life. They know that life is not just a bloody popularity contest.'

There was a germ of something there: Sean was anxious that people realised he was not just a fly-by-night discovery. 'When one does something that gets as much attention as Bond, the presumption is that you came from nowhere to do it,' he said. 'I have the feeling the legend is that I drove a truck into United Artists, smashed somebody on the head, dragged Cubby Broccoli up the street and said, "Make me Bond."'

Even so, he was not shying away from his Bond contract. He was grateful for it. And now, there was a new James Bond film in production to be called *From Russia With Love*. And the fan letters poured in, from America with love, from Japan with love, from Italy with love, from Israel . . . and frequently promising a love that was extraordinarily physical even for what in those days was called a man of the world like him.

They offered love he was in no position to accept. Not that he had need of it – he and Diane were now what was called in the less discerning American press an 'item', and could afford to be so. In the new film, Sean would be making more money. Much more.

He had just moved from the mews home he and Julie had shared and had paid £9,000 for a much bigger house in the unfashionable West London suburb of Acton – a house recently vacated by twenty-five nuns from the Order of the Adoratrices. He was having builders in and the work was going to cost him another £9,000, the sort of figure that made people gasp in 1962.

Nobody seemed to have come to the obvious conclusion – that he was soon to bring someone there to share the house with him. But when he was asked to make the comments expected from a star surrounded by the most enticing female flesh assembled in one place for years, he behaved appropriately. As he said around about this time: 'Let no man say that a red-blooded Scot turns away from a beautiful woman's shape – beyond that I am being discreet.'

But the point of discretion was about to be changed. On 30 November 1962, Sean and Diane were married by special licence in Gibraltar. It was all very James Bondish, especially since in *From Russia With Love* he would fly to the continent . . . and marry in secret.

They chose the Rock because they didn't think that, following the enormous success of *Dr No*, they would get away with the kind of quiet ceremony they wanted in London.

Not that it all went so smoothly in Gibraltar either. Sean waited for Diane on the quayside – while she was waiting in mainland Spain for her passport. It was at the height of the period when Britain and Francoist Spain were jostling for control of Gibraltar and every bureaucratic hurdle possible was placed in the way of people trying to move from one country to the other. When it was discovered that an immigration official at Algeciras had forgotten to stamp Diane's passport, she was made to wait for a new one for as long as suited the Spaniards' nationalistic prestige. By the time the required stamp was affixed, she had missed her ferry to Gibraltar. But the marriage ceremony eventually went ahead.

No one knew that a wedding was on the cards and the two witnesses at the Gibraltar register office, taxi drivers called Gonzalez and Garcia, didn't know who or what they were witnessing. The people at the Rock Hotel where the couple spent their wedding night knew a little more and found a way to tell the world before Diane and Sean crossed over into Spain for a honeymoon on the Costa del Sol, not at all the kind of place stars would choose for a holiday thirty years later. But then this was just one of the trends that Sean Connery was going to set. It was also the first inkling of the fact that Spain was going to be important for him.

Back from their honeymoon, they set up home in Sean's Acton house. Soon after their return, Sean reported to his friend Victor Spinetti that they were awoken by a noise of banging on their bedroom window. Someone was throwing stones. When he looked into the road below he saw it was a former girlfriend, still in love with him.

Sean and Diane were as happy as they thought they would be, which said a great deal. Diane's five-year-old daughter by her first marriage, Giovanna, lived with them.

As for Sean's career, he told the *Saturday Evening Post*, 'For now I'm reasonably content with what I'm doing. After all, I can kill any s.o.b. in the world and get away with it. I've got the powers of the greatest governments in the world behind me, I eat and drink nothing but the very best and I also get the loveliest ladies in the world.' You could almost believe him.

There weren't many star-like attributes about him yet, although he played more golf when he had the time. And he smoked, using a gold cigarette holder. This seems not to have been a Noël Coward-style affectation picked up casually in Kingston while on the *Dr No* location so much as a genuine belief that if he smoked through a holder the dangers to his health would be considerably reduced.

'I'm not James Bond,' he would protest, 'I'm Sean Connery, a serious actor.' Diane would have appreciated it if the serious actor could have joined her again in the cast of *Naked*, which was now moving to the West End. But he was just too busy.

From Russia With Love, complete with its Maurice Binder title sequence, its Aston Martin, its assassination gimmicks and its girls was even more successful than *Dr No* and was the picture that confirmed that this was now a series and nothing was going to stop it. The picture also confirmed that Sean Connery, serious actor, was also, without any doubt, a star.

But what made him so? It is not enough to surmise that women found him so sexy they were willing to drop all their inhibitions should he, in their wildest fantasies, have made the merest suggestion that he would be willing to take them on.

It was not even enough to say that it was because he was such a good actor. A thousand good actors could win prizes at drama school and never achieve stardom.

Of course, it had a great deal – a very great deal – to do with the way he communicated to an audience with a kind of celluloid chemistry nobody could possibly analyse. But even that is not enough. Nor is it sufficient to say that he was a combination of all these things. Much more, it was the simple fact that he *worked* at achieving all those things. It was as if he consciously stood by the kitchen range and stirred them all together.

What made Sean Connery a star was that when people saw *Dr No*, they couldn't wait to see him again. 'One of the Xiest pictures of all time,' declared *Films and Filming*. If 'X' meant 'O's on the cheques, it certainly was. In America alone, it took six million dollars – more than enough to justify a second picture.

From Russia With Love was about to satisfy not just the makers, but the audiences, too – until they were begging for more.

6

WITH LOVE –

AND A FEW PROBLEMS

From Russia With Love did all that anyone could have wanted it to do. The movie, about 007's personal war with an imaginary espionage–criminal organisation called SPECTRE, consummated the public's love affair with both Sean Connery and the Bond films. For the men and women lining up outside movie theatres, the two were interchangeable. Anyone else playing Bond would have been greeted with as many hoots of derision and disbelief as would a Santa Claus minus both a beard and his red cloak.

Unlike most sequels, the picture was a lot better than the original. The sets designed by Ken Adam were much more lavish, the costumes more extravagant. Sean himself was given a cheque for £1,000 to spend on his new Savile Row wardrobe. That was considered such a lot of money at the time that it, too, made the newspapers.

Terence Young insisted on the Savile Row 'investment', even if the stitching and cutting that went along with the labels inside the jackets would be lost on audiences who could have been fooled by a well-made outfit produced by a good local tailor or a branch of Marks & Spencer. But Young took the same attitude as had Florenz Ziegfeld when he insisted that the costumes worn by the girls in his 'Follies' shows should be made of the best silk and produced by the best couturiers – even if no one beyond the footlights could possibly notice. 'No,' said the man who inscribed the legend, 'under these portals walk the most beautiful girls in the world' over the stage door of his theatre, but I know – and they know.' Young thought Sean would feel more like James Bond if he dressed like James Bond.

For the same reason, all the gadgets handed to him by the Service's innovative expert Q, played by Desmond Llewellyn, had to work in real life. Those were the days before anyone had seen personal helicopters which resembled aerial bicycles or wristwatch radars or rocket-firing wheels on an Aston Martin – all of which would be expected in James Bond films from then on. As the films became more expensive, the gadgets became more audacious. But they did always have to work. Otherwise, it was argued, the screen Bond couldn't have felt quite so confident and quite so believable in front of the cameras.

Llewellyn, now approaching his eightieth birthday and ready for his next Bond film, established a character that played a brief but important part in the Bond film. Audiences waited expectantly for the moment when he would produce the slim attaché case (which was fascinating in itself) containing the latest equipment.

Q he became simply because Terence Young was worried about calling him by his full name, Major Boothroyd. There had been a Major Boothroyd in *Dr No*, but he had been played by Peter Burton. The director didn't think it would work to say, 'Send for Major Boothroyd,' and have a new face appear. Instead, although Boothroyd was officially still his name, M says: 'Ask the head of Q division to come in.'

From that moment on, Llewellyn was Q, and Q he remained, getting a little older in each film, no matter who was starring. But without him a Bond film would not have been complete.

It took two days to film Q's one and only scene in *From Russia With Love* – mainly because the briefcase and its gadgets *wouldn't* work at first. In real life, they had to go off instantly, and had there been those delays, James Bond would have been no more – without ever getting out of the Aston Martin.

In *From Russia With Love*, the attaché case contained twenty rounds of ammunition and fifty gold sovereigns, a knife that at the push of a button was released to do its worst and most deadly, a teargas bomb disguised as a tin of talcum powder (but guaranteed to explode if the case happened to be opened the wrong way), and the *pièce de résistance*: a folding sniper rifle with telescopic infra-red vision.

Another convention was Q's lack of patience. 'Do pay attention, Bond,' was almost as familiar a line as Sean's introduction, 'My name's Bond ...'

There was also irritation for Desmond Llewellyn himself. 'And that was because of Sean's acting. He *would* fiddle with all the gadgets, and since I myself didn't understand a word of what I was saying, it was very off-putting. I kept thinking: For God's sake, I wish he would stop fiddling so that I could remember my lines and what I am supposed to do. But he was absolutely in character and I think that helped.

'If it hadn't been for Sean, I don't think that Q would have been quite such an irascible character. For Sean used to give, you know, that insolence, an air of "couldn't care less". Sean's attitude was always, "For heaven's sake, get on with it. I want to go and have a drink." '

What was even more interesting was the effect that the role of Bond had on Sean's character. 'I had the feeling that even when filming had shut down for the day, Sean was continuing to play Bond. He looked like him and I think he behaved like him.'

But he was welcoming, too. 'I was invited to his table during lunch at Pinewood and we seemed to enjoy each other's company.' Llewellyn did not see it as a kind of *noblesse oblige* on Sean's part. It was just one symptom of the rapport among the company. 'Oh, Sean was a great mixer. I think, in fact, he was more at home with the technicians than he was with other actors.' Others have said the same.

Anna Korda, voice coach on the movie, remembered just what a good mixer he was. 'Actually,' she told me, 'I think I'm the only woman who ever turned down a pass from Sean. It happened in Istanbul, but when I rejected him, he was wonderful about it. He didn't persist and we became great friends.'

Once more, Sean's relationship with the *screen* Bond Girl was all that anyone could ask. Daniela Bianchi played the role of Tatiana Romanova, a cipher clerk who claims she is ready to defect and lures Bond to Istanbul to pick her up, only for him to find she has been not exactly on the level. It didn't really matter that Miss Bianchi was not much of an actress – what she was supposed to do, this former Miss Universe did. Daniela didn't quite reveal all and Sean's red-blooded seduction techniques were left largely to the imagination. You got the rough idea, but people who had heard of the director's search for accuracy might have considered the timely scene changes a little unfair.

Even in their lovemaking there was sufficient gimmickry to impress the gadget lover: in this case, a two-way mirror above their bed.

There was also just a smidgen of lesbianism to add spice to the dish and a whole thesaurus of *double entendres* that could have upset the censor had he only been more attentive. A classic line has Tatiana apologising for her small mouth, only to be told by Bond: 'It's the right size – for me, that is.'

An unexpected bonus was the casting of Lotte Lenya as the less-than-beautiful SPECTRE chief. The former wife of Kurt Weill, who had starred in his *Threepenny Opera*, took to the James Bond experience as the professional she was.

What made Lenya's role as Rosa Klebb so interesting was that she personified the conflict not just between SPECTRE and Bond but between SPECTRE and SMERSH, the Soviet intelligence outfit for which she had previously worked.

Robert Shaw, who might just have made a Bond himself, played Red Grant, another of the villains, whose fight with Bond on the Orient Express is powerful to say the least. It was Harry Saltzman's idea – he had come to the conclusion that Bond films had a licence to be violent and dreamed up the fight as one of the best ways he could think of to demonstrate the fact.

As Red Grant, Shaw is in such peak condition that when Rosa Klebb rams a few pounds of steel knuckleduster into his bare stomach (all he is wearing is a towel) he hardly notices. Shaw had to take special training to achieve the physical condition required. Both he and Sean had to learn Turko–Grecian wrestling for the fight sequences. Fortunately, since they were in Istanbul for the location shots, they were put under the instruction of the proprietor of a local gymnasium to pick up the finer points.

It was a hard six months working on *From Russia With Love* during that spring and summer of 1963. But there were consolations, and not just those that came with the cheques being paid.

Sean was seemingly happier than he had ever been before. Not only was his career at a peak point he might never have anticipated but in his private life he had never been more at peace with himself. At thirty-three Sean Connery was experiencing the delights of fatherhood. Diane had given birth to a son. They named him, with no apologies or reference to Julie Hamilton and her own offspring, Jason.

Diane even brought Jason to join Sean filming in Turkey. She had company – the villain of the piece, Walter Gotel, had just become a father too and his wife Yvonne developed a close sisterly relationship with Mrs Connery. Both fathers would help them in joint bathing sessions – Sean with Jason and Gotel with his new daughter Carol.

These were the kind of interludes that relieved the drudgery of film-making, of which there was plenty. *From Russia With Love* seemed fraught with technical hitches. Part of the problem was the helicopters used for filming – they were, quite simply, not very good and had difficulty in taking off. Then there was the matter of the speedboats – which just weren't speedy enough.

After all that, Broccoli and Saltzman decided to upsticks and change the location before actual filming could begin. A spot on the Scottish coast in Crinnon was chosen, which gave Sean no heartache whatsoever. It did, however, mean even more delays which, in turn, added to the total budget.

Even Scotland wasn't trouble-free. 'It was a hair-raising location in many ways,' Walter Gotel told me. Terence Young, once more putting his own personal stamp on things, decided to take off in one of the helicopters which were now being used to survey the terrain – and then crashed into the sea off Crinnon harbour. The pilot was an experienced man and and saved both their lives by turning the plane on to its side, tearing off the blades in the process.

Producers are usually the people who complain about all the unnecessary waits that are involved in film-making, the ones usually demanded by the director and his 'artistic' staff. In the case of *From Russia With Love*, it was Cubby Broccoli who caused one of the delays – all seven days of it. The cameras were about to turn on the speedboat chase when Broccoli decided that the wind was blowing in the wrong direction for anything to look the way he wanted it to. It was also playing havoc with the various explosions that were expected to take place. Walter Gotel was supposed to throw the explosive bags overboard and James Bond had to dodge the fire, which he did very successfully – he had a double. But until the wind changed a week later, there could be no explosions, and no filming either.

Gotel says he remembers Sean with affection. 'He was absolutely great, I have to say. He has always had an innate charm and complete lack of conceit. It stares at you in the face. That is not to say he is not an egoist – all actors have to be egoists – but there was a sense of sincerity. I think charm has to have sincerity about it.'

At the time, Sean was mostly concerned about his work. 'We would sit for hours talking about the job in hand. There were no signs of strain about him at that time, nothing to indicate that he did not want to do any more Bond films. I am sure that at that time he did want to do more.'

In fact, even though Sean Connery realised as much as anyone else that the success or failure of *From Russia With Love* depended more on him than it did on any other individual, there were few big-star prima-donna reactions from him. He took direction from Terence Young as keenly as he had once learned how to hold the reins of his horse Tich on the Edinburgh milk round. He was never late for work either on location or on the complicated indoor shots at Pinewood.

He also spent a lot of time talking about the Mercedes turbo car he had just bought. 'He enjoyed his cars and that was why he bought them. He had no intention of just showing off.' But then he didn't have to show off. That was the wonderful thing about the new status he now enjoyed – and enjoyed is the correct word – he didn't have to do any of the things less successful people might do in a struggle for status.

Others however, thought he was changing and not necessarily for the better; that he was behaving much more like a star. Ken Adam who spent a great deal of time with him saw the change. 'He didn't suffer fools gladly at any time but now you had to handle him with kid gloves. He didn't like many of the things he was asked to do. He was apt to lose his temper. We all had one interest in mind – making the film work – but Sean at times would see red when he didn't think he was being treated properly. One could understand him to a certain extent – but one also felt that if he had accepted the job, he should see it through.'

Some people might have thought that Diane was the ideal status symbol for an actor at his level. She was beautiful and feminine, the perfect appendage for the masculine man that Sean was, and completed the image which his producers wanted to cultivate. Not only did they look good together, everything about them seemed interesting, loving and as far as their relationship was concerned, complete.

Diane was on the set most of the time, watching her husband working, seeing him jump in and out of bed with Daniela Bianchi. It didn't appear to upset her. As far as the cameras were concerned, Sean seemed to be having a wonderful time. It was part of the game and the game was earning their livelihood for them.

However, Sean and Diane's relationship was not as easy as it appeared to be. They were in the same business, which is often reason enough for concern. Unless they are close to superhuman, couples in that situation are inclined to adopt subconsciously as their anthem Irving Berlin's *Annie Get Your Gun* hit, 'Anything You Can Do, I Can Do Better'.

Early on, however, Diane began making noises to the effect that it was her *husband* who could be doing better. 'She was angry,' Adam recalled, 'that he became so successful in something that for her was less than art. She became almost vicious.'

Letizia Adam saw the strain they were under even at this stage of the Bond saga. 'I was there and I heard them,' she remembered for me. 'She was the more intellectual of the two and he was the one who was now the more successful.'

'It became very competitive between the two,' said her husband, Ken.

'Yes,' his wife agreed. 'But it was mainly because she was doing what she thought was the right stuff and that Bond was beneath him.' Beneath them both. 'But I believe they were very much in love and would have stayed in love,' she continued. Would have stayed ... had that sense of competition not been so obvious. It is perhaps a judgment made with the benefit of hindsight, but with that hindsight it is easy to recognise the germs that led to a greater sickness.

Victor Spinetti remembers an evening at their home. Diane was in a critical mood, reflecting on the way his career was moving. 'Look,' she said pointing to Victor, 'that is an actor.' 'My dear,' Spinetti answered, 'Sean is giving more pleasure from James Bond than all the great stage actors all over the world put together.' 'I was quite embarrassed,' he told me.

You had to be in their immediate set to see just how much Diane did appear to be begrudging his success. To the outside world, it appears, there were no symptoms of trouble. They still looked wonderful together, a fact that United Artists were delighted to exploit. A handsome man happily married to a beautiful woman is the best publicity that a studio could hope for. And there was no evidence yet that there was anything wrong.

Other people working on the set of *From Russia With Love* begrudged Sean's success less. It was in all their interests that the film succeeded. From the second film onwards, there was a strong sense of belonging to a team. 'It was literally like being part of a family,' said Ken Adam. In fact, it was like a family reunion. When filming started, actors, directors, technicians put arms around each other and said how pleased they were all to be together again.

'From the beginning, working on the Bonds, we were travelling the world together,' said Ken Adam. 'We became real friends.'

Even so, that was something of a privileged situation for them. Sean has never been a man to enjoy socialising just for the sake of it. 'He doesn't like social functions. They just have no interest for him. He would rather have been on the golf course or in the kitchens of friends like us.'

That was one thing Sean and Diane enjoyed: eating together with their friends, with Sean in the role of the head of the family, carving the roast. It was a middle-class English routine to which the working-class Scot adapted perfectly. In London they became part of an almost repertory company of dinner companions – Sean, Michael Caine and, ironically, Roger Moore.

Letizia Adam was certain that Sean enjoyed this new-found role of star, despite all his protestations and Diane's complaints that he should be thought of as a serious actor. 'It was also very obvious that he liked reminding people that he had come up the hard way and where his origins were. Absolutely.'

Sometimes, he brought those origins into conversation at the least likely moments. On one occasion, he saw a newly-polished handrail at the Adams' home. 'I would have made a better job of it than this,' he told them, recalling his days as a coffin polisher.

It was partly nostalgia, of course, but he thought it helped him in his relations with other people and in theirs with his. Nevertheless, it did not stop him assuming that role of star – in spite of himself, it sometimes seemed. As his co-performer Walter Gotel put it to me: 'There are some people who don't have to play the big star – they are that whether they want to be or not. It is plain to see. They can't avoid it, can't run away from it.'

There were, however, certain privileges that big stars have which are not open to other people lower down on the cast lists. Occasionally, he asked for his lines to be changed. 'And they were,' recalled Gotel. Sometimes, the director changed them. 'Sean didn't balk at anything he was asked to do and when lines *were* changed, it was usually for the better.'

Possibly the only person who did balk was Ian Fleming. 'He was on the set a great deal at this time,' Walter Gotel remembered. 'I have the feeling he didn't get on with anyone.'

But even stars like Sean Connery were ready to tease other people working with them. 'Not cruelly – it was just for a joke,' recalled Ken Adam. 'He wouldn't have done it if he hadn't thought it worth a laugh.'

He would have only done it to people he knew well, people who would regard it as part of that innate charm of his. Certainly that is how Walter Gotel has always seen it.

'It was an innocent charm,' he says. 'You could pick it up from his demeanour. It was more than just words.' And yet Gotel adds enigmatically, 'You couldn't call Sean a gentleman. He has extremely good manners, but a gentleman would never call a spade a shovel, and Sean would.' There was no contradiction in terms there: 'I think it enhances his charm.'

A gentleman, says Gotel, would not lose his cool as easily as Sean lost his. And during that period waiting for something to happen on *From Russia With Love*, there were occasions when Connery's cool was well and truly lost. He swore at technicians if he didn't think they were doing their jobs properly, and used words about Saltzman and Broccoli he might not have wished them to hear in those early days of the Bond saga. Over and over again, people say about Sean Connery: 'He doesn't suffer fools gladly.' Some defend this and suggest that no one should ever have to suffer fools, gladly or otherwise. Other people wonder if a big man ought to be really big and rise above his instinctive emotions or temper.

Walter Gotel takes issue with that argument. 'The great thing about Sean,' he told me, 'has always been that he treated everyone alike, stars and lesser people. In his book, there are no lesser people. And no one was expected to take that temper seriously. I don't think he ever meant to hurt anyone.'

Plainly, raising his voice and using words that might not appear in the manual of Her Majesty's Secret Service is part of Sean's natural makeup. And yet he has always been intensely shy. If he wasn't totally happy with the company in which he found himself he could remain silent and unresponsive – not out of rudeness, but more out of that shyness. As Ken Adam told me: 'You had to get him going and draw him out of himself, just the opposite of, say, Michael Caine.'

Whole evenings would sometimes go by with him saying practically nothing or merely mouthing monosyllabic contributions to conversations you had the feeling he wished he would never have to enter. Others would be telling the jokes, recalling the anecdotes, but not him. He could appear to be totally uncommunicative.

Walter Gotel noticed that about him. 'He would just lie down and obviously not want to talk to anybody. He wouldn't necessarily go to his own caravan, but would lie on a couch on the set or in an hotel room if we were meeting there. There *were* people who would take that as a kind of affront, but he wouldn't talk to anyone at all.'

As Sean himself once said: 'My view is that to get anywhere in life you have to be anti-social, otherwise you'll end up being devoured. I've never been particularly social, anyway, but if I've ever been rude, fifty per cent of it has usually been provoked by other people's attitudes. Though I do admit that, like most Celts, I'm moody. It's fine until people try to cheer you up with gems like, "Snap out of it" or "Come on, now".'

Nevertheless, there were always the *other* times, as Ken Adam's wife recognised. If you wanted to draw him into conversation, you had a choice of two topics – Scotland or people he didn't like very much. Those were subjects that could guarantee his participation in a discussion.

It was another example of that black-and-white personality of his. 'Sean was a man of strong likes and dislikes,' Ken Adam repeated. But there were other times when the act of drawing him out was totally unnecessary. 'His presence was so warm and lovely that you didn't care. He would sit in his favourite chair in our kitchen and just beam. He would listen.'

There was no small talk about him, and nothing superficial in any of his actions. That was something his friends picked up early on.

It was also picked up by passing journalists. Bryan Buckingham writing in the *News of the World* told how a girl approached Sean on the set of *From Russia With Love* and asked him if he wanted her to take her clothes off again. 'Of course,' he replied and the girl, 'eloquently curvy in all the essential places', obliged. As she stripped to a bikini 'that would have trouble covering three postage stamps', he didn't even bother to look at her.

But Sean was not totally inhibited. At a New Year's Eve party at the home of Ken and Letizia Adam, he made his contribution to the drinking stakes, particularly with his banker friend, Sir Iain Stewart. It was a time when Diane was away filming and Sean spent most of the evening sitting on the stairs engrossed in conversation with the financier. 'He drank a little,' Ken Adam remembered for me, 'but never too much. He wasn't a Peter O'Toole. One had the feeling he didn't like it all that much. He didn't need it.' But he was glad to let the laughs come and if they did, he was happy.

The laughs *were* always important. He was only interested in things that had an importance to them, which was why if he played cards at this time he had to win – and win for money. 'He never wanted to waste his time doing anything that didn't have a purpose,' was how Letizia Adam put it to me. 'He insisted on having the money, if it came to that.'

The film made a huge amount of money for Saltzman and Broccoli, to say nothing of United Artists. Sean didn't do too badly out of it either. No more £7,000 salaries for him. He was, without any doubt, a star and close to being given the accolade of superstar. He was happy as James Bond and there was every reason for his being so. When the time came for a third Bond picture to be talked about, he was happy to take out his fountain pen and sign on the dotted line.

The Bond role brought him enough security, it seemed, to last the rest of his life. Effie and Joe revelled in their son the film star, and Diane, with her own career blossoming, if on a lower rung of the international acclaim ladder, was doing nicely enough herself. She certainly didn't need to work for financial reasons – Sean was making more than enough for both of them. To almost everyone they met, the handsome couple were also the perfect couple.

Most people were keen to report on the fact that Sean kept very much to himself as far as women were concerned. But in her book, *Behind Closed Doors* the late Diana Dors told of the times he went to her house. 'Sean was always ready for any girl,' she said. It struck her as odd because he had the pick of any beauty he wanted during the day. 'Yet indiscriminately at my home, he would play around with any female who chanced to be there.'

Diana Dors was very much down on her luck at the time her book was published and before long would be dying. It could be that she found the story too tasty not to embellish. On the other hand she was not sued by her friend – possibly because he understood her position and felt sorry for her.

Something unusual for a film star was happening to Sean. Unlike almost any other actor who had sewn up a role and made it all his own, he was not only in demand for other work, but he was getting it. And not just in television or live theatre which he could have had for the asking, but in other movies.

During the making of *From Russia With Love*, Sean was invited to make a film opposite Gina Lollobrigida, the Italian actress who, along with her countrywoman Sophia Loren, personified Mediterranean womanhood as far as the outside world was concerned. The picture was *Woman Of Straw.*

In fact, *Woman Of Straw* was actually made simultaneously with the second Bond movie, with Sean doing retakes in his Savile Row suits in between the scenes in which he played a totally different character opposite Miss Lollobrigida. In *Woman Of Straw* he was a con man encouraging an Italian nurse to marry her employer (Ralph Richardson) so that they could both inherit his fortune.

Sean seemed at the time to be genuinely excited at teaming up with the woman known as 'La Lollo', for fairly obvious reasons. He hadn't been denied the charms of enticing looking women, but this one was fairly exceptional. When they met for the first time to talk about the film, he said he found her 'much more beautiful than she is in any of her pictures I've seen'. He couldn't have realised how, by instantly referring to *her* pictures, he was being much more generous to her than she would be to him. She was not planning to reciprocate.

In fairness to the actress, she did genuinely think that Sean was an unknown. She had not seen *Dr No* and had no idea what it was or who Sean was. Certainly she knew nothing of his previous work. She said afterwards that she thoroughly enjoyed the experience of working with him.

Nevertheless, if his statements about Gina's beauty were to be regarded as an omen, it was a remarkably inaccurate one. Signorina Lollobrigida might have been the perfect Bond Woman – she was already past being a Bond Girl had she wanted to compromise her star status by taking the role – but she also had a personality which, when put together with Connery's, resembled a match put to sandpaper. They sparked virtually at first meeting, but not at all in the way the producers would have hoped.

She had the temerity to ask him : 'Tell me, Mr Connery, what kind of an actor are you ?'

That was not tactful. Not only did Mr Connery reasonably believe that his career résumé was sufficiently well known to make the question superfluous, but it also inferred typecasting. Sean Connery was not a 'type'. Did not the very fact he was now making this film prove that ? His response : he walked out.

Sean was irritated by his co-star's demands for explanations for everything she was asked to do. At one stage, he turned to the director Basil Dearden and in a burst of extremely bad temper said : 'Either you're directing or she is. If it's she, I might not be in it.'

But the fighting seemed only a temporary aberration. Having decided that Sean *was* important enough to work with without endangering her own reputation, La Lollo behaved as perfectly as a co-star should. What she may not have been prepared for was a certain part of the script where Sean slaps her.

If there were any lingering doubts about his views on hitting women and in particular on *how* to slap a female, here was an on-screen demonstration. This was not one of those pantomimic slaps which cause a chorus of laughs every time there is an action replay on video. As one ought to expect from a man who believes in doing his own stunts, this was the real thing. No one was sure if Sean really intended the slap to be genuine or if Gina simply recoiled and caught the blow in the process. Whichever was the case, the Italian beauty couldn't move her neck for three days.

There are those who think that it was not an accident. 'But Gina was very fond of Sean,' says Ken Adam, who, like Sean, had been 'borrowed' for a non-Bond picture and served as production designer on *Woman Of Straw*. And Sean still said he liked Italian women. By extension, that could have been read to include Diane. She, meanwhile, was glad that he was branching out from his James Bond image. She might also have thought that a new producer would value his services sufficiently highly to pay him what he was now worth.

However, if Sean himself expected *Woman Of Straw* to help him to another fortune, he was mistaken. He had accepted Basil Dearden's suggestion that he star in the picture for what he thought were valid reasons : it would indeed help him to escape the typecasting that now seemed inevitable ; it enabled him to make a little more money ; and the film was being shot at Pinewood. What was more, it was only going to be a short project that would give him time to do his Bond work, too.

The problem was that he didn't have enough time for both. He was confused by the totally different work he was having to do simultaneously and he confessed that he didn't really concentrate properly.

Miss Lollobrigida, however, seemed to regret her earlier behaviour and now tried to help him.

In the end, it was actually the public who weren't able to concentrate. Inevitably, the publicity attack of the film was based on the fact that Dearden and his producer partner Michael Relph had secured the Bond star. And when the film was finished and appeared in the theatres, people still thought of him as just the Bond star. Unlike *From Russia With Love*, which had the unprecedented accolade of being premièred simultaneously in four London West End cinemas, *Woman Of Straw* went in and then straight out of the theatres.

The movie wasn't nearly as bad as was alleged at the time. The press, however, were less than enthusiastic. Most of the critics seemed to think that Ralph Richardson stole the honours – as he was entitled to do, considering the extent of his career to date.

La Lollo came in for her share of rather unflattering notices. The *New York Times* doubted that she was as 'irresistible' as her reputation had led people to believe. 'She stubbornly remains her placid, matronly self – hardly the type to draw a passing snort from an old lion like Sir Ralph. No wonder Mr Connery double-crosses her in the end.'

Not much was said about Sean, but he didn't escape unscathed. One critic, Ann Pacey in the London *Daily Herald*, described Sean's acting as 'as wooden as an old beam'.

Leslie Halliwell summed up the film by saying that it was a 'rather half-hearted but good-looking star melodrama which ventures into Hitchcock territory.'

'Venture into Hitchcock territory' was precisely what Sean Connery was now about to do as he waited for work to start on the third Bond picture. Hitchcock asked him to star in his next film, *Marnie*, and Sean was not one to turn down an invitation like that. No one would have expected him to do so, no matter how busy he was and despite the fact that he had hardly had a day off in sixteen months. But what they didn't expect was that he would impose conditions on accepting Hitchcock's invitation. That was never done.

The director, who was known in the business as 'the Master' might have thought he had reason to doubt his judgment the moment his lawyers came back with Connery's reply to the film offer. Sean entered territory where most film angels had dared not tread: he asked to see the script before agreeing to the role. To Sean, that was no more than what he imagined any big star would do, as was the $400,000 fee that he required. Hitchcock baulked at the demand to see the script more than at the money. He sent word back that not even Cary Grant demanded to see a script before making a movie with Hitchcock. 'Well, I'm not Cary Grant,' said Connery.

Maybe it was the sheer chutzpah of the demand that endeared Connery to the director. Much to the amazement of everyone on his staff he accepted the condition.

Later, Connery explained: 'Cary's big enough to be able to insist on changes after a film starts. But I can't. So I must be happy with it before I begin.'

He said that the director took it all very well. 'Hitch was wonderful to work with. I knew we'd get on fine when I arrived in Hollywood and found he'd had two bottles of my favourite Scotch put in my room.'

That was something of a revelation for Sean because he had been warned that 'the Master' tended to treat his actors with contempt. Hitchcock had gone on record for calling actors 'a load of cattle' and the image had stuck. 'But I found just the opposite. I think it amuses him to keep up the pretense, for he gets ribbed about it all the time.'

What Sean liked about Hitchcock was his instinctive approach to his work. 'He gave very little direction, didn't even look through the view finder, because he had always worked out what he wanted. He could control the rhythm and tempo of the picture just by being there and making little adjustments and suggestions.'

Had there been a few more adjustments and suggestions, the picture might have been improved. Perhaps everyone expected more from it than they got – and Sean Connery to be a little better in it than he was. In *Marnie* he looked exactly as he had looked in the Bond movies – the same haircut (or toupee), the same attention to wardrobe, which might have been made by studio tailors in Hollywood but could easily have been produced in Savile Row. But that didn't mean that Sean looked or indeed was comfortable.

Sean himself was only concerned with what the picture would do for his own reputation. He had asked for script approval partly because he appreciated that the time had come when he was in a position to do so. Also because he wasn't going to risk damaging the career he had worked so hard to build up. He wasn't going to conform to the usual practices of the Hitchcock industry any more than he was going to stay at the hotel the studio chose (he liked the small motel he had chosen last time) or be seen at the events they wanted him to attend.

'I just don't have time for all that jazz,' he explained. 'I've been working continuously for a year and a half and I don't see why I can't grab my relaxation where and when I can. For the first time in my life, I can *ask* to read a script and if you had been in some of the tripe I have, you'd know why.'

He insisted that he wasn't growing conceited, which was precisely why he had turned down the suite at a luxury apartment hotel in favour of the motel. It was also why he had been driving a Volkswagen until recently instead of the Bond Aston Martin and Bentley (The Mercedes was an aberration). 'If I wore hats,' he said, 'I think you'd find I still take the same size.'

Meanwhile, Connery made the most of working with one of the only remaining legends of Hollywood. He took advice from Hitchcock which he might have laughed at from any other director. When Hitchcock saw that he had a habit of protruding his lower jaw, he told him: 'Mr Connery, I don't think that people really want to see your dental work.'

Diane enjoyed the idea of being married to a Hitchcock star. She flew to Los Angeles to be with Sean while filming progressed and seemed to revel in the status he merited – not least of all, the home rented in their names in Bel Air, the world's most expensive housing estate. There were reports that she bathed nude in the swimming pool. The fact that these were never confirmed said something for the security of the premises – another definition of having arrived with the thud of an express train.

But it was Hitchock who had the power and authority – and all his actors knew it. Tippi Hedren, the female lead playing Marnie – a girl with serious psychological problems arising from the discovery as a child that her mother was a prostitute and the girl's subsequent murder of one of her mother's 'clients' – found out the wrong way.

Hitchcock had fancied Hedren as the next Grace Kelly, and she was consequently dressed to look like the woman who a decade earlier had starred in the director's *Dial M For Murder*. The differences were that Tippi Hedren was a better actress and had a much more voluptuous figure.

Her appearance fitted in beautifully with Hitchcock's idea of Marnie. She looked ice cool, perfect for the girl she portrayed who was as frigid as the weather outside her mother's terraced house in Baltimore. The mixed-up daughter is also a thief and a fraud, but when she walks out on her husband, played by Sean, and her new-found wealth, he goes in search of her – only to discover that it is all the result of those childhood experiences.

She played the part well, but Hitchcock wanted everything done his way. When she asked for permission to go to New York for a weekend, the director refused. Her reaction – to call him a fat slob – found its way back to his office quicker than you could slam shut a clapper board.

After that, Sean found himself playing the role of peacemaker and intermediary. If the director wanted his female star to do anything, he would give the message: 'Tell Miss Hedren to move to the left.' To which she would reply: 'Tell Mr Hitchcock I *have* moved to the left.'

It didn't alter Hitchcock's affection for 'cool blonde women'. As Sean noted: 'What's wrong with that? I mean, it could have been cool blond men.'

The lack of chemistry did not do much to help the picture and it was not one of Hitchock's best films by any means. But in one regard it worked splendidly. Sean was probably not ideal casting – playing a top businessman from Philadelphia was not an obvious role for the kid from Edinburgh. Nevertheless, this was the film that showed that Sean could get away with playing someone other than Bond. It was a more serious role, and the violence and blood had nothing to do with the character he himself played.

Taking Hitchcock's instructions on the set did not mean that Sean was a good boy throughout the filming period. The publicity men wanted him to open the new MCA building in Beverly Hills, a tribute to the agency to whom more stars needed to doff metaphorical hats than any other. They thought Mr Connery in his London-tailored finery would be just the sort of figure they needed for the ceremony. Sean thought otherwise and went off to play golf.

With Hitchcock's help, Connery could afford to indulge himself in the sport that he had taken for granted in Scotland but which in the United States was not for the poor. He wasn't yet making golf an obsession, but he had already been elected an honorary member of the very exclusive Bel Air Country Club, which was known to have a prejudice against actors and show people, but which seems to have enjoyed his talent for the game as much as he enjoyed playing it.

One day he lobbed a ball onto the roof of a house near the fifteenth fairway. He walked over to the house, knocked on the door to ask for his ball back – and was greeted by a dour Mr Hitchcock wearing his slippers.

The mere fact that he had been allowed to play at the club and that

Hitchcock could laugh at the request to have his ball back gives some idea of just how far he had moved on in his world.

Had the picture itself reflected that, he would have been grateful, but it wasn't difficult to work out that it hadn't really clicked. Nevertheless, the director held no grudges.

And the film did succeed at the box office. This was what Hollywood at the time liked to call psychological drama and there was a lot to enjoy in it. Hitchcock said at the time that he was in the business of creating fear. 'I still get a thrill from scaring the pants off people,' he told Connery as he limbered up for the first day's shooting. 'People enjoy fear. It's rooted in all of us. The child on a swing goes higher and higher until it gets so high he catches his breath and stops. People on a roller-coaster scream, but they get off giggling.'

Hitchcock was pleased with Sean's work and gave him a radio alarm clock to prove it. Later, Sean discovered it only worked in America – even with a transformer it lost an hour a day in Britain. But it was the thought – Hitchcock's thought – that counted. The director had penned a note to the present: 'Now you'll have to come back.'

There was another, seemingly more valuable gift. The technicians presented him with an inscribed gold watch, said to be worth $3,000. There doesn't appear to be any significance in the fact that both the technicians and the director gave him timepieces. Indeed, throughout his career no one has suggested that his punctuality left anything to be desired.

Hitchcock wanted him for another part and Sean probably would have taken it, if only to prove to himself as much as anyone else that someone really important knew he was capable of more than Bond. There were, however, not to be many more Hitchcock movies and it never happened.

What did happen, however, was that the Connery stakes were now upped considerably. He could claim a fee up to $400,000 a picture and that really was big, big money.

Sean was no longer saying that he was down to his last quid. 'Nowadays,' he told the *Saturday Evening Post*, 'I'm down to my last bag of rubies.' But, then, it was gold they were focusing on in the next Bond picture.

7

GOLDFINGER

The ingredients of the Bond pictures were by now very well defined: Bond himself looking good, fighting and loving well, a group of girls who had to be prepared to strip down to their underwear – and from the rear to even less – and to promise a little more than is actually ever given.

There had to be a villain as finely drawn as any black-hatted character in a Western, but preferably, if not always, with a middle-European accent, a gaggle of gimmicky gadgets and the kind of sets designed by Ken Adam that boggled the eye as well as filled a sound stage at Pinewood. There also always had to be a location straight out of the pages of one of the classier Sunday supplements.

Almost coincidental to all this, there was also a plot, which frequently was subservient to the distractions on screen – quite convenient, since it would be possible to mix scenes from any one of the films shot in the past decade without causing too much havoc.

Then there was the violence, the near-sadism, the sardonic humour (singularly lacking in the original stories and inserted much against Fleming's own will on instructions from Terence Young). Bond always dispatched another victim, rubbed his hands together and went back to kissing the girl of the moment.

The final ingredient was perhaps the most important of all: the film made a lot of money at the box office, and had people who had given up the habit of going to the movies lining up outside theatres for an hour or more at a time to get a ticket at a frequently elevated price. If the critics liked it too, that was a bonus. But it was a bonus that was handed out quite generously.

The third Bond picture, *Goldfinger*, met all the requirements. What the picture proved was that Bond – or was it just Connery as Bond ? – could get away with things that would have been unthinkable in any other movie. It was that mixture of near-sadism and humour: never better or more graphically demonstrated than in Bond's argument with one of the villains. When the man falls back into a bath of steaming water, James throws a plugged-in electric fire into the morass, just to finalise matters. It is an instant electrocution kit, which Bond enjoys to the full. As the villain is transported to a place more likely to be worse than better, James mutters, 'shocking . . . simply shocking'.

Most of all the picture proved that the audiences liked what they saw. Sean himself said at the time: 'In *Dr No*, the character was established. By the end of the second film the audience had thoroughly got hold of him. After that, the interesting thing was to surprise people who thought they knew how he was going to react to a situation. You'd play the reality, play the humour, have a bit of playful repartee with the audience and do something unexpected.'

The movie was shot on location in Switzerland this time (one can imagine the producers drawing up a list of countries for Bond films and happily ticking them off as they get used up) as well as in the United States and Pinewood.

Goldfinger has since gained the reputation of being the archetypal Bond picture – with a romp in and out of the haystack with Honor Blackman and a more definite plot than most. In this case, it was James Bond personally taking responsibility for halting a raid on Fort Knox led by the larger-than-life German nasty Herr Frobe, who, from the moment he tries to cheat against Bond on the golf course and is beaten by an opponent playing his own game, is clearly on to a loser.

As far as Sean and his producers were concerned, the film could just as easily have been called *Goldmine*. In fact, this was to be the most successful Bond picture to date. But it didn't start out that way. Nobody doubted after the experience of the two earlier pictures that it would make a lot of money – Terence Young, for one, was convinced that it would do so, and wanted a share of the loot. If *Goldfinger* really was going to represent that goldmine, he said, he was not prepared to dig without having some of the nuggets to take home with him. Fine, said Broccoli and Saltzman, and promptly replaced him – with the *Colditz Story* director Guy Hamilton.

Sean, on the other hand, *was* satisfied with the financial arrangements. The money that he earned for the picture might have been thought somewhat excessive for 1964 – there still weren't many people picking up the one million pound fee that Elizabeth Taylor had exacted for *Cleopatra* – but he was canny enough to know his own value to the operation and stuck out for a figure that made many gasp. He had also got what Terence Young had failed to have lined up – a percentage of the profits.

Getting the money sorted out was the start of open warfare between star and producers. Everyone working on the *Goldfinger* set heard the rows and saw the glares being exchanged between them. But, contrary to the accepted view, Honor Blackman, who played number one Bond Girl Pussy Galore says it was not Broccoli who was making life difficult for the players. 'I thought that Harry was the one who put the pressure on. Cubby was acting as a teddy bear.'

Ken Adam agrees with that conclusion. 'Saltzman played the heavy,' he told me. 'Cubby liked to be one of the boys.'

Frequently, the rows that people working on *Goldfinger* heard were between Broccoli and Saltzman themselves. Broccoli loved the sex in the Bond pictures. Every time a girl exposed a bit more bust than she or any of her predecessors had before, he was happy. Saltzman was more concerned with the gadgetry.

That would have been all right, had not each of the men come to the conclusion that it was the aspect that he preferred which had made the pictures so successful. Each now was beginning to believe that they would have done even better had there been no partnership and they were working on their own. But it *was* in their interest to keep together and neither their rows nor the ones with Sean hindered the movie's success.

Sean hoped that the money he earned from the picture would give Diane food for thought as she continued her campaign to persuade her husband to think of doing something more 'serious'. But it didn't work. She hated his Bond image and wasted no opportunity to say so.

Ken and Letizia Adam told me how conscious they were of the tensions on the set of *Goldfinger*. They heard the couple screaming at each other between takes and after hours. It was not the kind of story that hit the headlines at the time.

The closest the newspapers got to it were a series of rumours that Connery was getting bored with the Bond role. But by the time they surfaced, Sean had signed a contract for three more Bond films which guaranteed him not only a large fee – up to that time Peter Sellers had been the only British actor to get the same sort of money – but also put officially in writing the fact that he was free to make other pictures at the same time.

There were offers for him to make a couple of pictures opposite Susan Hayward, but she was at the stage in her career when not only did she insist on being *the* star, but her pictures were all of the same genre: all about gutsy but very feminine women who allowed the tears to well up in their eyes at roughly the same time that members of the audience were taking out their own handkerchiefs. That was not for Sean Connery.

His wife, however, might have been better pleased had he found this a more tempting proposition. Sean was not helped by Diane's presence on the set, but it didn't show. He was fortunate that her attitude extended to the *kind* of work he was doing, not the way he had to do it. The first Mrs Fred Astaire was so incensed by the fact that her husband had to dance with other women, no matter how decorously, that she extracted a promise from him that he would never kiss anyone on screen, which is why Ginger Rogers rarely gets more than an arm around her waist.

Sean had no such inhibitions, even if Diane was actually sitting behind the camera as he fondled Shirley Eaton in her black bra or interrupted Nadja Regin in her bath or even romped in the hay with Honor Blackman.

Honor Blackman had made a name for herself as the female lead in the highly successful television series *The Avengers*. Now she was similarly attired as Pussy Galore, the lady who leads a flying circus of other women pilots.

But it was the activity in the haystack that made people sit up and think. Blackman told me that she herself had wondered why the steaming hay didn't actually catch fire as she and Sean seemed to do with each other.

As she put it: 'There aren't many ladies who wouldn't vote for lying in the hay with Sean.' And that's what they did, even at times when most actors would be expected to be replaced by other performers. 'There were close-ups to be shot so we had to stand in ourselves. But Sean behaved himself.'

Plans for the movie were well advanced by the time they actually met. 'In fact, we didn't meet until a champagne reception was held to announce that I would play Pussy Galore. He was a stranger then, so it's amazing how quickly I got to know him. I don't remember ever not being at ease with him.'

But there was always a special ingredient that appealed to her. 'He had the sexiest eyes I've ever seen,' she told me. 'So twinkly. I suppose it's a wickedness in the eyes. You feel he's so virile. You believed he was capable of doing everything – and he did everything.'

But when I asked whether he did everything with her, her answer was something of a let down. 'I'm just kidding. We didn't socialise. I was married; he was married. And oddly enough, apart from having old Sexpot there, the most interesting thing about being in the film was playing with Gert Frobe.' Frobe played Goldfinger, the villain of the piece.

There were, though, she added, 'laughs all the way'.

All this could give the impression that Sean, perhaps even despite himself, really was playing James Bond off the set as well as on it, as Desmond Llewellyn had said. If Honor Blackman did think this, then there were others to prove otherwise. 'I think,' said the publicist Jerry Juroe, that Sean was always one of those actors who wanted to get out of the nice clothes he wore in the film and just be himself.' It was as if the clothes represented Bond and he wanted to be just Sean Connery. 'He loved to put on a jacket with an open-necked shirt, an old pair of trousers, and that was it.'

Stars are, by their very nature, spoilt creatures. It suits the studios to make them so. In most cases, pandering to their every whim keeps actors and actresses in a good mood and thus helps the smooth running of the picture. Dressing them in their finery helps the image they want to create – which is why the publicist is so important to them. But Sean was not going to conform, and refusing to dress the part off-duty was a demonstration of the fact.

Sean hoped that Hamilton would make Bond less suave and more classy. Honor Blackman told me she knew there was a difference between Hamilton's approach and that of Terence Young – even though she hadn't worked with the original Bond director herself. 'Guy Hamilton was not a larky director. He was very serious. With him, you had to play things straight down the middle.' But that wasn't difficult. As she told me, 'the scripts were so good.'

The director brought in Paul Dehn, one time film critic of the *News Chronicle*, to adapt the script that had already been prepared for Terence Young by Richard Maibaum and hoped they could meet Sean's specifications. If they couldn't, it didn't matter – he was under contract and it was the director and the producers who had to be satisfied.

There was much about the picture that would have fitted equally well into a Terence Young movie, but Guy Hamilton put his stamp on *Goldfinger* all the same. For instance, it was Hamilton who suggested that Desmond Llewellyn should get even more annoyed with Bond's treatment of Q.

There was the scene where Q gets up to greet Bond. 'No,' instructed Hamilton, 'you can't stand the fellow. Treat him with absolute contempt.' The lines helped. When Q shows Bond the Aston Martin, James says: 'It's very handy for nipping round the corner for a drink.'

'It wasn't invented specially for that,' Q replies, suddenly giving the impression that he could do the job much better himself.

'Sean helped tremendously with getting that scene working properly,' Llewellyn now recalls. 'He was always suggesting things. He wasn't just saying his lines. He was very helpful in lots of little ways. He would add to the script the whole time and a lot of his asides were not in the script. Many of the speeches in which he seemed to be saying about me, "Oh no, that bloody man has come to annoy me again," came from Sean himself. I know he did the same for other people. He made gestures that really helped me very greatly.'

Llewellyn, who modestly says he never played anything worthwhile apart from Q, feels a degree of gratitude for that. 'He never made you feel inferior or just a small-part actor. You very definitely felt a part of the team. There was never any star quality about him. We were both just actors. I never felt that James Bond turned his head. I think he is a most charming person.'

As in *From Russia With Love*, Q's instructions were faithfully researched and put into operation. This time, thanks to the Aston Martin organisation, Bond's car – later sold at auction at Sotheby's New York centre for $300,000 – was equipped with rotating number plates, machine guns behind the headlights, an ejector seat which provided a wonderful solution to the age-old problem of what to do with boring passengers, smokescreens and oil emitted from the rear and a device which some thirty years later was actually put on the market in an attempt to trace stolen cars – a tracking device. Audiences watched open-mouthed as one gadget replaced the next – all ready for use in a 1960s version of a chariot race.

Everything about the picture was exotic – even the methods of killing people. The Bond movies were unique in that the secondary love interest was usually bumped off, no matter how loving and how attractive she was.

Shirley Eaton had come on the scene via a set of equipment not provided by Q – had the good Major Boothroyd been in charge, it might have been more foolproof. She is seen, standing on the balcony of Goldfinger's hotel, armed with a pair of binoculars and a radio transmitter – feeding the villain information through what is supposedly his hearing aid about the cards of the men with whom he was playing poker.

Bond takes the mike from Shirley Eaton and then takes her to her bed. Later, when Shirley does remove her black bra, it is for her to be covered, nude, in gold paint. Who would have thought that by covering a woman with so much paint, her pores become blocked and she is unable to breathe and that doing so is as sure a way of killing her as pointing a Beretta at her heart? Bond, of course, knows – and recognises the symptoms of the lovely girl's demise.

This was an age before AIDS, when the term safe sex meant doing it without your husband or wife finding out. Just the same, Sean already saw his part as having developed beyond the stage where he happily hopped from one bed to another for the sake of it.

But no one could claim this was reality. In *Goldfinger*, the sun was always shining or the moon always bright and the Ken Adam sets as pristine as the all-white world in which Rogers and Astaire really did dance in those old films.

It was *Goldfinger* that introduced Sean to serious golf – not serious in the way of rivalry with friends such as Daniel Massey, but serious as in playing for money. It was no longer enough just to knock a ball around or even think he had enjoyed a perfect game. Now he played to win, and the stakes were demonstrations of his status in the game as clearly as the figures on the cheques he received from Saltzman and Broccoli indicated his standing in the film industry. But his dedication to the game started more as a form of professional research in order to prepare him for his confrontation with Goldfinger on the golf course. Ken Adam confirms the impact that learning to play the game 'properly' had on Sean. 'I think he developed his passion for golf only while working on *Goldfinger*. He may have played well enough before then, but this was when he began to take it very seriously indeed.'

And he added: 'I found that that whole generation of actors, Sean and Bob Shaw for instance, wanted above all to win. They were not very good losers. But then Sean has no superficial sides at all. He is always very straight in everything that he does. Money is very important to him – particularly bearing in mind his poor origins.'

Sean was now sufficiently committed to the game to be a member of the Stage Golfing Society, which cost him twelve pounds a year in dues. But for that one pound a month, he could play at some of the finest courses in the land – even Wentworth. The only problem was that there were no privileges at weekends.

Desmond Llewellyn recalled one of those Pinewood lunches at which – and this made it notable – Sean shared a table with Cubby Broccoli among others. The conversation turned to golf as it inevitably would. Ted Moore, the director of photography, asked Sean if he were playing that weekend.

'No,' he replied.

'Well,' countered Ted, 'how about a game on Saturday?'

'No,' replied Connery. 'I can't play on Saturday. I only really like playing at Wentworth and I can't play Saturdays.'

Moore was incredulous. 'Why on earth not?' he asked.

'Because,' Sean replied, 'I'm a member of the Stage Golfing Society and we don't play on Saturdays.'

'You can pay a green fee,' Moore suggested. Sean wasn't impressed, to say the least. Unnecessary expenditure was not on his agenda. On the other hand, this was in sharp contrast to the generosity Llewellyn, for one, experienced. 'When ever I've met him in a bar, Sean's always the first to offer to buy me a drink, but I think he watches the baubies, as they say.'

But he didn't stint on the lessons he took so that he could play well in *Goldfinger.* James Bond had to be able to hold a club and putt his way around a course as easily and as comfortably as he wore a good suit or handled the silverwear at a society dinner table.

This time, there were no secrets about the lessons, and there was no one to rival him – except Gert Frobe in the film, and he didn't have to be as good as Bond. He took lessons now as much to please himself as to satisfy Guy Hamilton.

The producers saw how Sean moved on the golf course and were suitably impressed. He didn't merely address the ball, he made love to it with the same skill with which he made love to his women.

The professionals at the Stoke Poges Golf Club, which doubled for the so-called Royal St Mark's links in the movie, gave him hints and the occasional more stringent lesson, to ensure that when he practised he was practising correctly. He was. He played the game on camera just as James Bond was expected to play it.

He had picked up golf the way other people pick up viruses, and it became an obsession he was never to lose. From that film on, he made money every time he played, sometimes £100 a hole, sometimes more. As Ken Adam had noticed, there was no point in winning if there wasn't something to be gained from it.

Frobe is cast as the main villain in *Goldfinger*, but one mustn't forget the man who overshadowed him throughout – Harold Sakata as the wonderfully-named Oddjob, a man who could do wondrous things with his bowler hat. In that, he was confirming another Bond tradition – literally the oddjob man who does the dirty work in a way that could never be achieved simply by hiring a chap through the classified columns.

But it was Goldfinger himself, Auric Goldfinger to be precise, who was Bond's target. When he played golf, Gert Frobe knew what he was up against on the course and the cast knew what they were up against with Gert Frobe. As Honor Blackman told me, Frobe was a subject of much discussion on the *Goldfinger* set. 'No one could understand a word he was saying.' Which was why a decision was taken to dub his voice – by an anonymous actor who sounded remarkably like a young Anthony Hopkins.

Outside the studio, Connery found himself defending his antagonist. He told a woman journalist how much he appreciated Gert's work. 'Who's she?' asked the writer. Sean walked away in disgust – a frequently-adopted reaction.

Other women writers treated him differently. According to Ken Adam, Oriana Fallacci, the eminent Italian journalist, flew into London to interview Sean and decided that the best way of making any headway was simply to flirt. She liked tough men and thought that was the best approach. 'But,' said Adam's wife, 'he is not a toughie, but just wonderfully built.'

The flirtatious approach may not have worked, but they got on just the same. 'She was very intelligent,' Ken recalled for me, 'and Sean loved kidding around. That became almost a pastime for him. There was always an atmosphere of kidding at that time.'

When the mood was right, Sean was in the forefront of it all. 'He was a great tease,' said Letizia Adam. 'He knew how proud Ken was of his sets so he'd say things like, 'I don't think the camera caught that corner over there.'

It was doing things like that which made the rapport between them all so good. 'There is no question about that. That sort of thing doesn't happen any more. Stars are so concerned about their image that they never play around nowadays. Sean wasn't like that. He enjoyed a joke and I think that helped give him confidence, too.'

Almost annoyingly for an actor who claimed he wanted to get away from the image that the role had created for him, the picture was as much of a critical success as it was a box office triumph. 'Who else could play the part now?' asked Ann Pacey.

Such a question – a statement with a question mark attached – would have given many another actor more pleasure than he would have imagined possible. But he was not another actor, and Sean did now get seriously worried about the typecasting to which he had committed himself, for half the time at least. It struck him never more strongly than when he walked into one of the better Manhattan restaurants and was addressed by the maitre d' as 'Mr Bond'. 'I could have had his head for hors-d'œuvre?' said Sean. But that was unfair. Like it or not, Sean had created that confusion in the public's mind himself. Years after playing Tevya in the play and film *Fiddler On The Roof*, the Israeli actor Topol was stopped in the street by a well-meaning passer-by. 'Excuse me,' he said, 'didn't you used to be Topol ?'

So he tried *not* to worry. *Goldfinger* 'sort of demonstrates what I believe is a subtler, more discriminating Bond than you have seen in the earlier films,' Sean told Leonard Mosley in the *New York Times Magazine*, at the time of the picture's opening. 'All the girls still want to make love to him, but he doesn't need to make love to all of them. It's a process of development.'

When *Goldfinger* opened in Paris, the city went slightly crazy – in whatever sense anyone likes to make of the term. Sean attended the première – something he now said he would never do – and for once went along with the entire publicity gimmickry of it all. The Champs Elysées was completely closed to all traffic except for Sean driving the James Bond Aston Martin. The publicity the motor company got as a result of the Bond movies was equivalent to what an entire year's PR budget would have achieved except that they didn't have to spend anything beyond lending the vehicle in the first place.

Crowds five- and six-deep lined the pavements and broke through the police cordons. Letizia Adam was there for the première and for once was worried about Sean. 'I kept saying to myself, "How is this man going to cope with it all?" After all, this was Charles de Gaulle. This was Brigitte Bardot.'

When he arrived at the cinema, he virtually fell into the arms of his 'chums', the people he had got to know on the set while making the movie. He didn't do more than acknowledge Broccoli and Saltzman, but to people like the Adams, he muttered, 'Thank God you're here. You're ... well ... normal.'

In London, the *News of the World's* Weston Taylor said: '*Goldfinger* isn't simply the best vintage of all the 007 films. It's the year's best piece of escapist hokum in motion pictures.'

Playboy magazine was so overcome with the film – and the opportunity to feature full-colour spreads of Bond Girls wearing far less than they did on screen – that it named Sean Connery the star of the decade. That had never happened to a non-American before. The British critic Penelope Gilliatt said, somewhat ambiguously it might be thought, that the film was 'a dazzling object lesson in the principle that nothing succeeds like excess'. Judy Crist, meanwhile, called it 'a diverting comic strip for grown ups'. Indeed it was.

There was certainly plenty of activity in *Goldfinger*, although no one explained adequately why saving *America*'s gold reserves was a job for the *British* Secret Service. Admittedly the whole world economy was likely to be undermined, but Fort Knox *was* in America, wasn't it? In the 1990s the idea of England even winning at international soccer raises guffaws all round. Yet in 1963 it was still feasible that it could be up to Britain to save the planet. That this notion was acceptable not only to an American movie company but also to audiences across the Atlantic said a great deal, too.

What, of course, Broccoli and Saltzman, and through them Sean Connery, were selling was a fantasy no more fantastic than when men and women in the old Hollywood musicals walked down Fifth Avenue and suddenly burst into song with all the other pedestrians joining in as a chorus. The Bond films offered a world that was bloody and knock-about and fast and sexy. As Broccoli himself was to say: 'Our violence is carefully plotted. We don't do it promiscuously, we do it tongue-in-cheek.'

Broccoli and Saltzman worked closely with the censors in various countries, trying to assure the kind of certificate which would guarantee them the dollars they were seeking at the box office. 'We scale things down a lot because of the visual impact,' Broccoli pointed out. 'You may have noticed we avoid using the big screen.' That of course was to change.

The public lapped it up. The film that cost two million pounds to make took twenty three million at the box office in the first year. Such profits were not talked about lightly in the film industry. And, looking at his next bank statement, Sean couldn't take them lightly either.

What is more, despite the earlier rows on the set, these seemed happier days in the Connery household.

Possibly to show how happy the family were together, Sean did what he always swore he would not do – posed for pictures with the two children, bouncing Jason on his knee.

He even revealed the sort of detail so beloved of gossip columnists – that his favourite occupation was grinding up special babyfood mixtures for Jason. Mind you, he did love cooking. He even gave the recipe for the famous Connery casserole – taking 'a piece of proper beef' to which he added very thinly-sliced carrots and 'very, very fine' onions.'

Sean did not appreciate these sorts of demands on his privacy. Jerry Juroe told me: 'As he became more disgruntled with his own situation in regard to the Bond films, I think his attitude was partly due to his being very upset at the whole situation.' In short, he could let many of his frustrations out on the PR machine. 'But it has to be said he has done his share of publicity over the years.'

Christmas 1964 was the perfect family occasion, with Diane, Sean, Giovanna and Jason eating their turkey and sitting around the tree opening their presents.

Diane appeared to be accepting her role as the star's wife. But it didn't mean she liked it. As she said at the time, 'It's not worth arguing. Perhaps the easiest way to illustrate the difference between my two identities is to tell you what happens when I ring my bank manager. If I ring as Miss Cilento with a single account and then again as Mrs Sean Connery with a joint account, you can measure the change in attitude because it is in thousands of pounds, even though I was quite well known and could manage quite well before I married Sean. But it is because of him that I am now not just Mrs Sean Connery, but Mrs James Bond at the same time. It's not only confusing – it can be humiliating.'

As Ken Adam and his wife had noted, the humiliation was sometimes palpable. The previous September they had been in Rome, where Diane was filming *The Agony And The Ecstasy*, the story of Michelangelo. For the first time in years, it was Sean now following *her* around, sitting in on *her* interviews, waiting for *her* to finish a take. But it wasn't going to last. He was about to undertake the first role since *Dr No* that most definitely didn't make him a James Bond look-alike.

The star of *The Agony And The Ecstasy* was glad of the opportunity to meet Sean during the Rome filming.

'I greatly admire Sean,' Charlton Heston told me. 'Maybe we have something in common because we are both Scots, but I think he is a wonderful actor and I only wish we had had the opportunity to work together.'

For the moment, Sean was happy to let Diane be the focus of attention. The woman who was by then one of the senior Hollywood columnists, the English-born Sheilah Graham went along for the ride.

Diane talked to her about the film she had just finished, *Rattle Of A Simple Man* and said that she hoped she and her husband would soon be in a movie together – possibly *The Adventures Of Moll Flanders*. For the moment, however, they couldn't co-ordinate their diaries to allow it to happen.

'We like to work together,' said Diane and there was every reason to believe that was true. They still went to places together and still looked good as a couple. When Sean next went to work in California, Diane said, she was going to go with him. 'We'll go together and we'll work together.'

The newspaper columnists were reporting a rivalry between the

Connerys whether one existed or not. When Diane made *Once Upon A Tractor* the following year, more than one writer said that in the film there were so many gimmicks, so many chases and so much love interest with co-star Alan Bates that she outdid Bond.

Kay Gardella made the point in her *New York Post* column: 'In his role of Bond, the romantic Connery always fights through to victory and gets the girl. Does Diane get her man? Well she not only winds up in his arms in *Once Upon A Tractor* but after completing the TV special, she and Bates immediately began rehearsals for a new play, *The Four Seasons*.'

If this all seemed a little hypocritical from the girl who criticised her husband for wasting his talent on James Bond, she took refuge in the fact that the film, made for television, was intended to plead the cause of the United Nations. However, Diane said, 'Perhaps I should have read the script more carefully. Who would have thought that a TV programme about the United Nations would require so much action and so much strenuous physical activity? But it was fun to play and I'm glad I had the opportunity.'

It was also the actors' duty to let the public have the opportunity to see this busy, active, attractive couple. Diane and Sean fulfilled their duty in this regard.

At the London première of the Rex Harrison movie, *The Yellow Rolls Royce*, Sean and Diane did what was expected of them: they dressed up for the occasion and attended it, just as Broccoli and Saltzman wanted them to do. Sean may not have liked doing the film star bit, but he looked good doing it.

After all, he was an international star, recognised wherever he went. (In Italy, he was known as Mr Kiss-kiss Bang-bang.) And people were talking about him across that very British, very significant divide in what was only the second decade after the Second World War. The man who now wore in private the suits made for him in the Bond pictures, was something of a symbol that the class barrier could be crossed. It wasn't just that at the ball following the 1965 Royal Film Performance, a former coffin polisher could be dancing with his wife, the glamorous Diane Cilento. The crossing of the barriers was even more publicly visible: the Queen Mother told a bowing Connery that she thought *Goldfinger* was the best movie she had ever seen. It was a fine accolade but not one to be taken too seriously. Her Majesty, a keen judge of horse flesh, has never been known to regard the cinema as an essential part of her life.

Sean normally didn't bother to go to see his pictures. The *Goldfinger* première in Paris was an aberration (he was to say that the only time he saw *Goldfinger* after that was on video with his granddaughter, thirty years later). Back in the 1960s, he explained why he wouldn't go into a theatre to watch himself at work. 'It was always pandemonium,' he said.

His own immense talent, to say nothing of his good looks, had got him his success. But without audiences causing pandemonium he would have remained the 'serious' actor he always said he wanted to be most of all – and would possibly still be chasing the agents for work. Sean was ready to admit that Bond had made him rich – or at least was going to make him rich enough, he said, for him to retire. But that wasn't his interest at the moment. Still in his early thirties, he was much more concerned with what new offers were coming his way. There were several, all guaranteeing him a six-figure sum. His only real problem was the one familar to the very rich – tax.

He worried about the whole Bond ethos. He was in a state of conflict. It was perfectly true he didn't like the attendant fuss, the publicity machine, the demanding nature of the work, but he liked the money and he liked the fact that the public followed the films so affectionately.

A James Bond fan club had been set up and was busy sending shop girls and secretaries the latest photographs of Sean Connery, while at Oxford University there was now an all-male Bond club 'dedicated to maintaining the traditions of Bondsmanship'. Whatever that was, it wasn't likely to please the feminists preparing to go into battle against what in the 1970s would be called the male chauvinists. But that, of course, was precisely what Bond was – the king of the male chauvinist pigs. It was just that no one was saying so.

Ian Fleming was certainly a male chauvinist. He was also doing very well out of his Bond books, each of which was republished to coincide with the release of the relevant film and were selling in their millions in paperback.

Even though he didn't make the third film, Terence Young wasn't doing badly out of it all either. At forty-eight, he was in such demand that he was finding it difficult to juggle his diary engagements and decide which pictures he could afford to take.

But Sean was the one who was obviously being successful and becoming rich. People were beginning to charge him with being cocky. Now he turned down interviews and made rude comments about critics.

The *New York Times Magazine* had by now woken up to the 1961 *Sunday Express* article by Susan Barnes which quoted Sean's views on hitting women. The magazine particularly enjoyed the statement that

Sean liked the writer because she was feminine 'and all feminine women are adaptable'.

If that seemed arrogant, one could also detect something else about Connery now – a lack of that modesty that had seemed to endear him to so many of his colleagues and friends up to that time. Asked by Barry Norman in the London *Daily Mail* about his international fame, Sean replied: 'I am not surprised. I expected it. I'd been around a long time.'

He had thought it wise to bide his time. 'I knew everything would fall into place.'

Even so, there were still vestiges of the life he left behind; the one long before he had first become so sure that the pieces would fall into place. He might now be wallowing in a luxury unknown to all previous generations of Connerys, but he appeared to accept it all as his just right, no more than he deserved after all the work he had put in, largely for the profit of other people.

So he wasn't excited about the Mercedes or the Jaguar or the treatment offered by servants at the luxury bungalows to which he would be dispatched by the film company. What did impress him was the ability to have a bath whenever he wanted to. He said he still never got into a bath without wondering at the delight of doing so in such pleasant, private surroundings – without either having to empty it himself afterwards and hang it up on the wall outside his tenement or having to pay sixpence for the privilege of lining up outside a municipal cubicle with a rolled towel under his arm.

In 1964 Ian Fleming died of a heart attack, and Sean was asked for a tribute. He told the truth: 'He was a dreadful snob,' he said, 'but a marvellous fellow.' The first part of that was well known, but not so many people knew that Sean thought the writer was particularly marvellous. Nevertheless, he owed him a lot.

Fleming had created James Bond, but it was Sean who brought him to life – on film at least. In his *New York Times Magazine* interview with Leonard Mosley, Sean said: 'At first, it was I who had to model myself on the James Bond that Fleming and the scriptwriters had shaped for me. But now I am making Bond more and more like me, instead of the other way round. And I'm a chap, nowadays, anyway, who still likes all the girls but doesn't necessarily have to *have* all the girls.'

He was, he said, trying to make Bond grow up a little. 'I would never deny that Bond made me,' he said, perhaps in contradiction to previous statements in recent years, 'and I'll be everlastingly grateful to him. But that doesn't make me a Bond slave. I can cut the shackles free any time I want to. And they aren't made of steel chains any longer either, but smoothest silk.'

But Sean wasn't about to give credit to anyone else for having got where he had. 'Everything I've done has had to be accomplished in my own cycle,' he told another interviewer at about this time, 'my own tine, on my own behalf and with my own sweat.'

That was not a statement calculated to give much pleasure to Messrs Broccoli and Saltzman. But then that didn't bother him very much at a time when he was beginning to wonder whether he had got such a good deal with the Eon Productions organisation after all. They still laid down the policy about what was and what was not permissible in the world of which Sean was now king.

But now there were going to be changes in his life. Work was beginning on the new image he had created for himself in *The Hill*.

That new look was so complete, it was difficult to recognise him. He not only used his Scots accent – so effectively so that when the film was released in America subtitles were used to translate what he was saying – but no one who didn't know would connect him with Bond. He had a short, Government Issue haircut – and a moustache. He was like one of those talented impressionists who don't depend merely on their voices to convey a new character, but who by a tweak of the eyebrows suddenly *become* the person they are impersonating. Voice and accent are one thing, but actions change everything. Quite suddenly, Sean Connery was a chameleon.

It was as though he was using the new image as a kind of dividing line to show that this is where Bond stops for the time being and where Sean Connery, serious actor, begins. In truth, this was more like the real Sean Connery – or perhaps more like the old Sean Connery – than anything he had done in recent years.

Through *The Hill* not only did he show he was capable of a total contrast in roles, he also saved his career and made the next Bond picture all the fresher for the experience. Sean didn't so much *shake* off his James Bond image as *take* it off. In the same way that he took off one of those white tuxedos, the better-known Bond persona was simply and carefully cleaned, pressed and hung up in the studio wardrobe, ready to put on again when it was next needed. And cleaned and pressed was what it had to be – *The Hill* was an altogether dirtier job of work.

He was wont to say that this was the kind of movie with which he was most happy. Diane certainly felt so. This was no comic strip. It was a full-blown horror story that was all too realistic.

It had begun life as a play script called *Breaking Point* earlier in 1964, written by Ray Rigby and Ray Allen who had become known for working on an altogether different kind of military story – the black-and-white television comedy series, *The Army Game*.

Breaking Point had been discovered by the American-born film producer Ken Hyman, at the time he was representing the Seven Arts Organisation in England. Hyman then spent the following six months trying to turn it into a movie. First of all he needed a screenplay. Ray Allen would have been his first choice, but had gone to America, so Hyman asked Ray Rigby to do it. Rigby had never written one before and didn't even know how long it should be. Hyman told him to try for 220 pages which could be cut in half. 'He double-crossed me and turned in 220 *brilliant* pages.'

Having got his screenplay, Hyman tried to sell it to a major studio. One by one, all of them turned it down. There wasn't much of an international market for films about prison 'glasshouses', even less for a British film about them. Eventually, on his third try, MGM expressed some interest – to the extent that their senior executive Red Silverstein furnished him with a list of ten actors whom he would consider for the star role. Among them were Burt Lancaster, Kirk Douglas and Tony Curtis. Despite the fact that this was a totally British story, MGM wanted to make it with an American leading man. It made sense to them : there was more money to be made with an American in the main role.

But Hyman wasn't to be thwarted. He had seen *Dr No* and had the brainwave of making Bond wear battledress. Except that it wouldn't be Bond and he didn't want Bond. He wanted Sean Connery.

Sean's agent Richard Hatton read the script and loved it. After further delay, a meeting was finally arranged with Sean. Hyman had so little faith in the chances of Connery accepting that he took his then fiancée, Caroline to the dinner at the White Elephant – a normally thoroughly unbusinesslike thing to do.

'Sean was his usual dour self,' Ken Hyman remembered , 'until he discovered that Caroline was Scottish. I really think that was the thing that persuaded him to do *The Hill*.'

It was, as things turned out, an inspired choice. So was offering Sidney Lumet the chance to direct.

Lumet had established his reputation with an outstanding examination of the jury system, *Twelve Angry Men*, and had just completed the haunting Rod Steiger film, *The Pawnbroker*, about the depressions of a Holocaust victim. With *The Hill*, he would be telling a totally different kind of World War Two story. He couldn't understand why

Ken Hyman had chosen him to direct. 'Why should you want an American Jewish director to work on a British film set in the North African desert about a Scottish sergeant major?' he asked. Hyman muttered something about *Twelve Angry Men* and added, 'We all got along wonderfully.'

But getting the picture moving still wasn't easy. MGM said they wanted it to be made in colour. Ken Hyman said fine and proceeded to make it in black and white. MGM wanted music by Dmitri Tiomkin. Hyman said yes, but there was no music at all. Finally, Silverstein said: 'You've also got Trevor Howard, haven't you?' 'Sure,' said Hyman – only to hear that the actor had signed to make *Von Ryan's Express* with Frank Sinatra at the same time.

Sean experienced none of the problems with Ken Hyman that he had been having with his other producers – but then he had gone into the movie partly to be rid of Saltzman and Broccoli, whom Hyman knew well. 'I found him bright, co-operative and full of suggestions that were always worth listening to.' Suggestions for dialogue, for movement – 'nothing onerous for the director, nothing to annoy the producer because it involved a great deal of expenditure'.

Oswald 'Ossie' Morris, the cameraman, recalls the actor's professionalism which, when a project like this is involved, has to be the most important consideration of all. 'I got on with him so well,' he told me. 'Some actors can be a great pain. He's far from that. I have only the greatest admiration for him.'

He left the cameraman and the director to get on with their work – something he did less and less in later years. 'He did not suggest camera angles or anything like that. But Sidney Lumet is a very powerful director, very much respected by actors. And when one is so respected, an actor like Sean Connery would make his presentation to the director and leave it at that.'

Sean, meanwhile, was developing the kind of relationship with Lumet that he had enjoyed with Terence Young. He was a man he could trust, whose opinions he could seek and, in turn, accept. Sidney Lumet wanted a great deal of rehearsing and Sean was willing to go along with it.

Originally, Sean wanted to play the part of the warrant officer, a tough, professional soldier who will tolerate anything – bullying, even murder – just so that the place runs smoothly. But the studio wanted Trevor Howard. So Sean didn't get the role. Before long, the part went to Harry Andrews.

Connery decided he would rather play the Scots toughie at the centre of the story: a Scotsman, if not from Fountainbridge then at least from the Gorbals in Glasgow, caught up in a military system that inwardly he himself admires and which has made him what he is. But he is an obstreperous character, more difficult than even Sean himself now was in real life with Broccoli and Saltzman. This is a man who was once a warrant officer, but has now been demoted to the rank of private for striking a superior officer. He has been broken in other ways, too. Sent to a military prison somewhere in the Egyptian desert, he becomes the leader of a cell-full of rebellious inmates who, as punishment, are senselessly made to march up and down a man-made hill in full battle gear in the heat of the desert. He has to go on parade – even when his foot is broken by the sadistic staff sergeant, played by Ian Hendry.

It was a film filled with masterly performances: Harry Andrews quite brilliant in the part for which he had never been intended. Ian Bannen conveys convincingly the warmth of the sympathetic staff sergeant appalled by Hendry's behaviour, and Michael Redgrave says all that needs to be said about the weak, ineffective medical officer too frightened until it is too late to do anything about the way the prison is run. Ossie Davis – who had difficulty in getting a work permit – as a black soldier who has had enough, Alfred Lynch playing the soldier who actually dies as a result of his treatment and Roy Kinnear in the role of the resident coward are all superb, but it is Sean Connery who rises above them all.

Clearly, he set the pace. He was the one who led the climb up and down the hill. He was athletic, and did it seemingly without any effort. As Ossie Morris recalled for me: 'It was really very hot and yet there was no way the actors could have doubles do the work for them.' So, as though they were on the punishment schedule themselves, they had to endure much of the torment. Sean was no more exhausted by it than if he had just played a game of tennis, which next to his golf was something of a passion.

It was the overweight Roy Kinnear who had problems. 'We thought he was going to collapse,' said Morris. 'Because Sean did all the physical stuff without questioning anything, everyone else thought they had to follow.'

The film cost $1,200,000. The schedule was quick – shooting took no more than just over forty days. It was shot in good weather on location in Almeria in Spain, and the interiors were photographed at the MGM studios at Borehamwood. Today, Ken Hyman says that the success owed more than a little to the picture's star. 'Sean was absolutely pivotal to its working out, but he didn't get rich out of it. He loved the material. I think he was very excited about working with

Sidney Lumet, and he's so bright he knew it would enhance his career as an actor. He had the glamour of the Bond role and I think he wanted to enhance his career as an actor – and I think he did it.'

But it was a two-way thing. The producer and the studio also benefited from that 'pivotal' performance, which was due, as much as anything, says Ken Hyman, to the 'total confidence he had in Lumet. He hung onto his every word. He wasn't overawed by Sidney but was totally respectful of what he did.' In the years since it was made, Sean has more than once told Lumet that he was as proud of *The Hill* as of anything he has ever done. 'And so am I,' Ken Hyman told me. 'I made a lot of money from *The Dirty Dozen* but this makes me much more proud.'

Ossie Morris thought Sean felt much the same. 'You could see that he was pleased with it. We would all have lunch together and the one thing we never talked about was Bond. You had the feeling he wanted to forget it.'

Certainly, there was much to remember about *The Hill*. As Ken Hyman added, 'He looks so marvellous on the screen that he doesn't really have to say anything. He could have been a silent film actor. With only a look, he could register what was needed.' Which, considering the problems the Americans had with his accent, was a distinct advantage.

Shortly before his death in a tragic riding accent, Roy Kinnear told me: 'We were all about the same age, had round about the same sort of experience, although I had been to drama school which Sean hadn't, but there was no doubt who was the real star of that picture. It was Sean all the way. And that wasn't just because we were told he was the star and because he was making more money than the rest of us put together. He had the star personality, and also the star acting ability. He was wonderful. I don't think I have ever been so mesmerised by a performance as I was by his.'

The critics echoed this. Leonard Mosley, writing in the *Daily Express* noted: 'He gives one of the most disturbingly effective performances of the year.'

As Mr Mosley, one of the most respected critics of the time, wrote in the introduction to his piece, 'Anyone who thinks that Sean Connery can't act – and I admit I was one of them – should go and have their withers wrung by this devastating film and then apologise to Mr C.'

It was, he agreed, all so very different from Bond. 'Quite frankly, I think that as 007 in those Bond films, Connery is a cheap edition of what author Ian Fleming had in mind. He never looks or sounds like the polished man of the world. I suspect that he couldn't steal a stamp from a village post office, let alone burgle secrets from the Bolsheviks.'

And most damning of all: 'I also believe that no really glamorous and sophisticated girl would ever fall for his gawky mannerisms and his sexy technique.'

Well, experience had already proved that point to be wrong. All the women who had worked with him and all the women writers who had penned pieces about him, had nullified it a hundred times over. But, as he did not point out, there were virtually no women in *The Hill* and the man's man reacted accordingly.

So did the film industry. It was selected as the British entry for the 1965 Cannes Film Festival. *The Hill* was giving him a new lease of life before, it could be argued, he really needed it.

Leonard Mosley also wrote in his piece: 'But in *The Hill*, he isn't pretending to be a fabulous master spy but a genuine hulk of flesh, blood and bone. The tension he creates makes you sweat, so fierce is the drive he puts into his part.'

Not everyone liked it. The movie, in America at least, has become an acquired taste. *Newsweek* wrote: 'Above all, *The Hill* can be seen as a dissection of discipline, coming to perfect focus in a scene in which Connery and Harry Andrews mindlessly scream regulations at each other. But writer Ray Rigby and director Sidney Lumet could not leave well enough alone. They go up and down the hill from parallel to parable to platitude.'

At the suggestion of Ken Hyman, Ray Rigby turned his screenplay into a novel. *Life*'s associate editor Frank Kappler liked both the film and the book and was amazed things happened in that order – usually, films are made from books. 'Anyway,' he wrote, 'it's a hell of a book-or-film, and I use the fiery word advisedly, for *The Hill* in any medium is a couple of hours in an inferno Dante never dreamed of.'

In the film, Kappler actually liked Ossie Davis best of all. He 'manages to project the motivation that underlies his actions – possibly because it is pretty basic. Roberts, acted by Sean Connery on temporary release from Bond, emerges on film merely as a decent Joe.'

The critic for *Time* magazine, as influential an international journal as any by which he could have wished to be praised, saw *The Hill* and noted the watershed Sean had crossed. The magazine's anonymous critic wasn't so sure about the film itself. '*The Hill* seems unlikely to move mountains as a message film. The cold, cruel military mind has been tried and convicted all too often.' But about Sean, there were no doubts in the writer's mind. 'It can be said, however, that *Hill* provides a significant change for Sean Connery fans everywhere. Rough as a thistle, sporting a moustache, he lends muscular presence to a conventional he-man role and stirs up a hint or two that what has heretofore been sealed in Bond may be the screen's new Gable.' This would be a comparison made again and again throughout Connery's career.

What none of the critics hinted at was that there was a very good reason why he put so much into that part. He was determined to show – to himself every bit as much as to producers who, in any case, knew he was a walking, talking key to the bank vaults – that he didn't need James Bond.

By doing so he was simply following a pattern that almost every other member of the Bond team was also practising. People working on the Bond films were so close that they had their own vocabulary, which they used when referring to Sean and also when talking about themselves. After *The Hill*, they would talk of 'doing a Bond, then doing a civilian; doing another Bond and following it with another civilian'.

In the belief that there was still a mystique about the way Bond was presented, the series' producers banned television exposure. They were worried that television coverage would weaken the box office impact of the films. They certainly hadn't yet considered selling the movies for television showings – and the whole concept of home video was still a pipedream for someone sitting in a laboratory. Not even Q had yet had the idea of giving Bond a cassette to put into a machine which would generate pictures of its own on a television screen.

But eventually, Sean and his producers weakened. They agreed to a programme that would be narrated by Connery, would include clips from all three Bond films and would, it was said, try to explain the very mystique of the Bond story that the producers were trying so hard to protect. It was going to be sponsored by Pepsi Cola and would just happen to be ready in time for the next Bond movie, which was widely expected to be the story that had caused Saltzman problems – *Thunderball.*

Meanwhile there was something of a thunderball in his private life at this time. In 1965 Diane, then aged thirty, announced that she was going to leave the house in Acton with the two children, seven-year-old Giovanna and two-year-old Jason. It was said to be a trial separation as a last resort.

Why had it happened? To Diane, it could simply have been a sense of disappointment. When she had said earlier that she wanted more than anything to work with Sean, she was telling the truth. Sean and Diane had, without committing themselves in writing, agreed to make a new Twentieth Century–Fox film in Australia called *Call Me When*

The Cross Turns Over. Plainly, as far as Mrs Connery was concerned, the cross had already turned over and had caused a huge explosion in its wake.

But *Thunderball* was now going to start earlier than planned. The change of work schedule meant they wouldn't be able to make *Call Me When The Cross Turns Over.* Diane was desolate. The separation seemed an inevitable final attempt to salvage the marriage.

Diane told everyone she had had enough. The goose that had laid the golden egg had turned into an ugly monster as far as she was concerned. But for reasons no one was willing to explain, it had all come to a head.

In fact, it was Sean who did the leaving and among his intimates it was not surprising that he did so. No one was yet giving reasons but, as we have seen, professional rivalry wasn't proving to be a satisfactory basis for marital bliss.

There was no suggestion that there was anyone else on the scene. There were so many beautiful women on the Bond set, that the overall temptation was somewhat muted. Had Diane shown any jealousy – and as we have seen, it appears that she had not – he might justifiably have replied that it was all a bit like being a doctor : he had seen – and touched – it all before.

8

A FINE MADNESS

It took ten days for the separation to be made public, during which the kind of pandemonium that Sean had talked about surrounding this film premières broke out around the Connery household. Diane was besieged at home and wouldn't leave the house or answer the phone. As usual, Sean was keeping very much to himself, doing his work, retreating to his caravan, most certainly refusing to give interviews.

And yet was it all over? The trial separation did seem to have come to an end soon after filming of *Thunderball* began. The external location shots were set in the Bahamas and, after being apart for weeks, Diane flew to the islands to be with the man who was still her husband, bringing the two children along too.

The film company, ever mindful of the value of good publicity, were pleased to see that Sean met his family at Nassau airport before driving off to the bungalow set aside for them at the Garden of Eden, the sort of place that likes to boast that it has film stars to stay.

Hardly surprisingly, the world's press were at the airport to see a deeply sun-tanned Sean holding Jason with one arm and clasping Diane, who was wearing a fetching striped sweater on top of a white skirt, around the shoulder with the other.

It was an idyllic setting – if only you could keep the locals away from the man who, like it or not, was known only as James Bond. For try as he may, Sean Connery and James Bond were one – and on this trip more than ever before.

Letizia Adam says that she saw how little Sean enjoyed the confusion between the two names. She didn't drive, so he took her in his car to one of the local markets to buy chickens and other staples. 'Everywhere he went, they would call out, "Hello, Mr Bond. Mr Bond!" I can tell you he didn't like that at all. He went crazy.'

She told him: 'Sean, you owe your success to those people. What do they know if you are Mr Connery or Mr Bond? You owe them everything. They buy the tickets.'

Two hundred American college kids also claimed their rights as ticket buyers when they waded into the water to surround the boat Sean was using for one scene, declaring, 'You're our leader – and we're your people.'

When they were got out of the way and when the cameras shut down for the day, he had a chance to reflect on just how idyllic this country was – particularly if you were a multi-millionaire, who, according to the local regulations, didn't have any income tax to pay. There were more banks than there were corner shops and everything was expensive – four shillings for a bottle of tap water. Yet whisky at one pound a throw didn't seem that much more.

The Connerys' bungalow cost sixty pounds a day, which also gives you some idea of how long ago 1965 was. In those days that was a lot of money. So was the four shillings that taxis charged as soon as their metres were switched on. The newspapers at the time couldn't get over that. Four shillings! That proved how expensive it was to be in that part of the world, and how sensible it was of the film company to rent Sean his own Ford Mustang. Apparently, renting a car in those days was also a James Bondish thing to do.

None of that was considered a good reason to go to the Bahamas to make a film, but anyone seeing the white sand, the blue sea and the golden sun would get a pretty good idea of why the location was going to work.

Sean could only hope that it was also a suitable setting to get his marriage back on course. Things always did look better when the sun shone, didn't they? While Sean was working – he began every day at the traditional studio starting-time of 6.00 a.m. – Diane cooked, swam, played golf and lay in the sun. But she was bored 'up to her neck with this whole Bond thing'.

Sean and Diane were not quite the centre of social activity the film company had expected and hoped for. They kept very much to themselves, although there was a party given for them by Anita Ekberg and her husband Rick, who was in the film himself, playing a CIA agent.

Diane was going so far and no further in discussing their relationship. 'Neither Sean nor I mean to allow ourselves to be packaged by this business,' she said, which in a way screamed out loud what was actually happening.

'This industry can take hold of you and wrap you up like a piece of meat, and then you are left with about twenty per cent of your time for yourself and your family. It is not enough and neither of us will allow ourselves to become that involved. We are not going to let ourselves be merchandised.'

You read between the lines and came to the right conclusion. But there was little public sympathy for their cause, not much from other members of the acting profession and none at all from Eon Productions. It was an old story – contract players complaining that they had been exploited by the movie moguls who had turned them into their virtual slaves. The moguls' response was that it was a very nice form of slavery indeed and most lesser mortals would give ten years of their lives for the chance to live in that kind of bondage. And the word didn't have to have a capital 'B' – it applied to thousands of different stars in thousands of different roles.

But Diane was not impressed with that argument. 'I am through the other side now of being Mrs James Bond and although it happens, it cannot upset me any longer. Sean and I have our own lives to lead in our own way.'

One of the Bond Girls, Luciana Paluzzi, took it upon herself to douse all the doubts about Sean's relations with his wife. 'Can't you see they are very much in love ?' she asked. 'Otherwise, they wouldn't care enough to have fights.' That was a somewhat un-British way of explaining the fights that everybody working on *Thunderball* now knew about.

Others who heard what was going on were less sanguine. 'Diane could be very tough,' Ken Adam told me. 'Competition between them was still one of the contributory factors. But it was much more serious than that. It became a *Who's Afraid of Virginia Woolf* kind of relationship. Letizia and I have now been married for forty years and we argue. But it was not like them. We heard the rows and they were vicious.'

The Adams lived in a bungalow adjoining the Connerys on the inappropriately-named Love Beach. 'The relationship between them was more than just strained – you could hear it almost all the time.' Fortunately for the couple – and for the producers – none of the journalists around at that time picked it up. The studio's screening was very effective.

How much notice Diane took of Claudine Auger, the former Miss France who was the new Bond Girl, Domino, is not easy to work out. According to members of the team, Claudine was on the scene both on and off the set, although there is no evidence of an affair. She was, after all, only twenty-three and married to a much older man. But photographers were quick to snap pictures of her sitting on Sean's lap on a deck chair between takes, both of them in swimming costumes.

When filming switched to Pinewood, Sean visited the flat Claudine rented in Park Street, off London's Park Lane. Nevertheless, as far as the public was concerned, the only time the two stars were with each other was on the set or when they posed for publicity pictures.

Anna Korda was voice coach on the movie. 'We had so many girls, one more beautiful than the other,' she told me. 'I think he was the one who used to do the chasing. Otherwise it would have bored him.'

But he didn't give any impression of being bored. 'We were in the Bahamas. It was a dream. Really wonderful. He was very easy going, and so gorgeous! He was very popular. He talked to everybody. On English crews, we were all very pally in those days.'

Because he was surrounded by so many beautiful women, he had choices to make – between the ones he would regard just as, to use the biblical phrase, good to look upon, and those to whom he could relate in conversation. The extremely attractive Letizia Adam says that she got on with him principally because he regarded her as very different. 'He treated me as a chum'.

She was one woman who could speak to him as a mate. She would tell him if his wig, made specially for him in London, wasn't fitting properly. Early on in the shooting of *Thunderball*, she pointed out that she could see the joins – something that hadn't been noticed by the makeup girls or even by the director.

'I told him to scream, shout, do something – because it wasn't right.' This was one occasion when he needed to neither scream nor shout. By now you didn't argue with the star of a James Bond picture if you wanted peace.

It was on Claudine Auger that most eyes were directed – when they couldn't get close enough to Diane and Sean.

Claudine, who floated into the Bahamian shore on the back of a turtle for her entrance, said that she knew what she had taken on with the film role.

'The Bond women,' she declared, schooled no doubt by the Eon publicity department, 'are the women of the nuclear age. They are free and they make love to whom they want without worrying about it afterwards.

'In this film, we have this love scene underwater – for the first time in a movie, I think.'

The inspiration for that underwater scene came from Terence Young, once more directing and more than putting his stamp on a Bond picture. He took it upon himself to keep his two stars cool between takes in the heat of Nassau by passing glasses of champagne to each of them.

It didn't cool the ardour seen by the audiences. Making love under the Caribbean waters was about the only thing that hadn't been thought of before and was a scene just waiting to happen. Connery and Auger made it happen without any great problem, in itself something of a triumph. It was not easy to make love wearing breathing equipment at the bottom of the sea – not quite so low down as it appeared – but they made it look very effective. Especially when Mademoiselle Auger's bikini top floated to the surface.

Before they performed their underwater magic, they had to be seen on a raft in mid ocean. The take was constantly ruined by passing speedboats. Terence Young called for the boats to get out of camera shot but to no avail. Then Sean used his best Fountainbridge vocabulary and diction, and managed to persuade them without very much difficulty.

After all, every moment spent away from what they were supposed to be doing cost money. About one million pounds were being spent on the equipment alone. There was a giant hydrofoil to skim across the ocean at ninety-five miles an hour and a two-man diving bell worked fifteen fathoms down in the briny.

There was also a device that has come to be just part of a day's work in the air–sea rescue business today but which was put into action for the first time in *Thunderball* – a device that could snatch a man into the air at 180 miles an hour. The man wasn't real, but the device was. It proved just how useful to humanity James Bond could be.

Sean looked good doing all those things that were real, but a double was used for some of the really dangerous stuff – as much as anything because the insurance on a leading player who performed crazy, dangerous stunts would have been prohibitive. For those occasions, one of the most eminent stuntmen in the business, Bob Simmons, was on hand – playing both Bond and one of the adversaries.

In the scene where James socks a woman – this time no pretence about hitting a female differently from the way he would strike a man; no open-handed slap this but a rounded, heavy punch – the woman was no lady. It was Bob Simmons. Sean enjoyed that immensely.

In *Thunderball* Bond's assignment is to prevent SPECTRE – nearly bankrupt despite benefiting from the proceeds of the 1963 British Great Train Robbery – from holding the world to ransom after hijacking a NATO Vulcan bomber armed with two atomic weapons. The main villain of the piece is SPECTRE's Number Two, Emilio Largo, played by Adolfo Celi (a substitute for Ernst Stavro Blofeld who in *From Russia With Love* was seen only as a lap and a pair of hands holding a white cat as beautiful in the feline world as the Bond Girls were in theirs).

A finely-observed convention had developed that might have registered subliminally with audiences but was never stressed. Had it been broken, on the other hand, the image might have been destroyed: Bond was never seen covered in blood.

It was no more unrealistic than any of the other things Bond did, but even though he was hit often enough, he was never bruised and never were there more than a couple of drops of the blood about his person. A torn sleeve on his Savile Row jacket was about the worst thing he could suffer. In *Thunderball* he was shot in the leg, but apart from a slight smearing of blood there was little to show for it. Being roughed up was not something he allowed to happen to Bond. Besides, Sean, the former Mr Universe contender, could have seen any attacker into hospital had he wanted to. Sean seemed to have in mind a responsibility not to spoil the image, which had evolved between the beginning of *Dr No* and the end of *From Russia With Love*. In the first picture, he was slightly gauche, but he always moved perfectly. Like Fred Astaire who had people staring in wonderment even when he played pool, Sean was a co-ordinated mass. Yet he wasn't quite comfortable until the second movie reached its climax.

Desmond Llewellyn saw it. He recalled Sam Goldwyn's reputed definition of a man's star quality (everything Sam Goldwyn said has to have the word reputed in front of it) – that he had to have 'balls that jangle like temple bells'. Well, Sean always had balls that jangled like temple bells. Even when he killed someone, he did it with a panache that put him in the King Solomon temple class.

In *Thunderball*, one of the villains is killed with a spear. Twenty years later, there would have been blood, gore and groans. All Bond said before rubbing his hands and walking away was, 'Well, I think he got the point.'

When Diane went back home after seven weeks or so, their marital problems resolved or unresolved nobody could yet tell, Sean was left alone in the Bahamas to get bored, play golf, and be introduced to Nassau society. The trouble was that it was becoming more and more evident now that the man being invited to the parties in which the men all wore dinner jackets and the women the most fashionable cocktail dresses was James Bond, not Sean Connery. By inviting him, they were playing a Bond game themselves.

It seemed at times that, other than Diane the only person who could tell the two apart was Sean himself. To him, Bond was totally different not just from himself, but also from anyone he had ever known in real life. 'From an actor's point of view,' he said in a kinder, more reflective moment than many, 'Bond presented terrible problems. He has no mother. He has no father. He doesn't come from anywhere. He hadn't been anywhere before he became 007. He was born – kerplump – thirty-three years old.'

He went on: 'At this point, there is nothing more I can get out of Bond as an actor, but because of my contract I'll be making two more 007 films.'

That was not to say he was shutting his eyes at more after that. But there would be a price. 'If they want me to do more it will be a million dollars and ten per cent of the gross.' Then, he said, he 'might talk about it'.

The kind of man Sean was in real life was the subject of as much intense speculation as the marriage of which he was or was not a part. Jean Rook, the late *Daily Express* columnist who liked to call herself the First Lady of Fleet Street, did what all women columnists got round to doing sooner or later and started to analyse what there was about this man. 'I've interviewed every great sex symbol from Paul Newman ... to Guy the gorilla before he was stuffed. If you laid their libidos end to end they still wouldn't macho up to the sexual impact of Sean Connery,' she wrote.

'At six foot three inches and around two hundred pounds of prime, lean Scottish beef, Mr Connery looks like a cross between the Monarch of the Glen and the sharp side of Ben Nevis.'

But he was being very sparing about displaying those two hundred pounds. Not that he was being asked to take his clothes off or anything, but the fully-dressed Sean Connery had determined not to be one of those film stars constantly in the public gaze. If he could be quiet and uncommunicative among friends, in crowds he was now going to be a non-person altogether.

When *Thunderball* had its première (or rather premières; in London, it opened in two West End cinemas simultaneously) he was absent. Was this because he and Diane wouldn't appear together any more? Mrs Connery was still living at the Acton house – so where was Sean? No one was saying, but they *had* been in Hollywood together the previous week and that seemed to have dulled some of the speculation. The reason Sean wasn't going to the première, it was later revealed, was that they had both seen the picture in America 'and he didn't want to sit through it again'.

He was keeping his promise not to go to 'pandemonium' events. United Artists let on that they were disappointed that he didn't come to the première. It was the first inkling of the disappointment both sides were feeling for each other.

The studio, however, would have reason to pocket its concern and take comfort from their balance sheets. The film took $1,130,000 in its first week in New York and in its first year rang up no less than twenty-eight million dollars in America alone – a fabulous figure for a time when you could get into an American cinema for a dollar or less. The total income from James Bond films to date, it was reckoned, was 150 million dollars. They had cost altogether ... ten million dollars.

In December 1965, he was declared the world's top movie money-spinner. It was the second year in succession that the New York-based *Motion Picture Herald* had selected him ahead of Elvis Presley, Julie Andrews and Sophia Loren. John Wayne was number ten in the list that year.

All that was not, surprisingly enough, music to Sean's ears. On the contrary, it made him feel a victim. He wasn't being paid enough for the work he did or for the fortune he was making for his producers, even though £300,000 or $600,000 was a whole lot better than his original Bond fee.

Now Sean wanted his pound of the flesh being gathered by his producers. He wasn't yet making any public statements but people in the business knew that he and Broccoli and Saltzman weren't exactly getting on.

He had more confidence now that he could manage without Bond. *The Hill* had without doubt confirmed that. While he was working on *Thunderball* a copy of the film was flown over to Nassau specially for him, and he was surer than ever. People working on *Thunderball* noted that he now had fewer inhibitions talking to other members of the crew about his rows with Broccoli and Saltzman over money. A few of the more privileged heard the rows for themselves.

'He would talk about them all the time, complaining about how they were exploiting him,' Ken Adam told me.

'He talked about it in his dressing room, I remember,' said Anna Korda. 'But it certainly never affected his work. He was much too professional.'

Then, for one interview, the guard slipped. 'I've fed too many, too long for too little,' he said to Sheilah Graham, which gave you some idea of what was going on in the boardroom before the next script came in.

The producers weren't too happy among themselves. Sean said he imagined Saltzman and Broccoli sitting at their table glaring at each other and thinking, 'That bastard's got my other thirty million dollars.' There was no evidence that they had said or felt anything of the kind, but there was plenty to show – and much, much more to come – that Sean Connery, top box office favourite of the year, felt he hadn't made such a good deal after all. One could have muttered words about comfortable purgatory, but it wouldn't have appeased him.

The truth of the matter was that the sophisticated James Bond, used to playing at the most fashionable casinos in the world and being welcomed by fawning caddies at the top golf clubs, was playing an altogether more complicated but also much older game: cat and mouse.

Sean wanted the producers to think about what they were demanding of him. 'Each picture takes six months,' he said, 'That doesn't leave too much time for anything else. I'm expected to do one Bond a year.' But he now put his foot down. 'It will now be one every eighteen months. Otherwise I can't do the things I want to.'

As he told Sheilah Graham, 'Don't get me wrong. I like the part. But unless I get the million pounds and the percentage I am asking for, they'll have to find another boy.'

What he was going to do was take a break, do a film in Hollywood and then perhaps what he wanted to do more than anything else – go into Greek tragedy.

In another interview he said: 'There was conflict from the beginning. You could never tell when you were going to start and never tell when you were going to finish and that put me in a very, very vulnerable position in terms of wanting to do other pictures.'

Ask him what he hated most and he would be consistent: it was still to hear people in the streets calling out, 'There's James Bond.' It was happening more now than ever before and he wasn't in the mood to contemplate how much he owed the role or where he would be if people did now stop calling it out. That was why, more than ever, he made sure he didn't wear his toupee when he went into the street and why if it were possible to grow a moustache without affecting the Bond schedule, he was going to do that, too.

Another thing that annoyed him was the constant reference, particularly in America, to him as the 'English actor'. After all, he hadn't spent all those years in Fountainbridge simply to be called an Englishman.

'The Scots,' he declared, 'have nothing in common with the English. The Scots are Scottish. Period. And I don't like the English at all because I am Scottish. Period.'

Who was he getting at? Did he have no English friends? Those who categorised themselves as just that could have stood up to be counted and rounded on him. But they didn't.

There was a huge dichotomy between what James Bond had done for Sean Connery and what Sean wanted to do with his own future. Sometimes, you had the distinct feeling that he was going to use the Beretta – changed in later films to a Walther PPK carried in what experts knew as a Berns Martin holster – on anyone who suggested that he was being typecast.

Somehow, it wasn't enough to think what *The Hill* had done for him and to contemplate more of the same in the months and years to come. He was identified as James Bond. Worse still, like a man in jail for a sentence he hadn't committed who begins to believe the case for the prosecution, he was afraid he might begin to identify himself as James Bond.

Not everyone could understand his reaction to everything *Dr No* and all that followed had brought. To lesser mortals, this was stardom, success and wealth beyond imagination – and they were right. But it wasn't nice to feel exploited, and to believe that although you yourself were getting all that fame and money, others were getting more – and at the expense of your own future prospects.

By the end of November 1965, Sean was telling the world what he really felt, and that was complimentary to neither the films nor what he thought they stood for.

The pictures, he told Peter Bart in the *New York Times*, were 'like comic strips. The producers constantly have to come up with bigger and better gimmicks. That's all that sustains the pictures. How far can they go? I think that they'll have to switch the routine completely to survive.'

And he didn't like all that was being associated with Bond. 'The whole thing has become a Frankenstein's monster. The merchandising, the promotion, the pirating – they're thoroughly distasteful.' James Bond attaché cases (that was inevitable). James Bond toys, sweaters, underwear and James Bond dolls with spikes protruding from their shoes. They were all on the market, all licensed by Eon Productions – and all, Sean thought, making a fortune for the company on his back. 'It's all a lot of rubbish. The quality is appalling.'

That could have been taken as something of a suicide note as far as his career was concerned. Did he want to get out of his contract?

Reading what he said certainly made it seem that way. There were still two more Bond pictures to make and he had confessed he wasn't looking forward to them.

The rows between him and his producers were getting worse and he wasn't hiding the fact. He told Mr Bart: 'I am fighting for money and time. I want to get as much money as I can. And I want to do them in as little time as possible, so I can fit in other things that mean more to me.'

Undoubtedly Diane wanted to hear that, but the producers could be excused for feeling less kindly towards him. One of the reasons for employing top stars was because they were considered reliable – a word that went hand in hand with 'professional'.

No one could fault Sean's acting or the work he put into each Bond picture. He certainly was professional. He never missed a day, never came late. But life would probably have been easier for Saltzman and Broccoli had Sean not constantly said what he felt and had not let them know that he would like to spend less time as 007.

In 1965 Sean returned to Hollywood to make a non-Bond movie called *A Fine Madness*. He also had plans to direct a Broadway play – which showed precisely where his mind and his career were going.

The idea of *A Fine Madness* was, once more, to get as far away from Bond as possible. In it he played a Greenwich Village poet. There were fights, including a fierce sock on the jaw for Joanne Woodward who was playing his wife (was this now becoming statutory in a Connery film?) and a run across a steel girder on Brooklyn Bridge, with Sean doing at least some of the running. What was incredible was not so much that Sean wanted to broaden his career so much, but that there were producers happy to allow him to do so. Usually, the problem with typecasting is that it is done by other people – studio bosses who don't want someone for a part who is closely identified with another role.

The critics in Britain didn't go for the film very much, but Sean said he had no regrets. It had been a good choice for him, he maintained. The New York papers had been kinder than their British counterparts – in fact, he reported back home, 'they raved'. That pleased him. 'I don't want to sound a super-egotist but I think it was was worthwhile doing. A film when it is finished is like a young bird leaving the nest. It can be shot down, but if you believed in it in the first place that doesn't matter. You get detached about it.' Maybe playing a poet had rubbed off on him.

In truth, there couldn't have been a lot to be happy about with this film. In recent years, the legend has grown that this was a fine picture that summed up the mood of the first post-beatnik existentialist generation. That is being too kind. Leonard Mosley said at the time in the *Daily Express*: 'If he wants to continue to be accepted as a serious actor, I suggest that he keeps out of comedy from now on.'

Perhaps it was more the point that comedies should have kept away from him. It left the distinct impression that the picture was chasing and then begging him to do more than he was prepared to offer. The film started off somewhat reminiscent of a Doris Day–Rock Hudson-style comedy which had gone out of vogue a few years before. It then degenerated into something quite different – exactly what was not so easy to say. It was a dreadful movie and Sean did his career no good at all by involving himself with it.

True, he didn't look a bit like James Bond, which might have pleased him. But by now it was easier to imagine him as 007 than as a quirky poet who cleans carpets for a living – until, that is, the soap in one overflows onto the rug in an executive's plush office; Sean himself is fairly oblivious to the problem – at the time he is making love to the man's naked secretary.

Once more Sean found himself having problems with his producers – and Broccoli and Saltzman were nowhere to be seen. This time, it was Warner Bros whom he claimed had 'screwed' him. So he sued Jack Warner, a man who had had his problems with actors before and who took it all as part of the game. James Cagney – 'the professional againster', he called him – and Bette Davis had both fought Warner over their contracts. But for Sean it was the first time. It would not be the last.

The matter was settled and Sean was happy. That did not mean, however, that he was willing to go along with all the producers' ideas. Once more, he was being difficult about publicity, the very lifeblood of commercial film-making, saying that 'This personal publicity business has lost all sense of balance.' He didn't want to follow his colleagues in agreeing to personal profiles in fan magazines. 'The actors utter these inanities, then go to some movie set and pose for pictures in some mockup kitchen. The magazine then explains, here's Sean Connery, a real homebody frying eggs in his own kitchen.' After his early experiences doing just that at home, Sean Connery wouldn't now allow a photographer within a hundred yards of his own kitchen, or even, had it been within his power, a hundred miles of it.

He hated every bit of the film-star thing, even though that all-consuming machine continued to lavish love and money on him. He declared – as most big film stars do declare from time to time – that what he really wanted to do now was to become a director. 'I can't be the virile hero for ever,' he said, almost as an aside.

'I'd rather be thought of as a good actor than a matinée idol,' he added.

Nevertheless, he didn't mind making the most of a few of the perks of being that matinée idol – like keeping for himself about twenty of the Savile Row suits made for his movies. He looked good in suits and there were times when he liked to wear them in private. Those that he didn't want he gave to his father or his brother Neil, who, once a few alterations had been made, were quite the best-dressed men in Fountainbridge.

In 1966 it was Neil Connery who fell victim to the exploitation machine – with Sean himself a not unconcerned bystander. The younger Connery was invited to make a screen test. Now, he knew he got it on the strength of his brother's reputation, but there was absolutely no reason why he couldn't go into a film career on his own and be a success on his own.

What he did not realise at the time was that the film, to be made in Italy, would be a cheap spin-off of the Bond pictures. He was not the only member of the cast to have a connection with Sean, or at least Bond. In it, too, were Daniela Bianchi, who hadn't done a great deal since *From Russia With Love*, and the woman who appeared in *all* the Bond pictures but quite plainly was not a Bond Girl, Lois Maxwell, the ubiquitous Miss Moneypenny. To add further respectability to the whole, there was also Bernard Lee who had come to be identified with the snearing, impatient 'M'.

No one claimed that the picture had anything to do with James Bond. The very name wasn't even mentioned, but you would have had to have been living on a desert island for the past four years not to have got the point.

The dialogue, again without even mentioning the name James, let alone Bond, left very little to the imagination. In one scene, Lois Maxwell tells Neil: 'If you were in the Secret Service for long you would kill your brother's reputation both as an agent and as a bedmate.' And in bed Ms Bianchi tells him unambiguously: 'Your brother was never like this.'

Neil's brother, of course, had the advantage – for all the criticism, all the unpleasantness – of Eon and Saltzman and Broccoli, to say nothing of Fleming and Terence Young *et al. Operation Kid Brother*, as the Italian movie was called, had a director called Dorio Savetello whom Sean threatened to ... well, he didn't have to spell it out. Even so, the director asked Sean to pose with his brother for publicity pictures. Studying his reaction could not have been a pleasant moment for Signor Savetello.

For his trouble, Neil was paid even less than Sean had received for *Dr No*. All he saw on a cheque was £5,000, which only added to the embarrassment it had all caused. Sean tried to buy all the prints, but the director saw immortality at risk and refused. As might be imagined, it was not a picture that set the Tiber alight in his own country and was hardly seen anywhere else.

But Neil didn't feel all that perturbed by the affair. He went back to work as a twenty-pounds-a-week plasterer on a building site in Edinburgh and back to his council home at night. If he became a star through the film, he would be absolutely delighted, but until he was able to join the Martini set himself, he was content spending his evenings at the pub drinking Scotch and playing darts. Was he afraid of being laughed at by his mates? They wouldn't dare, he said, 'because they know I'd thump them if they did.' And he added stoically: 'If this film thing doesn't happen, it won't worry me. I'm not the worrying kind.'

Somehow or other, directly or indirectly, Sean would constantly find himself in scrapes involving members of his family. They weren't always a simple matter of sorting out contractual details. Sometimes, they happened on what seemed the happiest and most innocent of occasions.

In 1966 the writer Larry Gelbart invited Sean to a party at his Hollywood home. Among those present was Connery's friend and erstwhile producer, Ken Hyman, who was now busy on *The Dirty Dozen*. Another guest was one of the stars of that movie, Lee Marvin, 'a real pistol', as Hyman describes him.

There was a buffet, with plenty to eat. That didn't interest Lee Marvin because there was also a great deal to drink – and Marvin faced with a bar was like a kitten shown a saucer of milk. He was as drunk as only Lee Marvin could be, or so his reputation went. It was in this condition that he spied an elderly woman sitting in the corner of the room.

Marvin swaggered towards her, looking totally in control, but in fact, as Ken Hyman told me, 'so drunk he didn't know what town he was in'. The eighty-year-old lady thought he was going to have a fairly innocent conversation with her, but instead he flung a sexual comment at her that would have frozen any female a quarter her age. The words themselves weren't exactly insulting, and he might even have thought he was being complimentary. In fact, he was very, very rude.

The lady wasn't hurt – because she didn't hear a single slurred word of what the actor had actually said. 'Excuse me,' she replied, 'what did you say?'

So Marvin repeated his comment. At that point another guest whispered to him, 'She's Sean's aunt.' That was when Connery heard what was going on. As Ken now relates the tale, 'Out of nowhere comes Sean.'

All Ken could think of at that stage was the filming of *The Dirty Dozen* and his own star's appearance. He rushed to Sean, endeavouring to separate him from his laughing, drooling quarry. But Sean was in full, outraged flight, and there was no stopping him.

Hyman knew that he wasn't going to be able to deflect Connery from his aim of bashing Marvin's brains out. There was little chance of preventing a confrontation of some kind; the best he could hope for was a compromise.

It was more in desperation than expectation that he tried to reason with Sean – not an easy thing to do in the full heat of battle. 'Hit him in the *body*, PLEASE,' he begged. 'Please, don't hit him in the *face*, Sean. Sean ... SEAN! He's got closeups tomorrow.'

And he added: 'I got to the point where I was about to say, "Sean! Hit me! *I* haven't got *any* closeups." '

But before he did, Sean collapsed in a heap with laughter. 'You fucking producers,' he said and couldn't control himself any longer. The old lady at the root of the incident just smiled – and was still none the wiser as to what had almost happened.

Like the state of affairs between Connery and Eon Productions, Sean's relationship with his wife was now not so much under control as in a state of guarded truce. On the surface, the marriage seemed to be perfect. Even the newspapers had now forgotten the time they headlined Diane's supposed leaving of the matrimonial home. Now those same papers gladly featured photographs of Sean kissing his wife and children as they left Heathrow together for a holiday abroad. In 1967 there was no apparent reason to do otherwise, which shows how successful Sean was in keeping his personal affairs to himself.

That was why he and Diane were planning to move from Acton. There was no privacy. Things would be easier in somewhere like Grosvenor Square or Knightsbridge, he said, not because it suited his station in life more – although it would do – but because there was more anonymity there. He wanted to get away from that public glare, which was why he had already bought a house in Spain. Before long, he would be spending more time there than he would in Britain.

The Connerys did buy a new London house – not in the super

luxury of Mayfair but in the upper-middle class suburb of Putney, home to, among others, the Lord Chancellor, Lord Hailsham. Sean hoped the Lord Chancellor could keep the press away.

It had to be said that the journalists were getting all they needed from the things he was more happy to talk about in public – like when he was elected the most popular star in Britain in December 1967. Lee Marvin was second, Michael Caine third, Julie Christie fourth and John Wayne fifth. Elizabeth Taylor came in at number eight and Richard Burton was tenth.

He was gently cultivating the image that brought him to that sort of popular acclaim – not, when he could get away from it, by the usual press stunts (heaven forbid!), but by doing the occasional television programme – although not as an actor. His television output for 1967 consisted of *The Castles Of Scotland* and *The Bowler And The Bunnet*, a programme about the Clydeside shipbuilders, then severely under threat (the bowler was worn by the bosses, the 'bunnet' or flat cap by the workers), which he wrote himself. They were both documentaries for Scottish Television. He was as distressed as the television company was that other members of the independent television network didn't take up the option of running the programmes. What did that say about the magic of the Sean Connery name?

As far as he himself was concerned, it was all a contribution to his native country, and rightly seemed to be appreciated by his fellow Scots. The programmes certainly didn't make him any money. Nor had his previous year's opus – his narration of *Peter And The Wolf* for Decca records. A whole batch of classical actors had previously done that. It pleased Diane immensely.

Nothing he did was allowed to escape the public's attention. When he went to see the comedians Buddy Hackett and Shecky Greene at Las Vegas, the world was told that he almost fell off his seat laughing at them. It was a moment when he had allowed his mind to go off duty. Had he known there were people around watching his every giggle, he would have walked out.

When the public was told that his favourite singers were Ella Fitzgerald and Shirley Bassey, it was because some studio official, his or her heart in mouth, had the temerity to ask him so that some questionnaire or other could be filled in.

There were other things that more readily tickled the public's fancy. He was asked to stand for Parliament as a Scottish National candidate. But at that moment, he wasn't seeking a political career, he said. Even if he had been, it would have involved a huge financial sacrifice.

In 1967 it wasn't Scotland that he was helping, but Israel. Five months after the Six Day War, he was in Tel Aviv to help launch Israel's Variety Club and personally handed over a cheque for £103,000 to the first Chief Barker of the club, Chaim Herzog (who sixteen years later would become president of the state) for the purchase of 'sunshine coaches' for both Arab and Jewish children.

Sean stayed during his visit to Israel at the Dan Hotel in Tel Aviv, at the time the best in the country's biggest city. Staying there at the same time was the British historian David Pryce Jones.

'Sean was sitting at the bar with Stanley Baker,' Pryce Jones recalled for me, 'when two perfectly nice little boys wearing skullcaps came up to him and asked diffidently for his autograph. Sean looked at them and in a very loud voice said, "Piss off." Their father, whom I had seen encouraging them to go up to the great star, seemed not to believe his ears.'

But if the reason for that trip made him happy, other foreign events were less satisfactory. Sean sued a French newspaper for libel, the first of a whole string of examples of his belief that litigation was the solution to wrongs inflicted upon him. This time he challenged the assertion by *France Soir* that he had lost his sex appeal and had grown a paunch. He showed that his waistline had gone up by only an inch since the first Bond picture. Presumably, there were all manner of females ready to go into the witness box to testify that he was as sexy as ever.

On the other hand, people were not slow in taking *him* to court either when they thought it necessary. In October 1967, magistrates at Hendon in north London fined him fifteen pounds for speeding. The officer making the complaint: one Sergeant James Bond.

The fifteen-pound fine was not a blow to him. In fact, he said that the trouble with his kind of money was that 'you lose sight of the fact that it *is* money.' So he went on writing an income tax cheque for £15,000 – a figure that staggered readers of the *Daily Express* in 1967.

Since he was doing so well, it was more important to him than ever to show that he admired other people's work. The cult British film at this time was a short, near silent picture called *The Plank*. Sean went with a group of friends to see a preview.

'Afterwards,' Ronald Fraser remembered for me, 'we all went into The Intrepid Fox pub in Wardour Street and Sean and Eric Sykes were engrossed in conversation. Someone said, "Look Sean's in very deep discussion with Eric over the film." I walked by and Sean was saying, "See, I can't seem to get my hand round the club." He was talking about golf.'

Golf had already become an obsession for Sean, but he wouldn't have minded taking it even more seriously. If he could take six months off from *everything* else, he would become a scratch golfer and go on the pro circuit.

Golf was one of the things his money had bought. Money, he told David Lewin, was important. 'I still can't get over the fact that when some producer signs a dinner bill of eight pounds for six people he is spending in one go more than my father had to live on and bring up our family on for longer than a month.' Joe, he always said, had worked 'for sweeties'.

That was why he appreciated his own sweeties. But that shouldn't be taken to mean he was tight with them. 'I'm not stingy with money, just careful,' he said. 'And I have respect for its value because I see how hard it is to earn and how difficult to keep.'

And when he spent the stuff he never ceased to wonder at the things it had brought him. He had a sauna installed in his basement and a shower that was capable of shooting hot and cold water simultaneously. Such were the marvels and mysteries of science to a man who still remembered that sixpenny entry fee for the public baths.

He did try hard to make it seem as though money was not the all-important god. 'One doesn't do everything for money, of course. But one should be paid what one is worth. Money gives you freedom and power to do what you want.' And he was now thinking about what it was that he did want. 'I want,' he told David Lewin, 'to use the power I have now to be a producer.'

It was, of course, a not too subtle swipe at Broccoli and Saltzman. 'What I am really tired of is a lot of fat slob producers living off the backs of lean actors.'

Now with *You Only Live Twice* he was opening up the gates to experience all the old aggravation. It was clearly going to have to be worth his while.

The fact that it was came as a result of a new deal between Sean and Broccoli and Saltzman. It was to be the last of the Bond movies under his contract. He contemplated the fact with considerable relish.

As he planned that last movie, Sheilah Graham thought the time had come to speak up for the producers. 'What,' asked the American columnist 'if the first Bond had been a flop? They would have lost their investment in the film and in Sean. When he makes other films, he proves he is a good actor, but they are not as successful as his Bonds. He should relax and enjoy his success and good fortune.'

Besides, Sean was a 'pleasant, happy person – when he isn't discussing his producers.'

The financial situation was sorted out for the time being, and star and producers agreed not to shout at each other too much in public. It was not a recipe for a successful outcome, except for one vital ingredient – neither side could accuse the other of being unprofessional.

Sean Connery in front of the cameras behaved as though he were making a picture on which his entire reputation depended. Lewis Gilbert was now the director and Sean took his instructions like a newcomer anxious to make a good impression. He continued to make his own suggestions and, like his predecessors, Gilbert accepted a number of them.

You Only Live Twice was partly shot in Japan. Desmond Llewellyn spent ten days in Tokyo with the *You Only Live Twice* squad.

'Sean was pretty well fed up at that time, so he kept to himself as much as he possibly could,' Llewellyn remembered. 'You didn't see very much of him. He had had this bust-up with Cubby and Cubby had had his own bust-up with Saltzman, but it never affected what he was doing or the atmosphere on the set. He took it all very seriously. It was very much easier working with him than it was with Roger Moore.'

And that was clearly demonstrated by the way he worked with the man playing Q. 'Because much of what I had to say was just gibberish to me, he would, if necessary, feed me my lines. Roger was a bloody nuisance. *He* would say something like, "You're not going to get this right, are you?" and then when I did get it, he'd put up an idiot board with "Bollocks" written on it. Sean wasn't like that.'

For Sean the make-believe rows with Q were probably moments of relief. The Japanese location brought its own difficulties, again mostly concerning the publicity machine and the reporters caught up in it. He was getting more furious every day with the way he was being treated by the media. It was the talk of the whole Eon operation. One member of the crew muttered: 'One good scandal would probably restore things to normal.'

'It was quite intolerable,' Llewellyn told me. 'I know that any time he went to a loo, there was someone finding a way to see what he was doing.' Some even climbed on to the skylight to take pictures of Sean below. When Sean saw what was going on, the language was choice. 'What the fucking hell are they doing?' was among the milder things he said.

It was at the Hilton Hotel in Tokyo that he actually had a confrontation with a gang of reporters. He had left off his toupee (once again explaining that he didn't want anyone to think of him as a matinée idol), was dressed in the sort of trousers that make the word 'casual' seem like a description in a Savile Row tailor's catalogue, a blue open-necked shirt and a pair of sandals.

One of the reporters who had protested about being kept waiting at the hotel for six hours before Sean arrived, looked at the less than suave figure before him and asked: 'Is this the way James Bond dresses?' Sean replied: 'I'm not James Bond. I'm Sean Connery and I like to dress comfortably except for formal occasions.' He did not tell him that he had bought a job lot of trousers for three dollars each from a New York store.

The fuss continued all the time the movie was being made, and in the end, he had security guards watching practically his every move. But at times, to his credit, he did try to ignore it. He was, he said at the time, contemplating 'nineteen weeks of swimming, slugging and necking'. He wasn't going to have to do a lot of acting, he said; all that was required was the 'constitution of a rugby player'.

The final product was yet another confrontation with SPECTRE and the man known as Number One, Blofeld, who this time shows he has more than a lap and a pair of hands – and a white cat – and reveals a scarred face which beneath the makeup looks remarkably like that of Donald Pleasence, adding a new, sinister look to the series. *You Only Live Twice* was a story of war in space and Bond escapades in Japan, the centre of operations for SPECTRE who have just engineered the swallowing up of an American spaceship by their own giant craft somewhere in the dark blue yonder.

It was an appropriate subject for the era of the first space walks – Buzz Aldrin made his pioneering stroll from Gemini 12 while the movie was in production – and one not included in the original Fleming story. Like other Bond films to follow, the picture included a supposedly dead James Bond – and even a Bond funeral at sea – and the kind of gimmicks that got more audacious as the action moved on. This time, there was the one-man jet helicopter 'Little Nellie' with a car-carrying giant magnet suspended from it.

There were a number of differences in *You Only Live Twice*. One thing that up to then had remained inviolate was the crisp looks of Bond himself. In this picture, he dressed up as a Japanese fisherman in an attempt to find out what really was going on with the local SPECTRE operation. Not only that, he also actually went through a form of marriage in an ornate Shinto ceremony with the Bond Girl of the moment, Kissy Suzuki. It proved how far the Bond story had now advanced, that it could risk having as its leading lady a Japanese girl and not a European or American beauty.

Much of the change was due to the fact that a new writer was now involved. The children's author Roald Dahl, famous for his expeditions into the world of fantasy, was allowed his head. Dahl once told me: 'I didn't really give a shit about Bond, didn't like Saltzman and Broccoli and hadn't much to do with Connery, but once I had obeyed certain conventions, I was allowed pretty much to do my own thing and that I enjoyed. Just so long as Bond wasn't allowed to change his character and the girls were around without showing too much of their tits, everyone was happy.'

Ken Adam was happy too, with his most amazingly well-crafted sets of any Bond movie – this time including an operations room for Blofeld which, complete with giant screens and the usual knobs, dials and slides, was supposedly inside a volcano. What made it even more different was the presence under the cone of the volcano of a 66-feet-high silver rocket that really did fire and actually lifted fifteen feet off its gantry.

It was perhaps the best of all the Bond pictures and looked set to be so from the opening pre-credit sequence – in which James apparently meets his end in bed with a girl; an event that triggered the comment from another member of the Secret Service: 'He died on the job. He would have wanted it that way.'

The death and the subsequent marine burial were intended to put his enemies off their guard. The picture itself might have had the same effect with the press. Although some critics agreed that Bond was at his best, others were not so sure. The *News of the World* asked: 'What's gone wrong with James Bond's sizzling love life?' That is what happened when Sean restricted himself 'to a few embraces with assorted Oriental girls'.

Ann Pacey in the *Sun* confirmed the fact that she still didn't like Sean's work all that much. 'Bond,' she declared, 'you are getting to be a bore.'

Alexander Walker in the *Evening Standard* in London was even more condemning: 'The Bond formula has now been run into the ground and only requires a headstone.'

Everybody now knew the Connery name and if they still sometimes confused it with that of James Bond, it didn't seem to do anybody any real harm – except for Sean himself who kept repeating that he was being exploited and that he needed more money. So why make another Bond picture if he wasn't contracted to do so?

Even Broccoli and Saltzman now had to concede that things weren't going to work out. In 1969, they made *On Her Majesty's Secret Service* – without Sean Connery. It was not an experiment they were anxious to repeat.

9

ALL CHANGE

Other people in other worlds have talked about their Noble Experiment. In the 1920s and 1930s the term was used in America to describe Prohibition. That ought to have been a warning both for Saltzman and Broccoli and for Sean Connery.

The Noble Experiment at Eon Productions was to make a Bond picture without Sean Connery. Both sides thought that Connery and Bond could be easily separated from each other – and both came to regret it. James Bond without Sean seemed at Pinewood like *Hamlet* without the prince.

On Her Majesty's Secret Service was released in 1969 and followed the usual Bond pattern – with the fundamental difference that in the lead was an actor who had done little more than a series of commercials for BP petrol. George Lazenby made no impression at all in the movie and negotiations were immediately put in hand for another Connery Bond movie. But it wasn't going to be easy.

Money and typecasting are always the explanations given for Sean leaving Bond behind at this stage. Desmond Llewellyn told me: 'We all heard that he was worried about typecasting, that he wanted to go and play other roles, to star in more stage plays. Well, I fell for that. It wasn't until much later that I discovered that he and Cubby had been having these terrible rows over money.

'I think that if Cubby – who actually is also an extremely generous man – had sat down with Sean and with Terence Young, who I am sure fell out over money just as Sean had done, and said: "Look, there's a lot of money to be made here, let's all work together," things might have turned out differently. They were a very effective team.'

Sean had always had the advantage of the fact that in all Fleming's books there was never a single description of Bond's appearance. Sure, you knew where he went to school, what he did in the Navy, the way he treated women and villains (sometimes identically) and how he liked those Martinis. But the moment Connery had said, 'My name's Bond, James Bond,' he couldn't help but set the pattern. For that reason, he remains the *best* Bond for most people. It didn't make Roger Moore's job any easier and might well have contributed to the Lazenby fiasco.

There is, however, another theory: the best Bond is always the one you saw first, which in a way sounds like another 007 title. As Llewellyn said, 'There are people who saw Sean first who don't like Roger because he is too light. Others who saw the Moore films first don't like Connery – because he is too tough.'

Observers of the Connery domestic scene however are convinced that the real reason Sean left Bond was his relationship with Diane and her continuing influence on him; that another pattern had been set.

Sean, meanwhile, concentrated his energies elsewhere. In 1967, he had made the first of two theatrical ventures. He presented Leo McKern and Zia Mohyedden in a new production of *Volpone* first at his old stamping ground, the Oxford Playhouse (it is fascinating to note Sean's attraction to Oxford, a place that would seem to be the antithesis of most of what Sean represented), and then produced its six-week stay at the Garrick Theatre in London. It was, he thought, a wise move for a man who wanted to be taken seriously in the theatre.

Whether he was equally wise in going to see a doctor at this time in Oslo is another matter. The doctor was eighty-year-old Ola Raknes, who was a practitioner in 'cosmic orgone energy', which, allegedly helped people to achieve perfect orgasms.

Diane was no more pleased than Sean was when news of the visit got out. She told reporters: 'Sean is not in hospital. Not in that sense. He had to go to Oslo to see friends and discuss some business. While he was there he decided to pay a visit to Dr Raknes. He's a great admirer of his work and has read many of his books.'

Certainly, he wasn't unwell. More pointedly, she added he was 'not receiving treatment of any kind'.

If anything proved how healthy he was it was his regular visits to the golf course, where he spent part of his time organising an international tournament. 'A lot of people seem to think I'm wasting my time being out on the golf course when I could be setting up a picture,' he told the *Daily Express*, 'but I don't see it that way. I like the isolation of golf. I do a lot of thinking when I'm playing. And you meet marvellous people on the course. Golf, food and drink – that's what I enjoy. And the only point in having money is to indulge them.'

He now had more than enough money never to work another day in his life. But, despite all that about spending time on the golf course, he did continue to work. When he had a new film to think about he was as happy as when he signed for *South Pacific*.

Then there was another matter of great professional pride and self satisfaction: he and Diane were at last working together, and once more on a play.

After provincial try-outs in Oxford and Newcastle, *I've Seen You Cut Lemons*, a play by the Canadian writer Ted Allan Herman about a brother and sister suffering from insanity, opened in 1967 at the Fortune Theatre in the West End – starring Diane Cilento and Robert Hardy. Sean was delighted to be working with his wife again – as her director. It was a career first, his only experience to date as a director.

It brought him back to the stage, in a way that not only gave him a new insight but also relieved him of the pressures of working as an actor 'on the boards'. He said at the time that directing had a lot to commend it. He found the work 'quite extraordinary'. He also said: 'If you act in a play you have to sign for six months to a year. I get bored after the first six weeks. Being an actor gives me less and less unless it's something very unusual.'

As things turned out, he would have had to work far less as an actor in this play. Six months? He didn't even have a chance to work for anything like six *weeks*. The closing notices went up, and after five days nobody saw anybody cut lemons. It was another Noble Experiment – and it flopped.

A number of the Connerys' friends saw the brief attempt by husband and wife at working together as being no more than an effort to pull the crumbling marriage together. As far as any of them could see, it was a humpty-dumpty affair by now and there were few who gave much hope for picking up the pieces, let alone putting them together again.

But neither of the Connerys was admitting that their marriage was in peril. Diane for one thing was busy at work on something new. She was writing novels – and at the same time insisting that she and Sean were doing very well indeed together. Her second steamy novel was currently under way, and at their Spanish home in Marbella she would read what she had produced and he would suggest changes and new chapters. 'I sit at one end of the garden and Sean sits at the other. Then every so often we toddle over to each other to show what we have done.' Yes, she agreed, it 'sounds a bit gooey'.

It was calculated to hush the rumours of an impending separation. Diane posed for newspaper photographs sitting at her typewriter with a picture of her husband on the shelf behind her. It was also preferable to hearing the publicity stories that they couldn't avoid – like the ones about what happened to them when they made one of their rare visits to parties. 'It's very tedious. You get stupid birds who really expect Sean to slap 'em round the face and throw them across the nearest sofa *à la* Bond.'

Neither of them, she believed, had a film star mentality. When it came to work, 'We both have a conscience about doing something worthwhile.'

They liked, she stressed, to keep their private lives private – as if most people didn't know that already. 'We spend a tremendous amount of time together, but we don't go out, letting everyone see us holding hands. So it gets around we are apart.' And she added: 'I know where he's having dinner. With me. Anyway, even if I wasn't on hand, I wouldn't worry. I don't think about such silliness any more.'

And then she added, not a little defensively it seemed: 'If Sean got mixed up in anything serious he would tell me. There is that much honesty between us. We both believe that marriage should be conducted with a kind of dignity.'

That did not preclude *anything* happening. 'I do not think about the odd flirtation. I would expect Sean to behave wisely and with discretion. And if there was something serious . . . well, I would be the first to be told. By Sean.'

And if things didn't work out? 'Marriage should be true while it lasts. But I think it important to have an escape clause. With no ugly fights.'

But years later their son Jason would recall huge rows between his parents, which sounded very similar to the *Virginia Woolf* variety mentioned to me by Ken Adam and his wife. Jason would tell Judy Wade in the *Sun*: 'I used to listen to their rows. Even though I was up on the sixth floor, I could hear them arguing in Dad's dressing room on the second floor.'

There was no suggestion that she was thinking of her husband when she called her first novel *The Manipulator*, although the book certainly did have an autobiographical element. It was about movie people and was set at a film festival. The manipulator in question was a director whom she described as 'sexually warped'. The book itself was very erotic.

Was Sean's statement about his enjoying acting less another swipe at

Messrs Broccoli and Saltzman? Probably. But it had to be admitted that without Bond his screen career was not moving terribly fast or successfully.

For instance, the previous year, to the accompaniment of newspaper stories highlighting a 'historic meeting ... [of] two of the great sex symbols', Sean had starred with Brigitte Bardot in a Western, *Shalako*.

The idea of bringing them together had come from the producer Euan Lloyd, who had originally conceived the idea of having the roles played by Henry Fonda and Senta Berger, but the finance needed to get Fonda to do anything blocked his plans.

Now, when he put the notion to Sean, Connery replied: 'Bloody marvellous!' Having got Sean's approval, a script was sent to Bardot in St Tropez. She said she liked it too.

She told the world's press when the film was announced: 'Oh, I have never made a cowboy picture. I like to try something new.'

The 'something new' was the amount of publicity she generated for the film. Being photographed wearing a bikini in a recording studio while still managing to plug the film was worth a million dollars.

She even liked the idea of Sean getting the star credit. 'I can't even say how much I appreciate the moral rest it is for me not to play the lead for the first time,' she said. '*Shalako* is Sean's film. He carries all the weight on his shoulders. Usually in French films I did that with a few minor actors around me.'

In *Shalako* Sean played a Confederate Officer-turned-guide, who takes a party of European aristocrats on a hunting safari in an 1880s Indian reservation – only to find themselves in the midst of an Apache attack. Not surprisingly, the Indians see the interlopers, all dressed as if on a shooting weekend, as a distinctly hostile element.

It was the most unlikely setting for what indeed was a great cinematic coupling. In those days, Brigitte Bardot looked wonderful in any place a director chose to put her and Sean with long sideburns and his non-Bond rugged look was the ideal cowboy he might have been in *Maverick*. Even with the Scots accent.

The studio were fully aware of the enormous publicity potential. Not only would they get the two sex symbols in one picture, they would also get them on one horse – in newspaper pictures, at least. The idea of Connery in buckskin was not to be lost on editors. And Brigitte in a Western? 'The next twelve weeks,' declared the PR department, 'will be full of fighting, retreating, climbing, riding and shooting. Nothing like it has happened to her before in a film.'

It was soon apparent that little like it had happened to the other actors involved in the picture before, either.

Jack Hawkins, newly recovered from the cancer operation which deprived him of his voice, was hardly a shadow of his former self. Bardot played a French countess in a riding habit and top hat, and Honor Blackman a titled English lady who doesn't like being separated from her jewellery – which proves unfortunate since the Indians proceed to push every last bauble of it down her gullet, turning her into the most valuable corpse since Tutankhamun.

'Shalako' is the Apache word for rainmaker. Rain is the enemy of the *film*-maker, but in this picture, it would have been light relief. Honor Blackman told me that it was not a happy picture to work on. 'It certainly had nothing like the atmosphere of *Goldfinger*. I think it had a lot to do with the fact that Sean was going through a very difficult period in his life. And Brigitte didn't help either. She was surrounding herself with her entourage while Sean was otherwise occupied. Actually, she was very remote. She had never made a film out of France before and she was constantly making it very clear that she would never do one again.

'On top of everything else, Stephen Boyd was going through a strange period in his life – going round to everybody saying, "Peace". Eric Sykes was having trouble all the time with his hearing aid. We were all worried about Jack Hawkins' medallion, which hid the hole in his throat through which he tried to speak, and Sean was, as I say, otherwise engaged; he came and did his thing and then went off again.'

The fact that the film happened at all was something of a miracle. Brigitte kept threatening to walk out and had to be coaxed back. She was given a Rolls Royce and was treated with rather more deference than anyone had anticipated would be necessary.

The film got so-so reviews. Cecil Wilson wrote in the *Daily Mail* one of the most enthusiastic. 'You have not really lived until you have seen BB in this epic British answer to the American Western, wearing an immaculate top-hatted riding habit and galloping across the Spanish mountains into Sean Connery's arms.'

Sean himself received encouraging treatment from the press. Eric Rhode, critic of the BBC publication *The Listener*, pronounced Connery 'the best Western lead since the discovery of Steve McQueen.' He appeared, however, to have lost his sense of direction, even if his own fee was reputed to be half a million dollars. The film itself wasn't going to make any money, and it was one thing to rebel against Bond but quite another to make a series of movies that were not doing their studios any good. Certainly, it was not a recipe to make producers happy – or even, had he thought about it, to make Saltzman and Broccoli think of him as a commercial proposition again.

The truth of the matter was that there now seemed to be two Connerys. The commercial Sean was the one who made Bond pictures and was ready to fight his producers for every cent he thought he was entitled to get from their bank accounts. The serious actor gave every impression of not caring whether he made money or not.

Sean would have been happier if his home life had been more inviting. The disputes with Diane were complicated by the fact that by now he had met another woman.

Micheline Roquebrune was a French-Moroccan artist who had been born in Nice and was once again living in France. She was a year younger than Sean, was married, had two sons and a daughter, and was as different from Diane as a daffodil from a delphinium.

Diane could, had she wished, have doubled as a Bond Girl although we all know that nothing would have been further from her mind. Micheline was petite and very pretty, with a body that was very, very curvy and not restricted by the requirements of the film industry. It is easy to see why men considered her extremely sexy – which, it soon appeared, was precisely what she considered Sean.

She had no acting pretensions, thought that James Bond was just about the best thing on the screen (although she knew nothing about the cinema, to which she rarely went), and she loved golf.

In fact, golf was as important to her as it was to Sean – it was not so much a pastime as a passion. They had originally met at a tournament in Morroco, just as they were both receiving prizes. She won the women's award, Sean the men's.

They spent a few days with each other, although not much seems to have happened. Three months later, he told Micheline that he was in love with her. Then he moved out of the Putney house.

Sean and Diane had not yet publicly stated if they were separating permanently or not. Sean was also trying to work out a similar situation with his other 'marriage' with Broccoli and Saltzman.

In the meantime, as always, there was a 'civilian' movie. *The Molly Maguires* was an altogether happier professional experience than most for Sean, although there was still uncertainty on both marriage fronts. But it was one of his better pictures to date and the casting was far more appropriate than that of some of his previous films – although a stirring performance by a young, vibrant Richard Harris as one of his compatriots did threaten to overshadow Connery's work.

But he was good enough. This time, it was the Sean of *The Hill*, again looking like a man who had never seen a Martini in his life. He wore a moustache and spoke with what most Americans would judge was just the right accent for the part of the leader of a gang of Irish immigrants who terrorise a mining community in protest against the wages they earn and the conditions under which they live. The title came from the name the gang gave themselves when they dressed up as women to avoid detection (Sean managing to hide his moustache). That was why they were the *Molly* Maguires. But they were women who played Gaelic football, a cross between soccer and rugby which resulted in almost everyone involved suffering bruises, cuts and strain. None of the actors allowed stuntmen to do their playing for them.

It was a well-crafted story, with magnificent photography and some superb acting. It has been said that Sean rushed to make the picture having made his television documentary on labour relations. Certainly, he could relate to a bunch of men faced with the kind of problems he saw in Scotland even if his own family had, almost miraculously, remained untouched by most of them.

It awakened people's interest in perhaps getting Connery to consider once more standing for Parliament as a Scottish National candidate. But that was no more on the agenda now than it had been before. 'I would not be so presumptuous as to sit for any political candidacy without sufficient work and background knowledge in the actual sense. I suppose it would be easy enough to get lieutenants to spoon-feed you but I'm not familiar enough with all the details across the country. I'd get found out.'

But he remained committed to the cause of the Clydeside ship-building workers. 'I don't want to sound like a Communist on Clyde-side,' he said in 1969, 'but I think if they can solve their problems there, then they have the solution to all the labour-management problems in Britain.'

That was what *The Molly Maguires* was all about – labour relations. The fact that the film was set in America made no difference to the basic premise as far as he was concerned.

It was a subject not just close to his heart but practically engraved on it. Could that have been the reason why he resigned at this time from the Garrick Club? Certainly, he looked more comfortable – if that is the right word – in the Maguires' coalmine than in the black leather chairs of the club where he had not been seen for two years. If he couldn't go, what was the point in being a member? He explained: 'I am not in central London much, so I didn't really have many opportunities to go there.'

After seeing *The Molly Maguires*, he might have found a working man's club in the industrial north more his strong mug of tea. His affinity for the story showed, and the fact that it did was noticed. 'Sean Connery,' said *Time* magazine, 'who has admirable screen presence – grace as well as strength – gives a sure and intelligent contrasting performance ... even though it is almost an unwritten role and we never discover what's in his head or how he thinks his explosions will feed his family.'

The *Sun* in London – a broadsheet newspaper, not the tabloid that later bore its name – said of the film: 'It's a film that I am sure will get a showing in Russia – tremendously powerful, incredibly brave, extremely intelligent and made in the USA.' As for the acting of Sean, Richard Harris, Frank Finlay and Samantha Eggar, who provided what little love interest there was in the film: 'Never, ever, have they acted so well.' Sean 'proves himself better than the reputation he deserved but never got in *The Hill*'. That was perhaps a little unfair and depended on which newspapers you read at the time.

However, despite the good reviews, the new picture made very little money at the box office.

If things had been better between him and Diane, she would have been proud of the way he was doing the things she had pressed him to do for years. Micheline, who was occupying a great deal of his thoughts now, made no such demands. Would they marry? They had still to decide. The only thing certain was that Sean and Diane were separated now, even though there was still no plan for actual divorce.

That was just about the situation between Sean and the Broccoli–Saltzman partnership. The fact was not lost on the rest of the film industry. Columbia Pictures thought they had a nice wheeze that would both tickle Sean's fancy and send the Eon pair reaching for the smelling salts. They were planning a Bond parody based on the one 007 story which had got away – *Casino Royale*. But Sean wasn't interested. So Columbia settled for David Niven, Woody Allen and Peter Sellers, all having their go at the spoof anti-SMERSH epic. Sean was probably wise to avoid it.

There was another 1969 film that seemed sufficiently distant from Bond to make it acceptable. In accepting the role of Roald Amundsen, the Norwegian explorer in *The Red Tent* (also known by its Italian title *La Tenda Rossa*) Sean was doing his bit to bring the Soviet Union in from out of the cold – a perhaps not inappropriate term, since this was about an Arctic expedition. The picture was one of the first examples of artistic, if not commercial, co-operation between the Soviets and the West. Sean had a small role. Peter Finch was the real star in a movie that was worthy rather than exciting.

Sean had yet another new guise for the picture, which ran for four hours in the Soviet Union and, hardly surprisingly, was just about cut in half in the West. This time his hair was white – not at all Bond-like – and he wore mock ice-encrusted furs.

All he wanted to do now was to impress more as an actor. But the picture was a dismal failure. The question now had to be asked: like it or not, was it possible that Sean could only succeed while playing 007? He didn't allow the thought to cross his mind, although others did.

Nevertheless, there was something about him which stood out even in the midst of such an unmitigated disaster. Robert Rietty, who took charge of dubbing some of the Italian and Russian voices, told me: 'What struck me most about this picture was the sheer professionalism of Sean Connery. I had never seen him at work before and had only known him from the James Bond roles, but he was quite an astonishing actor.'

But he was happier with *The Anderson Tapes*, a 'caper movie' released in 1971. This time Sean played a newly-released prisoner who seemingly can't wait to get back inside again. He organises a heist in an apartment building. The plan is to burgle the entire building, sparing none of the flats. It wasn't the kind of block of flats Sean had been used to in Edinburgh. In one apartment, there was more money than in the whole of Fountainbridge.

Sean's character manages to steal the money, just as Sean stole the picture. (The picture was his all the way, although he and the cash would be separated by the time the final credits came on the screen.) Yet he had a degree of competition from Martin Balsam as a homosexual antique dealer and from Dyan Cannon as Sean's girlfriend. There were also enough television screens, tape recorders and video controls to make Q salivate (Sean was later to say it was an extraordinarily prophetic picture, since it came out just before Watergate). What also made it work was another actor–director partnership between Sean and Sidney Lumet.

Lumet and Connery still liked each other and worked well together. But it wasn't another *The Hill* and nor did it need to be. If you can accept the idea of a burglary being fun, this was it. To make things even more pleasant for the participants, it has gone on to make more money from television showings than it ever made in the cinemas.

As for Sean himself, he now had a little time to think of his next project – and did much of it at his Spanish home. The negotiations for another Connery Bond movie that had begun as soon as George Lazenby's *On Her Majesty's Secret Service* was released had finally paid off. In *Diamonds Are Forever* Sean very much had the upper hand. He not only had negotiated the best financial settlement of his life – not just the million dollars he originally hoped for but one and a quarter million dollars plus a share in the profits – and he had inserted clauses into his contract which gave him control over the timing of the picture. A day over the original length of the shooting schedule and the company would have to pay penalties. Mr Connery was not to be kept waiting.

Broccoli and Saltzman licked their wounds and contemplated how much better it would have been to have come to a similar conclusion earlier on. Sean had the satisfaction of knowing that he could beat the money men at their own game. The only thing to distract from that satisfaction was the fact that the substitute work he had found for himself in the meantime had done him no good at all.

Once more, he put his all into the picture – even if the 'all' had changed slightly. Now entering his forties, he was noticeably older than he had been in the earlier Bond epics. There was a certain thickening of the waistline and there was no doubt that what he had on top of his head came courtesy of a manufacturer based in London rather than of his god.

One might, however, have noticed a frequent smirk on Bond's face. It came not just from the sheer delight of having Jill St John as his number-one Bond Girl and not even from the pleasure of overcoming attacks by two of the most unlikely waiters ever to wheel in a dinner trolly. Of course, he had good reason to be happy, considering the money he was now earning.

The company did well with it, too. The formula was much the same. Bond was fighting all manner of adversaries, among them two quick-footed young ladies called Bambi and Thumper who both look as though they could go a few rounds in the ring. There is Bond busy killing villains, Bond apparently being killed – this time burned alive in a cremation ceremony which audiences had to know would never result in his own ashes being collected in an urn – Bond looking good, Bond making love and Bond delivering himself of some of the best of his wisecracks. When Lana Wood (sister of Natalie) introduces herself by saying, 'Hi, I'm Plenty,' Bond replies, 'Of course you are.' Yes, she goes on, her full name is 'Plenty O'Toole'. 'Named after your father, perhaps,' he quips.

There's the usual mixture of deception – this time Bond doesn't disguise himself as a Japanese but takes on the identity of a diamond smuggler. He doesn't seem too distressed at somewhat unfairly killing the real man when things get awkward.

When Plenty O'Toole gets in the way of a gang of thieves, they simply throw her out of the window of their top-floor hotel room, allowing her to fall into the swimming pool below. 'Exceptionally fine shot,' says Bond. 'I didn't know there was a pool there,' says the hood who threw her.

There were the usual moments relaxing with the cast, technicians and directors and, of course, the usual games of golf. Ken Adam played one with him at Denham.

'I had got very pissed off with the way Sean and all the other actors and technicians were golf fanatics. So I decided to take two weeks off and get lessons from a very good assistant director, who was a sort of golf pro, so that I could get a reasonable handicap and beat Sean.'

So he took the lessons and challenged Connery to a game. 'I seem to have been quite good. Every night I went to a golf driving range, but when the day of the match came, it wasn't so good.'

It rained. 'Sean was unbelievably nervous because he had given me quite a good handicap and he had to play the whole course with a five iron – although I didn't realise that a five iron was about the best club he could use.'

Adam was actually doing quite well – until about halfway through. 'That's when I fell to pieces. And Sean won.' They played for £100. Sean insisted that he paid up. 'He would have got very angry had I not done so. It was very important for him not just to win but to be seen to win properly.'

In the movie, there were all sorts of contemporary references. Bond escapes from his adversaries on a moon buggy. The multi-millionaire head of practically everything around lives secluded in the penthouse of his Las Vegas hotel – just like Howard Hughes.

It was the second time the Bond team had gone to Las Vegas, but this time Q reserved the most valuable gimmickry for himself – an unbeatable system for guaranteeing the jackpot on the fruit machines.

'Sadly,' Desmond Llewellyn told me, 'it was the only thing that didn't work for real.'

But having Sean back as Bond did work – even though as usual he rationed the number of interviews he gave and when he did speak to the press the one thing he didn't want to talk about was Bond, despite the fact that he *was* meant to be plugging a Bond film. 'On the subject of James Bond, he's considered the best three-second interview in the business,' quipped an Eon executive at the time.

As usual, the Bond Girls didn't get to know Sean all that well. Jill St John confessed that she didn't even fall in love with him. 'He's a super guy but I guess I didn't want to fall in love with him in case it

The following text appears within the movie poster image:

NOW THE SHOUTING BEGINS!

SEAN CONNERY IN

co-starring
HARRY ANDREWS
IAN BANNEN
ALFRED LYNCH
OSSIE DAVIS
ROY KINNEAR
JACK WATSON
and
IAN HENDRY
as Staff-Sergeant Williams

featuring
SIR MICHAEL REDGRAVE
as the Medical Officer

Screenplay by
RAY RIGBY

Produced by
KENNETH HYMAN

Directed by
SIDNEY LUMET

THE HILL

AN M-G-M/SEVEN ARTS
PRESENTATION

A KENNETH HYMAN
PRODUCTION

The Hill (1965) showed a new dimension of Sean Connery.

With Ken Hyman, producer of *The Hill*.

If you're going to play golf, why not let people see you enjoy it?

Still loving football: with the Celtic team in 1967.

...ean the action man: going to the Venice film ...estival means more than just watching movies.

He didn't do much playing but he looked good when he turned up at the Royal Albert Hall in June 1984 for a charity evening in aid of Muscular Dystrophy.

The film which expressed a lot of Sean's political sympathies, *The Molly Maguires* (1969).

Sean and Audrey Hepburn as an ageing Robin and Marian (1976).

The perfect partnership: Connery and Caine in *The Man Who Would Be King* (1975).

Sean wasn't the main star in *The Untouchables* (1987), but you wouldn't know it from this picture. Kevin Costner is on his right.

An Oscar at last (awarded for *The Untouchables*). The look on his face shows he knows it's about time.

In the habit: *The Name Of The Rose* (1986).

Above left With his future bride, Micheline, on the set of *The Man Who Would Be King*.

Above Like father like son – actors both. Sean and Jason in 1988.

Love story. Sean and Micheline at the end of his legal action against former financial advisor Kenneth Richards.

Above With Harrison Ford in *Indiana Jones And The Last Crusade* (1989).

Right As the Soviet submarine commander in *The Hunt For Red October* (1990).

Perhaps everybody's dream: coming back to old haunts a hero. Sean with Edinburgh children on his receiving the Freedom of the City in June 1991.

The mature elder statesman: receiving the Freedom of the City of Edinburgh.

spoiled our great relationship. He has magnficent qualities of honesty, openness and friendship.' In fact, she said – in case, perhaps, she had offended him – he was the greatest man she had ever met.

That sort of image didn't do any harm to the picture. 'Connery proves yet again that he is irreplaceable as Bond,' said the *Monthly Film Bulletin.*

Saltzman and Broccoli had come to the same conclusion, but this time negotiations for another movie broke down. Sean said he had had enough; this was really the end, he decided. From now on – to use a phrase that recurred constantly at this time – he was out of Bondage. Now Saltzman and Broccoli had to accept it. Connery didn't even intend to keep the money they paid him for *Diamonds Are Forever.*

All successful film stars move into other things, as the financial markets would put it. The more successful they become, the less likely are they to depend on a fickle industry to give them their millions for the rest of their lives. With the help of financial advisers, they put their fortunes in stocks and shares and they hedge their bets in what is, after all, a huge gambling operation.

Sean did it through the Scottish-sounding Dunbar Bank, based in Pall Mall. He was such a good investor that they invited him on to the board – along with his friend Sir Iain Stewart. The fact that he was now accepted in the banking circles of one of the most prestigious areas of London must have seemed to him the supreme triumph of the poor kid from Edinburgh. But then he had collateral that would have impressed the Rothschilds. The one and a quarter million dollars he got for the last Bond film went straight into the bank – and then straight out of it. The money, Sean decided, should go to help the one cause to which he felt closer than any other – Scotland.

Together with a group of Scottish industrialists and other leading personalities from the country, including racing driver Jackie Stewart and the Vice Chancellor of Strathclyde University Sir Samuel Curran, who became chairman, he set up the Scottish International Educational Trust – a means, he thought, of helping young Scots to get the kind of break he had had himself. He thought this would give youngsters the chance to study and then qualify for the professions, and Scottish educational institutions the wherewithal to succeed in a competitive world where they could otherwise have easily gone under.

To cement the deal, he arranged for the European première of *The Anderson Tapes* to be staged in Glasgow, with all proceeds going to the Trust.

As far as Sean was concerned, it was game, set and match with his adversaries at Eon. He had fought Broccoli and Saltzman to the death for the money he said he required and then showed that he didn't need it for himself. So there!

He also had the satisfaction of knowing that his two major opponents were themselves on the threshold of a divorce from each other. However, the 'alimony' one would have to pay the other had not yet been worked out and they were still officially in partnership and were still very much planning the profits they were going to amass together from the next Bond picture.

The fact that Sean wasn't going to use the money from the movie for his own purposes was a point in his favour and was the talk of the industry for years afterwards, although there were few others who followed his example. Sean, however, had proved a point: he was still justified in commanding a number of noughts on his cheques that demonstrated his position in the movie business, but nobody said he had to keep the money if he didn't want to. The British Inland Revenue didn't do too badly out of him, either.

Fresh from *Diamonds*, he made one of those dark movies that couldn't have been further from Bond had they been conceived and shot in outer space. *The Offence* was a tough, unremitting examination of the police force, and showed how far down the road the British film industry had travelled in that regard since *Dixon Of Dock Green*.

Sean, with that tell-tale moustache and the kind of haircut that would have made 007's barber want to go away for a rest cure, played a detective not afraid to beat a suspect to death. He was hedging his bets a little on this one. Because the charge was child molestation, there was a chance that the people in the stalls would be with him.

'I honestly don't know whether the public will take the film at its deepest level,' he said at the time.

Because of the doubt – but also because he thought it all worthwhile, even wearing a short, mock-suede coat and a tweed hat searching the moors for clues in bitterly cold and damp weather – he took no fee and agreed to work simply for expenses.

Sidney Lumet again showed that he and Connery could get on to the same wavelength as easily as a prize comedy duo on the radio – except that there was no more humour in *The Offence* than there had been in *The Hill*. Again, Sean had Ian Bannen for company in a Lumet film – this time playing the suspect. Vivien Merchant, then Harold Pinter's wife, with whom Sean had played in *Judith*, also starred.

I interviewed Vivien Merchant at the time she made the film. 'It was not a nice picture,' she told me. 'It was hard, hard work on a film that had no light touches whatsoever. But there was one for me – Sean Connery. I only knew him as James Bond and didn't relish working with him. But it was a heady experience. What a presence!'

What made the picture remarkable in the Sean Connery career was that it was made by Sean's own company, Tantallon Films. Now, he was playing the producer at last, although that wasn't officially his role and Denis O'Dell had the production credit. Nevertheless, there was a lot of Connery input. It gave him the chance to see what life was like on the other side of the camera.

During the making of *The Offence*, the problems on Sean's horizon were more personal than professional. His marriage with Diane really had come to its end now, although their lawyers had not yet drawn up any documents for them to sign. There were also other worries for Sean: in Edinburgh, Joe Connery was suffering from cancer. He died before *The Offence* was completed.

Sean was intensely saddened by losing the one man who had been such an influence in his Fountainbridge days. By the time of Joe's death, he had found his parents a new home in a more salubrious Edinburgh suburb. But not too salubrious – Newlington was not that far from Fountainbridge and their old connections. They were able to breathe and enjoy the simple comforts of life, while feeling distinctly at home.

There had always been a great deal of mutual love and respect between Sean and Joe. The elder Connery, who never earned in his whole life a fraction of what Sean made in a month, was the kind of man's man Sean always needed around him. He was a drinking companion as well as a father, and, most important of all from Sean's point of view, had remained loyal at all times to Effie, and even in the depths of the Depression had provided for her and the boys.

Sean was too fine, too precise an actor for him to show all the emotions he felt at the time; the intensity that was required for *The Offence* was not exactly hindered by bereavement. He is an actor who puts his emotions into his work and this was a powerful performance. Fergus Cashin's review in the London *Sun* was headed: 'CONNERY KILLS HIS 007 IMAGE'. 'Sean Connery,' he wrote, 'is terrific as the gnarled fuzzman ... It is the sort of film that grips from the first title shots and holds you so fiercely that you daren't spend a penny. I can't say more than that.'

It was not, however, translated into a big box office hit. Takings were so bad that Sidney Lumet broke off with the United Artists' New York office head, David Picker, the man who had not only been a close friend but had been best man at his wedding. UA were distributing the film and Lumet charged them with burying *The Offence* so as not to affect the hype they were preparing for the next James Bond movie.

Years later, Sean said that he had all his problems with producers because 'I simply don't *like* injustice. I won't be walked on. It really ought to be a pleasure for the film company to pay you for making the picture work.'

Saltzman and Broccoli thought the failure of *The Offence* was good enough reason to try to persuade Sean back to their fold. At about the time that Sean was making *The Offence*, Eon were at work on planning the eighth Bond picture, *Live And Let Die*. Now it had been announced, Roger Moore was going to play 007. But it wasn't what either Saltzman or Broccoli wanted, and the amount of mail they had received from fans indicated that it wasn't what the public wanted either.

Totally unexpectedly, Sean got a phone call from the producers. They were prepared to cancel their agreement with Moore if Connery would come back. He could write his own ticket, and fill in the line on the cheque. 'Fuck off,' said Sean.

The story has never been told before. But Victor Spinetti was with his old friend when the call came. 'I heard it for myself,' he told me. Sean was absolutely delighted to be able to tell his old adversaries where they could put their offer. Moore stayed on the payroll and was to make six more Bond films, all of which made enough money for the producers not to want or need to look elsewhere.

Had Micheline been with him, she might have talked Sean into taking up the offer. She loved him as James Bond. But for the moment, she was not influencing him.

Once the new film was complete, it was inevitable that Sean would be asked his opinion of that first Moore Bond movie. 'I thought it was a trifle lightweight,' he said. 'But it is difficult for me to make an analysis which does not appear smug.' Indeed it was. Kindly, he added : 'I thought Roger Moore was very good and very funny. He is an old friend of mine and I wish him great success.'

What was interesting about Sean's comments was the fact that he had seen the movie at all – particularly since he so rarely bothered to see his own pictures outside the studio projection rooms. Other people in his position would have avoided it on principle. But then Sean's principles were usually of a different order – mainly to make sure people weren't screwing him.

It was also true that he rarely saw any films at all. The only ones he really enjoyed, he was to say, were the 'Carry On' series, news that would have gladdened the hearts of his old *Time Lock* producer and director, Peter Rogers and Gerald Thomas.

There was a message in those movies, he believed. 'I love that no-bullshit, very straight lavatorial humour. I find it's quite refreshing.'

As for his own career, he was an actor who, without the customary Bond to rely on for padding his bank account, was making a string of fairly undistinguished if – to use that word again – worthy pictures. There was the sense that he was losing his sense of direction in a fairly big way.

He still wanted to do things that were impressively artistic and to make movies that showed he was anything but the matinée idol he despised as much as he did 007. But, above all, he wanted to prove he could really act. That his current work brought in anything but fortunes was no reflection on his agent Richard Hatton, who had negotiated the best deals possible. Now, however, Hatton was giving up his agency and was going to produce films himself. Sean was agentless – and, some people believed, rudderless.

It was then that he met Dennis Selinger again, the friend from *South Pacific* days whose girlfriend Sean had 'nicked'. Both were guests at a gin rummy game-cum-dinner party Ken Hyman gave at his home. It was the first time the pair had really had the opportunity to talk since they had been rivals for the attentions of Carol Sopel. A great deal of celluloid had passed through the cameras since then. Selinger was now as busy and important an agent as Sean was a star. They talked about a lot of things at that dinner party.

The following day, Sean phoned Selinger and asked if they could meet. He then told him he needed a new agent. He asked Selinger, who had a reputation for being caring, considerate and exceptionally tough, if he wanted the job. He didn't really know anyone else, he explained.

Now it would seem an offer no agent worth his ten per cent could afford to refuse, but Selinger was cautious. 'I was blunt with him,' he recalled for me. 'I said he had to get back to work.' The agent is now in his seventies and, as president of one of the biggest international firms in Britain, still brings in the stars. What that blunt message meant was that Connery, stripped of the Bond image, had to create a new one for himself. He might be satisfied creatively with the kind of roles he had been playing recently, 'but they didn't bring him public attention and without that, there was no certainty how long he would continue.'

They were blunt words indeed. So was what followed: 'I said that he had to make at least three films a year. I took the same view as far as Sean was concerned that I had taken with Michael Caine – and that was to keep making pictures, as many as he could. If he made three a year, there was a good chance that one of them would work.'

Now that was something of a revolutionary suggestion in 1973. It was a time when actors, particularly big, glitzy actors who enjoyed the soubriquet 'superstar', were saying that they didn't want to be overexposed; an era when it was fashionable to let people see them more on the golf course than on the screen. Although he still enjoyed his own game of golf much more than most things in life, Sean had been busy enough and was not guilty of that. But he might have had reason to think that was the way he ought to go. Certainly, he had enough money not to need to work again.

But need was different to craving, and Connery still had that craving to act. But wasn't three films a year not just hard work but also spreading himself too thin? 'I didn't think so,' Dennis Selinger explained to me. 'He needed to keep in the public eye, and to do so he needed to make commercial pictures. But you can never be sure which pictures will succeed and which will not. With all the best ingredients, you can come unstuck without realising why.'

It wasn't, of course, a case of Sean deciding to slacken. But nothing he was doing was worthwhile. As far as agents are concerned, that was not working at all. Said Selinger: 'Nine months afterwards, Richard Hatton asked me, "How the hell did you get him to go back to work?" Which I took to mean that *he* couldn't get him to go back to work. All I did was say that unless he worked, there was no future in it for either of us. I think he finally decided that if he didn't go back, nothing was going to happen to him. Every actor wants to work. That's what they all aim for.'

It was a totally realistic albeit worrying diagnosis of the situation, and it worked. So did another instruction – avoid anything that looked like a James Bond replica. Sean knew that for himself, which was why he kept that moustache which now was as much a dividing line between his Bond and post-Bond career as any drawn from top to bottom down a blackboard.

'I was very surprised to get the call from Sean in the first place,' said Selinger, 'I wasn't expecting it at all. But once he was working with me, I hit on what I thought was important – I didn't overprice him.'

Sean Connery in a picture was going to cost a producer about £250,000 and a piece of the action. 'I knew that would be attractive to producers who knew what he could do. They weren't put off by the James Bond image. They knew there was more to him than that, but we had still to persuade people to forget him in that role.'

Selinger had been right about the exposure and the sheer volume of work. He was also right that they wouldn't all work.

The first picture made with the help of his new agent was an interesting idea that simply got ... well, too interesting. *Zardoz* was a peek 300 years into the future, but a future that looked more prehistoric than science fiction.

It was about a world in which nobody ever died, but where as a punishment people did age – sometimes by as much as an instant fifty years for bad behaviour. And since no one died, there was no need for reproduction – and, therefore, no sex.

Director John Boorman had originally had Burt Reynolds in mind for the role of Zed, but there were problems with Reynolds' availability as he was suffering from a hernia. When Selinger suggested that Sean was there waiting, Boorman was happy. Sean was too, as if he had been the first choice. He read the script overnight and phoned his acceptance the following morning. Strangely, he himself looked not a little like Burt Reynolds: the black moustache, the swept-back greased hair merging with the long 1970s sideburns.

Within a week, Sean was in Ireland preparing for filming. 'What gripped me especially,' he told the British writer Gordon Gow, 'was the direction the people in it were taking in this future existence, as opposed to space ships and rockets and all that. I'm not a science fiction buff. The idea of going to the moon is kind of interesting in itself of course, but I'm not interested in going there personally. What does interest me is the possible development of society in centuries to come. The way different levels and types evolve in the script is intriguing and refreshing and could well be true.'

Sean said they had 'a crazy time' making the film and there was no reason not to take him at his word. Sean seemed to spend much of his time with ladies exposing their breasts – the cinema had only three or four years earlier discovered the nipple and were making up for lost time – while Connery himself showed every hair on his chest. Those people who were not half naked walked around in rags and looked as if they hardly washed. But to prove the point that they weren't turned on by the opposite sex, they were instructed in what used to happen to their more corrupt ancestors in the bad old days. It was good enough reason to have the most graphic sex education lessons ever seen in polite society. There was, for instance, a detailed description and demonstration of the kind of stimulation required to give Sean's character, Zed, an erection – which, of course, he would now neither have nor need. So show more breasts, more thighs, more ... well, you got the idea straight away. Mr Connery, sex symbol of the age, was supposed to need none of it.

Most of the filming was done, on location in the Wicklow Mountains, of all places. One thing that was pleasant for Sean about this expedition was that it gave him a chance to introduce Effie to Ireland. She had never crossed the sea before and was fascinated to be in the country whose heritage had been such an influence on her late husband. She said she loved the experience. But there wasn't much else to be said about the filming. It was ice cold most of the time and the company was getting very close to running out of money – to the extent that there was no cash even to provide boots for the extras. Instead, they had their legs painted red and many of them were running around in their underpants.

Zardoz was not a good move on anyone's part – not on Sean's for making it, not on Selinger's for suggesting it. 'It looked good on paper but it didn't work,' the agent told me.

It was a worthy try, however, and Sean's co-star Charlotte Rampling looked as ravishing as he was undoubtedly handsome. But his fans couldn't understand what he was up to. They went into the cinema expecting something that at least had a semblance of James Bond about it and were distressed by a picture they couldn't begin to understand. Certainly, one thing was for sure: pictures like *Zardoz* alone were not likely to help him into a new career.

Neither was *Ransom*, his first movie of 1974. This was a less worthy effort altogether and probably failed simply because it wasn't very good.

In this, Sean played a security officer, the man in charge of the investigations into the kidnapping of a British ambassador in Scandinavia. It is he who holds out against paying the ransom demands.

Ransom was shot in Norway, and almost brought the local pilots' association out on strike because they complained that the film-makers had blocked up Oslo Airport.

Sean didn't cut either a particularly romantic or a happy figure at this time. Iris Rose, who now runs the Eon production office supervising the Bond films, was, ironically enough, working in a similar capacity on the *Ransom* set.

'I remember Sean sitting at the other side of my desk and barely saying a word,' she told me. 'If he had any great charm or magnetism I have to tell you it escaped me.' Not the usual reaction of women to the man, then or now – but then Sean Connery hadn't yet come into his stride again after the axing of the Bond connection.

Isabel Dean, one of Britain's most respected stage and television actresses, has a totally different memory of him. 'He was kind and very considerate,' said the actress who played the wife of the British ambassador in the film.

'We didn't really have a chance to get to know each other before the film started,' she recalled for me, 'but I remember how much he wanted to put me at ease. I remember him coming up to me and asking about the theatre and the last play I had done. I am sure he did it because he knew that was what I usually did, work on the stage, and he wanted to make me feel more comfortable.

'I watched him with other people and he was really quite remarkable. He watched other actors, too. Not to show how important he was but simply to put us at ease or perhaps to study our techniques. He was very nice.'

On the last day of filming, the director Caspar Wreade invited her to see the rushes, 'which was an unheard of thing for a small-part actor, particularly one like me who wasn't very pleased with her part. And to my horror, I saw Sean sitting there, too.

'There again, he made me feel very comfortable. Normally, one would feel very embarrassed. He didn't make one feel that at all. He made me feel as though I was playing the lead opposite him. He wasn't complimentary, just with his greeting he was so nice.'

Dennis Selinger admits that this film, like the very different *Zardoz*, 'didn't work at all'.

But there were no complaints from Sean about that or about anything else. 'He never complained to me – not once – about the work that he had done,' said the agent, 'although he would complain to me about his producers as was his wont. He was never very happy with anybody. Sean has always been suspicious of the people he was working with, that they weren't necessarily behaving with him as they ought to have done.'

What really irked him was the old question of hidden costs which ate into the profit of a film and his percentage of it (although that does not specifically seem to have been a problem with *Ransom*). 'It was what we all know exists, that creative book-keeping,' said Selinger. 'And you can never reconcile that, there isn't much you can do about it. As far as I was concerned, it was all part of the game. We kept him at a price that as far as the producers were concerned was reasonable but was also always good money for Sean himself.'

Had Sean been a producer himself he would have been more in control of the situation – and was sure his own book-keeping would have been much more fair.

That was why he *was* now aiming himself in that direction once again. He had an ambition to produce a new film version of *Macbeth*. But the 'Scottish play' was always a mass of problems and this attempt was going to be no different and never come to anything. The Australian feminist Germaine Greer wanted Sean to make a film about aborigines. His reply was not calculated to make Ms Greer take Mr Connery to her heart. He muttered something like they had been around for thousands of years, so why make a film about them now?

Sean's energies soon reverted to acting – what he really wanted to do still was act, and as he saw it, act properly. But he still had difficulties getting more diverse and challenging roles. As Dennis Selinger put it: 'He has always been like the old-time Hollywood actors, like Ronald Colman or Cary Grant. Whatever he did, his personality was so strong, he was always Sean Connery.'

He had no compunction, however, about making something decidedly more commercial. *Murder On The Orient Express* was seen as an almost last-ditch attempt to save the British film industry and did, it appeared, staunch the blood loss from Elstree and the other places for the time being.

In this, playing the British Colonel Arbuthnot, he was just one of a whole portmanteau of stars – including Lauren Bacall, Albert Finney, Ingrid Bergman, Vanessa Redgrave, Jacqueline Bisset and Martin Balsam – involved in a typical Agatha Christie murder mystery which succeeded mainly because of the popularity of the author.

Selinger had noted something about Sean's career that had to be taken seriously. Until he once more had a thumping hit, there was an enormous risk that the good he had done himself with the Bond pictures could be nullified. But for the moment, he could still rest on those 007 laurels. The press was content to allow him to do so. They treated him the way all stars are treated – they probed into his private thoughts and, possibly because he wanted to stay in the public eye, he was now answering questions he would have previously replied to in words of one syllable. What, for instance, asked one journalist, did he think of sex? A reasonable enough question, one might think, for the archetypal male sex symbol.

'The world revolves around sex,' he replied. 'But that doesn't mean that youngsters should sleep around willy-nilly. I'm all for trial marriages. The wedding of two virgins starts off with a high handicap.' And he saw it from a personal angle. 'I wouldn't mind a daughter of mine living with a man she loved as long as she took the pill. Then if it didn't work out, there'd be less chance of anybody getting hurt.'

He said that the Swedes and the Russians had set the world a good example in that regard. His motto: 'Keep Sex Sensible.'

As for his own romantic life, he was putting it on what both he and Diane considered a much more sensible footing. For the first time, it was revealed that all the wrangling over the years between Sean and

Diane over Sean's career paled to insignificance in comparison with the discussions about money. For months they had been thrashing out who got what – and how much of it there was.

Finally, in October 1973, it was Sean who was awarded the decree nisi ending the marriage. It was a change from the old film-star arrangement when the man agreed to spare the woman's sensitivities and allowed her to do the suing. But this was a different age. Nobody had to prove cruelty; there were no suggestions of adultery. Instead, British law now allowed divorce on the grounds of a marriage having broken down and there being no way of saving it. If it could be proved that for two years nothing had gone right between them, a decree was theirs for the asking. Sean said it had been two years and asked. Automatically the judge said yes.

But one wondered whether Sean had sued simply because Diane would not. Just a few weeks before the decree was granted, she was telling friends that she wanted to stay married. She never gave up hope that they would get together again. 'There is no need for a divorce,' she said before going on stage at the Duchess Theatre in London's West End where she was appearing in the play *The Collaborators*.

Now, though, she had no choice in the matter. Jeremy Tatham, Sean's counsel, told the court: 'The husband and wife not only wish for a civilised end to the marriage but wish to end the financial litigation between them forever.

'After fifteen months of negotiation, I think we have achieved this by capital sums which they would prefer not to mention in open court.'

What was revealed was that Diane got a capital sum 'in full and final settlement of all her claims against Mr Connery'. There was also a settlement for the two children, Jason and Giovanna. Diane retained custody, while Sean was granted 'suitable and amicable access' to them.

The real sufferers when any marriage collapses are always the children. The Connerys were no exception. Jason was to say: 'My parents' divorce didn't exactly put me off marriage but I think it made me wary. I realised just how much two people can hurt each other.'

It hadn't been an easy childhood for him and it wasn't going to be any easier in future. It taught the youngster a need for independence – whether he liked it or not. 'I wasn't living in a normal family set up. I don't remember great closeness to my parents or special family outings that we went on. I have never had any problem being alone.'

Sean recognised that Diane would take her own daughter under her wing and that it would be virtually the end of his own relationship with Giovanna, the girl of whom he had always been very fond. Jason was another matter. He was not going to allow the boy to drift out of his orbit.

As far as Sean was concerned, everything had been said that was necessary. But he added a postscript. 'As from this day, I will have no comment to make on my private life,' he told reporters, sounding quite as menacing as Bond fighting Blofeld. 'Nothing of my private life will ever be divulged to the press with whom I do not have an especially good relationship.' It was a shot straight from the hip; the Beretta was smoking. 'To simplify matters, I intend now to keep private matters private.'

It was a warning that would never be kept to the letter, but Sean's intentions was clear and he would deviate from them rarely. Having stated his position, his adversaries moved away like SPECTRE operatives making way for the moon buggy. They had been told.

Diane was given custody as Sean knew she would be. And his work didn't exactly make him an easily available Dad. But he did ensure that he wasn't going to be a shadowy figure from the past, one the boy would soon forget. He and his half-sister were sat down and the situation was explained to them. 'They seem to have accepted it,' Sean declared.

Jason and his half-sister spent most of the year with their mother. 'But I still love my father,' the boy said.

In the final analysis, why did the Connery–Cilento marriage go wrong? 'We both had careers and we both needed them. It was like putting two pints into the same pot,' Sean said.

Diane saw more than a little of Sean's Scottish roots in his behaviour. She remembered what he had said about hitting women and she still didn't like the sound of it.

'The view that women want to be roughed up is shared by men from a certain standing, a group who have set minds, crystallised ideas and beliefs. It's actually ghastly for women who have got to endure it.'

She had never had to endure it herself but she said: 'Sean's views *are* crystallised. Some people have beliefs and they are not able to change. If you become fixed in a belief, it's very difficult to change because that's your *credo* and that's what makes you you.'

His crystallised views had, however, affected her work. 'It was made very difficult so that it was impossible to move. I could not see how weird it was for women to work. But Sean is the type of man that if the wife works, she's not ... well, she can't ... as far as he is concerned that is not her position. As a person, I found it frustrating. If you have a free spirit, you can't compromise yourself to someone who is trying to squash you.'

However, Micheline now came on the scene again and, despite Sean's best endeavours, keeping the press away from the budding new romance wasn't as easy as he might have wished. Micheline didn't want to complicate her new man's life, but she did want to be with him.

The woman who had said it had been a case of love at first sight between them hadn't wanted to break into Sean's marriage. But now that it was public knowledge that everything was over between Sean and Diane, she hoped something more would develop. As she confessed in an interview with the London *Sun*, 'I'm a very determined woman.'

Now everybody wanted to know just how determined she was going to be. And did Sean feel the same?

10

THE MAN WHO
WOULD BE KING

No one doubted that Sean and Micheline would get married. Neither of them could get the events at the golf tournament in Casablanca out of their minds.

Micheline kept repeating how much she cared. 'Once I met him, he was no longer Sean the actor, but Sean the wonderful man.'

And she proved that Honor Blackman was not alone in finding a certain part of the handsome Connery face particularly exciting. 'What first attracted me were the eyes – those dancing eyes. The contact between us both was immediate and very strong. In fact, it was fantastic.'

Meeting Sean and falling in love with him convinced her to divorce her husband. They agreed that if she married again, her three children would stay with her.

With nothing in the way, she and Sean decided to wed, although early in 1974, Sean was still saying he didn't think it would happen. Not that he was making a lot of statements about that – after all, that was his private life and he was keeping it . . . private. In February that year, Micheline was saying no more than that marriage was a . . . very private matter. 'It's not for me to say.' 'I am very happy with Sean. I think everybody knows about us, don't you?' Most did, although it had only been hinted at up till now.

While he was sorting out his private life, Sean was also trying to get a grip of himself professionally. What Dennis Selinger had said was true: it was one thing to discard James Bond, but 007 had been a very powerful image for Connery and every actor needed that. Had he found a new image? The answer was that he hadn't. Now he was a film star who took what tempted him, but there was no definite pattern to it all. Even so, Selinger pressed him to continue with his policy of working hard. 'It wasn't a very original idea. It was what used to happen in Hollywood under the old contract system. It happened with Ronald Colman and Bette Davis : they made films all the time. You won't remember most of them. Nor would I, but it worked. Sean could always be relied upon to get work, because he was a bloody good actor. But until then he wasn't getting the money.'

Now the money was coming, too. But certain things could be relied upon. He was not a man to be trifled with. Even when he went to see a show, he expected a kind of consideration many stars believe should be reserved solely for themselves. In California he and Michael Caine were at the Comedy Store on Sunset Boulevard, a mile or so from where West Hollywood becomes Beverly Hills, trying to listen to a new comedian who was being constantly interrupted by heckling from a group of their countrymen – well, almost ; Sean wouldn't have liked to consider the English tourists as having anything in common with a self-respecting Scotsman like himself. He told them to be quiet in no uncertain terms. 'One more word out of you and I'll smack you through that fucking wall,' he said. 'Now give the kid a chance.' They did. It was not a memory of Sean Connery any of them expected to go home with.

In the mid 1970s quite suddenly and quite unexpectedly, he started talking about the last thing anyone would have expected him to consider. Something very strange was happening. To a casual observer, Sean Connery was exhibiting withdrawal symptoms – for James Bond. In 1975, four years after *Diamonds Are Forever* and following all those statements about being released from Bondage, Sean was talking about making a *new* Bond picture. Not for Broccoli and Saltzman, that was for sure, but for himself.

It would also be with the help of Kevin McClory who had wanted to make *Thunderball* in the very beginning before Saltzman set up with Broccoli, and who now won a lawsuit which gave him the rights to do what he liked with the story. He put to Sean that, even so soon afterwards, the Eon version of the story *Thunderball* could be recycled.

Sean was keen. He saw this as an opportunity to play Bond as he thought he should be played, to have an opportunity to lay the canard he only heard about years afterwards – Ian Fleming's aside to the Eon producers that he was looking for a Commander James Bond, 'not an overgrown stuntman'.

What appealed most about the idea was that McClory had suggested that he might like to have a go at writing the story himself – which he did. 'Once Sean wrote it he started to care about the character he'd previously got fed up with playing,' said McClory. There was also the possibility that the film would make 'a large fortune' for him. He was going to call it *Warhead*. But for the moment, it was getting no further than the drawing board, or Sean's writing desk. But like his idea for a new film version of *Macbeth*, it was taking root in his psyche and he wasn't going to let it go.

Ask him why, and there was a distinct feeling of a backtracking operation. 'There's an impression around,' he declared in the British *TV Times* magazine, 'that I have been constantly rebellious about playing Bond. This is not so ... the Bond character has brought me money and fame – and I'm not such an idiot that I regret either.' That was part of the strange dichotomy that was Sean Bond. He would forever afterwards be saying things like Bond was a monster that had all but consumed him, but he couldn't wait for the opportunity to play him again. Perhaps what he was really thinking about was the sweet revenge it would allow him on his old adversaries.

There was now a discernible change in his approach to what he did. He was no longer protesting that he was a serious actor. His work had proved that for him. In fact, more than ever before, he was being modest. 'Acting is a job,' he declared, 'like carpentry or building roads.'

But you couldn't own a house in Marbella or buy a home on the Chelsea Embankment if you were building roads, unless your name was McAlpine or something like that. Sean now had both. He had bought himself a new house on the Chelsea Embankment in London – a house that before the war had been the home of Joachim von Ribbentrop, the German ambassador who later became the Nazi Foreign Minister. Ribbentrop, the one-time champagne salesman, had also been an art connoisseur and his gallery in the house that Sean now bought for £35,000 would be converted into private screening room. So, as he had said, he had reason to appreciate what Bond had brought him.

It was interesting that nobody tried to say there had been long, serious Connery affairs. At one time, Shelley Winters said he gave her a mink coat – 'the first time a girl ever got anything out of a Scotsman' – but nobody took this story or any other terribly seriously. Which is perhaps strange : it might have been considered par for the course for a sex symbol. But he escaped most of the rumour mill. Now that people knew he and Micheline were living together, both in London and in Spain, there was nothing more to be said. There was no doubt where they would spend most of their time with Micheline's three children, and with Jason and occasionally Giovanna when they had holidays – in Marbella. Sean liked his Spanish home better than anywhere else he had lived.

What was more, he was learning Spanish – taking lessons even while in London. He had found a language school conveniently situated in offices above the Dunbar Bank. He found it hard, but his acting experience helped.

'It's a trick looking interested when you're bored,' he explained. 'But if you have to deal with other actors it's one you've got to learn.' But, he added, 'It's hard to concentrate when all you're hearing is "the blue pencil is longer than the green pencil." '

Sean contined to watch over Jason as though he himself was a male bird who had left the boy's mother to stay in the nest. There was a lot in his own upringing to condition his views on the way the boy should be brought up. There was no chance of Jason going to Fountainbridge to live, but neither did he want him to forget the family's Scottish roots. For a time, Jason was sent to Millfield, the most expensive public school in Britain, but he hated the air of privilege there just as he disliked the beneficiaries of that privilege, his fellow pupils. Sean sympathised and agreed to a change of schools – to Gordonstoun.

It wasn't like Fountainbridge either. But it was Scottish and it was tough – with its emphasis on open-air activities which, in their way, were not totally different to the things which Sean himself had got up to in the Edinburgh slums. He thought Gordonstoun would toughen Jason up. And so it did – apparently somewhat more so than it had managed with the boy's contemporary there, Prince Edward, who before long would leave the Royal Marines because life in the corps was *too* tough.

Jason did best at drama – making his stage debut at Gordonstoun, playing the role of Malcolm in *A Bedroom Farce*.

The theatre certainly provided a warmer regime than most of the other activities, for which Jason, like his schoolmates, wore his pyjamas under his uniform of grey trousers and blue jersey as a primitive kind of thermal underwear.

It was a difficult time for the boy. Not only was he away from home and away from his parents, but during holiday times he was shared between them, almost – to put things into a Hollywood context – like a star loaned out by a studio mogul to rival companies.

It didn't mean Sean was any less concerned or paid any less attention to his progress. In fact, Jason said he now saw more of his parents in the school holidays than he ever had before the divorce.

As for the school work itself, Connery senior didn't like the most frequently-administered comment: 'Jason has the ability but does not use it.'

'I used to drive Dad mad,' he said. 'I had all these opportunities he was giving me and it looked as if I wasn't using them.'

As Jason told the *Daily Mail*'s Deborah Ross: 'Dad would shout with rage and get aggressive. But only because he was worried I had no centre, no purpose. He found it very painful.'

Shortly afterwards, he would say: 'I often think (Sean) is jealous of my privileged childhood. But then he gave it to me.'

In March 1975, Sean finally revealed that four months earlier he and Micheline had married in a secret ceremony. People should have guessed as much. The last thing this most private of public people should have been expected to reveal was his marriage plans. After all, even his wedding to Diane had been a close secret before it got out.

And yet ... it turned out that this secret wedding was even more secret than his first had been. On 6 May 1975 it was revealed he hadn't been married at all – yet. In fact, the ceremony didn't take place until that very day. And on Gibraltar.

Announcing that the marriage had already taken place had been a ruse of the most strange and oblique kind – or a good or a bad joke, depending on which way you looked upon it. It could have been just that having talked about a marriage-that-never-was, reporters would be off the scent for the real wedding. Perhaps the newsmen should have smelled a rat. Was it really possible that Sean Connery could get married without their knowing it? The real ceremony, which was performed under a special licence from the Governor of the Rock, proved that he could not.

What was even stranger was the decision to hold the marriage at exactly the same place he had chosen for his first wedding. What Diane said about that no one seems to have asked.

Sean obviously had something good to say about his previous nuptials and saw no reason not to repeat the venue. What with his plans for the Scottish play and now this, Sean was demonstrating he had none of the usual actors' superstitions. Micheline didn't appear to have any either.

Once their honeymoon in Tangier was over, they settled into domestic bliss in Marbella. Micheline had ample opportunities there for her painting. Her prize exhibit: a portrait of Sean which now hung in the house and which she vowed would never leave it. Certainly, she would never sell it.

As for Sean himself and the decision to live in Spain, he made no apologies for deserting Britain, although he did provide reasons for his decision.

For the rich, he said, it was a different world in the 1970s. The big inflation was on the way and such things like house prices were, as we have seen, ridiculously cheap by later standards. But at its top rate in those days of Britain's Labour Goverment, income tax was ninety-eight pence in the pound and, which ever way you look at it, that was a lot of money to lose to the Chancellor of the Exchequer. Then, when he left the country, he was allowed to take no more than twenty-five pounds with him – which for Connery was roughly the cost of hiring the limousine that might have taken him to the airport, had he not had his own cars in Spain. (In more recent years, he has maintained that he has always paid British taxes – and those owed in the United States, too.)

As far as he was concerned, he was still spending more time out of Britain than he was inside it. Spain remained, as he said, the perfect base from which to work. There was plenty of golf for him and Micheline – it was a toss-up as to who enjoyed it more – at the Marbella course adjoining their home.

It seemed that sometimes he was as busy with the game as he was with his acting – which perhaps he had to be, considering his status in the sport. He had sponsored an open tournament at Troon in 1971 – with Bing Crosby, Bob Hope and Andy Williams among the celebrity players. He was also elected a member of the Royal and Ancient Club, apart from Crosby the only show business personality ever to be included. Then, along with star footballer Bobby Moore, he became a director of a new club, Woolston Hall in Chigwell, Essex. But the club was hit by a number of problems, including a fire, shotgun attacks on the home of another director and serious financial difficulties. The late Bobby Moore told me: 'It was an impossible situation. Neither Sean nor I could be expected to continue with the club, so we upped and left.'

It wasn't the only business interest which he gave up at this time. Apart from the educational trust and the bank directorship, which he treasured, he had divested himself of his company affairs, which, as far as he was concerned, seemed to offer little more than a means for his accountants to make money and in the process give him a fair share of additional headaches.

Now for the most part he was doing his own accounts, taking professional advice as and when it was required, but no more. But he had new help of which he was taking full advantage. Micheline clearly had a good head on her shoulders along with her other physical attributes. She still liked what he was doing – apparently a lot more than Diane had done – and was proving a deft business adviser. If Sean wasn't around when a crisis arose – and, as we shall see, they came along with increasing regularity – she was able to deal with the first shots and prepare Sean for the coming battle. Usually, she did it perfectly.

He knew what he was saying when he explained : 'We like to control it all. Then, if we make a mistake, it's our mistake.'

Micheline helped bring a serenity to Connery, which some people would have thought was almost a contradiction in terms : Sean and serene didn't go together. But he would now say : 'I feel free and happy and creative, and that's a great feeling to have.' There was a lot to show that that was indeed the situation. He still liked the odd moment to shut off from everybody around him and he didn't mind being separated from his new wife when he went off filming. 'I think it's important to be parted for a time, because whether you're acting, painting or writing, there's always a marvellous exchange when you come back. I couldn't ever be with someone night and day. That's how I am.'

And that was the personality Dennis Selinger now believed he had to project. And having convinced himself, he set about convincing the producers. 'I think they always knew what Sean had to offer, particularly now when he probably looked his best. He had always looked older than his years but very virile and producers liked that. But they wanted to know that other people felt the same thing. They knew he could fill theatres with James Bond. But when he failed to fill theatres with something else, they got worried.' The job of the agent was to stop the worries.

When he was working, Sean said he always preferred to be on location rather than in the studio, where there were so many distractions. 'On location, all you have to think about is the film.' A couple of locations gave him just such opportunities.

The first was in Marrakesh where he was to make *The Wind And The Lion*. In this Sean, Scottish accent and all, played a Berber sherif who engages in the quite reasonable pastimes of chopping off heads and getting romantically attached to the woman he has just kidnapped.

It wasn't intended, but there was almost a Bond-like quality to Connery's sherif, Mulay Hamid El Raisuli, Lord of the Rif, a man who took his violence and his passion equally seriously. When you saw the extraordinarily attractive Candice Bergen, then at the peak of her cool beauty, it was not difficult to understand why.

There was international intrigue a-plenty in the picture, particularly when Teddy Roosevelt sends in the Marines – the first President Roosevelt *always* had to be seen sending in the Marines – demanding the delivery of either Mrs Pedecaris (Candice Bergen) or the sherif's head. And then the Germans arrive on the scene. After that, there isn't much to do but watch Sean sneer, ride his horse, raise his sword and ... it really didn't matter what. It was all in the cause of good entertainment and didn't say a great deal for Sean Connery, serious actor. He still hadn't found a real role for himself that marked him out as a unique personality.

Sean described the writer–director John Milius as 'a very good writer, especially of the historic stuff. But he is so *busy* being butch and Hemingway and samurai and all that, it gets in the way of his direction nowadays. But his invention as a writer is wonderful.'

Pauline Kael in the *New Yorker* wasn't so sure. 'When the actors begin to talk (which they do incessantly) the flat-footed dialogue and the amateurish acting take one back to the low-budget buffoonery of Maria Montez and Turhan Bey.'

His second film in 1975, however, gave a glimmer of what was to come. *The Man Who Would Be King* was directed by John Huston and it showed – a mixture of fantasy, adventure that was never quite realistic, comedy and suspense that only a master of the camera could achieve. But if it had been a long time waiting for a picture like this to happen, it would be even longer before there was anything quite up to its standard again. This was to be the best Connery film for ten years.

Fortunately for the fans, there was plenty to savour. In the movie Sean Connery teamed up with the man who was to become his favourite film pal, Michael Caine. In a way, it was a love story – Sean loved Michael and Michael loved Sean, but with the kind of love that two men can have for each other without any sexual connotation. You knew from the moment it started that this was a pair of actors, suddenly released from the constraints of anything they had ever done before, who cared about each other. More important, they cared about the film – and so did the audiences.

The fact that it worked said as much about Huston as it did about his stars. The movie was based on a Ridyard Kipling story, and Huston had bought the film rights from the Kipling estate more than twenty years earlier, had actually had scripts written and had sounded out Humphrey Bogart and Clark Gable – the Gable connection yet again.

Oswald 'Ossie' Morris, once more working on a Sean Connery film, had been involved right from the beginning. Huston had wanted him to be the cameraman when he originally had the idea to make the movie.

'Twenty years ago, I had a call from him and he said, "Kid, I've got a great story. *The Man Who Would Be King*. Ever heard of it?"'

Morris hadn't. Very few people had. It was one of a collection of short stories in the *Wee Willie Winkie* book. He said it was going to be Bogie and Clark Gable starring. 'Fade out, and ten years later, exactly ten years later, he said, "Kid, we're going to do *Man Who Would Be King* again – with Peter O'Toole and Richard Burton."'

Then another ten years went by, as he told me. 'I'd come in from shopping and there was a message to ring him at the Beverly Hills Hotel. "Kid," he said, "Wonderful news. We're going to do *Man Who Would Be King* again."' 'Yes,' said Morris, 'who with this time?' He told him it was Caine and Connery.

But first, the director asked him to go to Morocco to look at the location he had in mind in the Atlas Mountains. 'Huston always wanted the movie to be shot in the Hindu Kush of Afghanistan where the scenery was so marvellous,' Ossie Morris recalled, 'and one of the reasons why the first two films were never made was because the insurance companies wouldn't go for it. They thought it was much too risky there. Somebody convinced him that it could be done well enough there in the Atlas Mountains.'

The picture really got moving again when John Huston was thumbing through a portfolio of Kipling scripts with producer John Foreman. 'Why don't we do it?' he asked. 'Why not?' agreed Huston, and so the picture was made.

The marriage broker, however, was Selinger. 'Huston was talking about wanting to make that movie and I said that as far as I was concerned, there were only two people who could play the parts – Michael and Sean. One's a Scotsman and one's a Cockney, and that was exactly how it had been written.'

Dennis Selinger didn't have much of a problem in persuading Sean to make that picture. It was the perfect 'marriage' of Connery and Michael Caine, who were both his clients. 'It was a film I desperately wanted to do. It was my idea to put him together with Michael Caine and John Huston and it worked like magic.'

'Sean,' he remembered for me, 'loved it from the word go.' Selinger got Caine and Connery, accompanied by comic actor Graham Stark ('he does a wonderful Indian') playing the part eventually portrayed by Saeed Jaffrey, assembled to read for Huston. 'And there was no stopping it thereafter. They agreed they wanted to make the film.'

The Man Who Would Be King had Connery and Caine doing what they both did best – playing con men. Both are red-jacketed, pith-helmeted British soldiers in India in the days of the raj. They swindle and con their way into the territory of Kafiristan, which they see as a kind of Valhalla for their ambitions. Without really trying, Connery finds himself being worshipped by the monks of the country; a god who also becomes king – how he does it is really beside the point.

Caine is his aide-de-camp. They come unstuck only when the king tries too hard and is about to marry a local princess, which one might think is only right for a king to do. The princess, incidentally, was played by a young lady named Shakira, who in real life was Mrs Michael Caine. Her husband saw the funny side of it. As he said, 'I never thought I would end up being best man at my own missus's wedding.'

Dennis Selinger said that Caine's humour caught on. 'Sean gives the impression of being a very dour person, but he found Michael one of the funniest people he had ever met. They had marvellous fun together. Sean spent more time in Michael's trailer, just laughing with him, than he did in his own – and the relationship came over on the screen.'

Ossie Morris saw it for himself and was impressed. 'I used to do a lot of filming with Claude Rains – he was very professional, and professional people tend to be dull. I thought Sean, who was so very, very professional, would be like that, too, but he was tremendous fun.'

But once and once only, the professionalism gave way to over-enthusiasm. For reasons no one was able to explain, John Huston arrived on the set late one morning. Sean and Michael Caine were getting more and more irritated. 'Finally, they came up to me and said they wanted to block in the scene and rehearse before John came in. Then they said, "Why don't we shoot it once anyway and then do it again when he comes?" They were getting fed up – particularly because they knew that when he came on the set the last thing Huston wanted to talk about at first was the film. He had to warm up by discussing the international situation or the racing news – even in Morocco.'

The cameraman wasn't having any of their 'blocking in' idea. 'I think it was the only time I ever refused Sean Connery anything. But it was more than my life was worth to agree to that. John would have been very, very upset.'

And because of his professionalism, Sean threw none of the temper tantrums that other actors might have been expected to have. In the picture, he is involved in the only completely nude scene in his career – his posing in Edinburgh's art school apart. In *The Man Who Would Be*

King, he doesn't even have the comfort of a posing pouch – although he was seen on camera from the rear only. It is the moment of crowning when his own clothes are ceremonially removed to be replaced by the white robe of monarchy just prior to the crown being placed on his head.

'It was done very tastefully and there wasn't a murmur,' recalled Morris. You only saw him from the back but, of course, he had to strip completely and I could imagine all sorts of other actors making a terrible fuss, demanding that the set be cleared, walls put up between them and the electricians, that sort of thing. But Sean required none of that and it all went through in five minutes.'

There were even a couple of continuity girls around and he made no demands about them either.

John Huston was to say that watching Sean and Michael in action was like seeing 'a polished vaudeville act'. But vaudevillists who *acted*. Both of them. Nevertheless, you always had the feeling that Sean was boss (which was perhaps why he became king) and Michael was doing what he did only because of the strength of his mate's performance. Quite literally, Connery raised Caine.

There's even a sprinkling of freemasonry in it all. Caine steals Kipling's watch (Kipling is played by Christopher Plummer, and provides a useful mechanism for telling the story), only to discover he is a brother mason, and, therefore, has to find a way of returning it: mason did not steal from mason. But the real freemasonry was between the two stars who look as though they have never had a better time in their lives. Even when King Connery dies – a painfully long death, hanging on to a rope bridge that you know is going to collapse, singing as he goes to a far, far better place than this – there's the feeling that he's not failing to enjoy the experience.

Sean climbed onto the bridge himself at first, although the job of actually hanging from the rope over the ravine was given to a stuntman. 'But he was quite courageous,' Alex Thompson, the second-unit cameraman recalled for me. 'When you get on to a rope bridge in the wind, it makes waves and starts rolling about, but it didn't appear to worry him.'

The song he sang as he clung for life caused a few problems between Sean and Huston. He called the director 'a bit Machiavellian' and what happened with the number proved it. Huston wanted to change the song on the actual day of filming. Sean told him to try to do it himself. Huston thought about that. 'Let's leave it how it is, kid,' he said. As Sean remembered: 'I never knew whether he was trying something on to get me into a different mood, or just being contrary.'

Sean looked as good in his robes and crown – to say nothing of his beard and moustache, leaving a clean-shaven chin that added a sense of distinction – as he did in his scarlet uniform. It was all whimsy at its most fantastic and yet if you were in the mood you'd sit in your cinema seats, open-mouthed, feeling as much part of the action as anything going on in front of the cameras. You had to have that sort of faith to picture a Scotsman becoming a king in the Himalayas, and yet Sean made it easy.

Actually a real king came into the picture, too. One advantage of Micheline's decision to join Sean while he was making the movie (they, needless to say, also used the opportunity to play golf there together) was that she happened to know King Hassan of Morocco and asked if he could use his immense influence to ease the film-makers' path through the Mountains. It would involve Sean in a degree of horse-manship, through difficult terrain, but he worried about that no more than he had about sipping a Martini in one of the films he now didn't want to discuss.

The king, it transpired, then sent replicas of the medallion worn by Sean in the film to both him and to Caine – replicas in real gold. But with the gift came a bill for $15,000. The money was for the jeweller, who pointed out that causing a fuss might turn into a diplomatic incident. His bill was paid by John Foreman without any further trouble.

To do otherwise would have risked insulting the king. 'And,' recalled Ossie Morris, 'we had the distinct feeling that you didn't do anything there without the king's approval. Even the Arab extras weren't paid directly. The money went to their leaders, the sheikhs, and we had the impression that the poor extras didn't get very much at all.'

One of the real problems working in the area was the impact made by the strict Islamic code. There was nothing for Caine and Connery to do in Marrakesh one night except go to a rather seedy disco – which they then discovered was frequented solely by men. Sean turned to Michael at one point and asked: 'Do you mind if I dance with your driver? Mine's much too ugly.'

Alex Thompson agrees that the relationship between Caine and Connery was part of the secret of the film. However, the camaraderie didn't extend much further: 'He's a very pleasant sort of guy but he didn't mix very much with the rest of us. Big actors don't, on the whole. You know they're in the trailer while we're out in the blizzard.' Neither did he go through any Bond motions for fun, as Alex Thompson had hoped he would. 'Sean only goes through motions for money.'

One thing that was apparent to all who worked on the movie was how much both Caine and Connery admired John Huston. All of them would go to the rushes together. 'They were very interested in the picture and were hoping for great things.'

The spirit of fun in which they made their film showed. But at one stage, there seemed the distinct possibility that they might not have got their film out of the country – or the people who made it either. As Ossie Morris told me: 'We couldn't get out of the airport lounge on to the plane because someone came along and said that none of us – Sean included – had paid our hotel bills. You didn't pay anything direct to the hotel. You paid it to the government and for three hours, we were stuck there.' Once more, someone wanted baksheesh.

Sean wanted his cut from the film, too, which led to considerable legal problems. Allied Artists was the studio under whose aegis Huston made his film, and Columbia were distributing it in Europe. There was a five million dollar budget which would turn out to be anything but enough, and both Sean and Michael received a $250,000 fee in addition to five per cent of the profits. It was the profits that caused the trouble – Sean wanted what he considered to be his fair share.

When they started the work, Sean and Michael trusted the company and didn't allow themselves to bother so much with financial detail. But later on Connery would say – among the dozens of other things he said on precisely the same subject – 'It was a good movie, but the production was mismanaged and botched because of the Mickey Mouse company whom I eventually had to sue, and we bankrupted them. Michael and I did two weeks of rehearsal for nothing and then two weeks of exploitation for nothing, and then they just stole us blind.'

It would all end in tears – those of Allied Artists.

Sean also wanted his cut from the poker games he played. It was a game he perfected while working on *The Man Who Would Be King*, Alex Thompson remembered. 'He was a very canny player,' he told me. 'He's a careful player who plays with his head.'

The winnings were important. 'He's a man with long pockets and short arms,' Thompson recalled. 'He won't spend a shilling where a penny will do. But then, of course, if you look at his background, you can understand it. He's also a hard worker.'

It was because of the importance of money that Ken and Letizia Adam were surprised Sean had turned to poker. 'He hated losing,' said Ken.

'I didn't know that he could part from money at the gate,' mentioned his wife. 'We used to gamble with Michael Caine and Roger Moore, but never Sean. He didn't like the gambling aspect and for him it's futile. Anything that has no purpose behind it didn't interest him.'

It was no more easy then or when he made the Bond pictures all those years ago than it is now to get to know Sean. People still say he doesn't suffer fools gladly. 'He won't take crap from anybody,' says Ken Hyman, 'no bullshit.' But then he still doesn't talk down to people either. 'He won't patronise anyone, and neither is he a bully. He treats everyone alike.'

But if anyone is rude to him, a producer or a waiter, he will react in no uncertain terms. He can storm at those who upset him like a bull being teased in the ring.

As Ken Hyman told me: 'Sean sees a line and if he sees someone deviating from it, he won't allow it. If someone says to him, "Sorry, that's the way it is," he won't accept it sweetly. He'll just say, "Bullshit. That's *not* the way it is." He knows his business, and sometimes other people are horses' asses.'

On the other hand, the image of the brusque, macho actor who will as soon slap a woman as make love to her isn't true either. There's a charm about him that might well have fitted Errol Flynn, another man's man and an actor of lesser talent but equal celebrity a couple of generations earlier. Flynn was the hellraiser whose activities outside the film studio were better known than anything ever suggested about Connery – and there were more of them. He also exuded charm and sometimes that was the more powerful attribute.

'We have been in a restaurant,' Ken Hyman told me, 'and Sean has gone from one end of a room to the other just to give my wife Caroline a kiss. That's an unusual thing from a film actor. Most stars would expect you to walk over to them. I wouldn't walk to him. I wouldn't want to intrude. By the same token, if Sean didn't like you ... forget it. Ice water.'

That is the trouble with a lot of the people who talk and write about the boorish Sean Connery. They only know about the ice water. Unfortunately, and probably from his own sense of self preservation, he won't allow anyone he doesn't know – and for him knowledge presupposes trust – to see that at times he is more like a cup of soothing, warm cocoa.

Once it was completed, the critics loved *The Man Who Would Be King*, and rightly so. They also liked Sean Connery. 'With every film he grows in stature, discarding all vestiges of James Bond which never sat too easily with him – to become a truly fine character actor,' wrote the always incisive Margaret Hinxman in the London *Daily Mail*, who was perhaps being a little too generous about his previous past-Bond work. In her piece headed 'Connery the King' which was not referring solely to his role in the picture, Ms Hinxman added: 'Dispensing with the toupee and the trappings of star glamour, he transforms Danny from a doughty Scottish soldier of fortune into a man who assumes the mantle of majesty as an unmistakable right.'

What was perhaps most notable about her review of what she described as 'this triumphant new John Huston film' was her own comparisons between the two protagonists. 'Caine's quirky Cockney characterisation has never been so succinctly employed. But it is Connery who continues to be amazing.'

The remark about his Bond feelings was, as we know, not wrong, except that this was really the only post-Bond movie that the public liked, too. Even so, it never recouped anything like a Bond box office and what it did make was anything but a precedent for what was to follow. But it was true, Sean Connery was growing in stature and his fees were growing along with him.

Taking Dennis Selinger's advice in full, there were two more Connery films the next year. One of them Sean always said was among his favourites. *Robin And Marian*, with the lovely Audrey Hepburn as his co-star, imagined what happened when Robin Hood and Maid Marian, freed of robbing the rich to feed the poor and of having to be nice to the wicked uncle at court, entered middle age.

Originally, the picture was going to be called *The Death Of Robin Hood*, which Sean said he would have preferred. He explained: 'They should have stuck with that title because that is what it was about, and people were disappointed because from the new title they expected some stirring adventure. The whole thing was very much anti-mythic. The guy comes galloping back after eighteen years away on the Crusades and he shouts, "Hi, I'm back!" and of course no one cares much any more. And he's getting up each morning in the forest, and creaking and groaning and coughing and taking a leak in the bushes and it's all too much for a man of his age.'

But perhaps it was simply a matter of Columbia Pictures thinking that the original title gave away the ending of the picture before anyone had walked into a theatre.

Richard Lester directed the movie that gave the impression of a cold and bleak Britain that had benefited not one little bit from Robin's endeavours. The script was written by James Goldman. There was comedy and pathos, which was rarely a happy mix in a Connery movie, and this was no exception. Once again, Richard Harris joined Sean in a movie, this time as the ageing, enfeebled king.

In truth, the nicest thing about this picture was the presence of

Audrey Hepburn as the mature Marian, bearing as little resemblance to Eliza Doolittle or the girl in *Roman Holiday* as Sean did to . . . well, it has to be said, to James Bond. It was not difficult to imagine Audrey Hepburn as having once been the delicious Maid Marian. But Sean in Lincoln green and looking like Errol Flynn? Not easy. When he and Robert Shaw, as the sheriff of Nottingham, go to it with swords, they seem to be fencing with their age more than with each other.

Even worse, there was the sense that Sean was playing a part that didn't fit in with the strong Connery image, particularly with his sense of self assurance. At one stage, he actually asks Marian: 'Do you love me?' Bond would never have doubted it. Neither would Connery. But his Robin wants it spelled out. 'Then say it,' he tells her.

There were moments of great beauty. This Marian has become a nun and Robin is not sure how sinful it is to take her. The answer comes in the love scene in a cornfield. And the pathos? Their love is sealed in death – from the poison Marian administers.

Sean liked Goldman's script, particularly the point where Robin has a moment of embarrassment: 'Waking up with a bit of rheumatism, he goes to have a piss and realises Marian is there and he has to cover up and go somewhere else.'

As Sean said to *American Film Magazine*, 'Here was a guy who was ageing.'

It was the end of the myth. 'He's not a very intelligent guy, and is at heart a boy, and that's how I played it.'

All of it was very different from *The Next Man*, in which a still bearded Sean – although this time it was a smaller, trimmer beard – seems to have decided it is time to go back to a decent tailor. This Sean Connery is an Arab – with no more explanation of the Edinburgh accent than he was able to give in *The Wind And The Lion*. As a Saudi Arabian oil minister he pre-empts the Middle East peace talks of the 1990s by at least sixteen years and dies for his troubles.

Not even Sean himself has tried to say that the picture was in any way outstanding, and most critics seem to think it was anything but. Yet it was such a polished performance that he managed to make the totally improbable seem credible – something he was doing rather a lot of these days. That took acting, even the kind of easy, I-know-I-don't-seem-to-be-trying-too-hard school of acting he was doing now. The hardest things are the ones that look simple and this was a measure of his success.

Standing at the OPEC meeting, sitting at the back of his limousine – an Arab in a Russian fur hat – travelling on a plane, you had to give it to him. He convinced you he had a peace plan up his Savile Row sleeves.

He made strong speeches in the film – although not as strong as the things he was saying about the press in real life. As usual, the journalists were his *bêtes noires*. But he was detecting a new tactic in their operational activities. Now they were ringing up Micheline, telling her things they alleged Sean had said and she would counter with, 'Oh, he said that, did he?' and give them all the quotes they needed.

In Spain that gave less trouble than in London. Spain was where Sean hoped he could escape the film-star gazers by behaving less *like* a film star. He wore an old brown jacket – the same one that he had worn in *Tarzan's Greatest Adventure* in the late 1950s – over a pair of tartan trews. It made him feel good to be taking the Scottish image with him wherever he went.

In New York, however, hiding was more difficult – the New Yorkers have never been renowned for their reticence. But a man quick to blow a fuse like Sean was immensely laid back when dealing with them. In an elevator at the apartment building where he and Micheline were staying, he pressed the '20' button. 'Twentieth floor,' hissed a woman knowingly behind him to her companion. He said nothing. Then, when they stepped out, the woman said: 'And she's not such a young chick, either.' It was one of those things he had to put up with and he liked doing so now no more than he had before.

Would it have been easier as an MP? There were those who more than ever wanted him to be just that. The British press were carping more than a little now that he had 'deserted' his home shores. His film career wasn't quite taking him where he wanted and he was feeling strongly about the way Scotland was treated. Wouldn't 1976, between general elections, be a good moment to do something about it? Harold Wilson had just retired as Prime Minister and what popularity the Labour Government had was blowing in the wind, to quote a song they were singing at the time.

Sean was more than satisfied with the way that the International Educational Trust was going, but the Scottish National Party was pointing out something they thought might have eluded him: just think what the voice of Sean Connery MP in the House of Commons would do for the country. Some of them were still thinking of the idea of James Bond MP, which didn't sound quite so crazy. But he wasn't interested. Even so, he had some definite ideas.

'We came to the conclusion that the quality of life in Scotland obliged people to take a powder ... When they go away, they make it work. So why not improve the quality of life in the place? The trust supports people who find they have a talent but no outlet for it.'

He was contributing what he could to the trust. All the money he earned, say, from television interviews went straight to it. He tried hard to emphasise just how important that was to him, how Scotland was engraved not just on his arm but on his heart; how he valued the idea of an education he had never had himself.

Yet word was spread that what he was doing was simply setting up a very convenient tax dodge. It would also have been a very expensive one, but that part seems to have escaped the attention of the detractors – people who said that Sean Connery was a great actor, a highly successful film star, but not a very nice man. Sean would not deny it. If newspapermen tussled with him he would be quite willing to say, 'I never said I was nice.' To Scotland and its educationalists, however, he was more than nice. He was a lifeline.

'I have been two years setting up this trust,' he said. 'It was a struggle to convince the Inland Revenue that one was not trying to evade tax; quite rightly, they have to stop all avenues of evasion.' Eventually, they were convinced – and so were those detractors. Meanwhile, *Variety* announced that Sean's own personal take from *Diamonds Are Forever* would finally work out at something like six million dollars.

But the trust wasn't the only idea he had for helping his home country. He wanted independence for Scotland – a place which he now said for the first time could become another Switzerland. 'If the SNP got any power, it should nationalise the oilfields and the bank,' he declared.

Even Dunbar Bank? Well, that wouldn't matter now. In 1979 he was to resign his directorship of the bank but still hold on to 102,000 shares. When the bank became part of a takeover deal in 1981, Sean's holdings became worth £835,000.

There was a good chance he would make more money from a takeover deal than anything since he had decided that diamonds were forever but Bond didn't have to be.

Even so, he was still talking about his own new Bond venture, now working with Len Deighton on the movie which was to be called *James Bond of the Secret Service*. Filming would take place very soon in the West Indies – or so it was said. People interested in that sort of thing were advised to watch this space.

Nevertheless, this *was* stiff-upper-lip time. In his only film of 1977, *A Bridge Too Far*, he was back in World War Two Army uniform, only this time in a more exalted rank than the one he had held in *The Longest Day*. Now he played General Urquhart, one of the leaders of the ill-fated Arnhem operation in the autumn of 1944 when the British

Airborne regiment were sacrificed to the Nazis – principally, it seemed, in the cause of showing that Field Marshal Montgomery could beat the Americans into Germany.

All the anger, frustrations and sadness of the operation were there, along with Sean in his khaki uniform, the beret placed at just the right angle, the toothbrush moustache, aiming his Army-issue pistol not a little like the way he had been taught to do for the 007 roles.

He wasn't the only big name in the picture. One critic said the film could well be given the subtitle of a 'A Star Too Many'. Ryan O'Neal, Robert Redford, James Caan, Michael Caine, Gene Hackman, Elliot Gould and Dirk Bogarde were among the others.

Those names – or rather the money they earned – complicated the issue. Sean heard that Robert Redford was getting two million dollars for his role, and complained. He wanted the same. As he said, 'At first I thought it must be a mistake. But then I learned it wasn't. Now, considering the size of my part in the picture, the salary I'd agreed was fair. But when I found how much the others were getting – for the same amount of work and with no more ability – it became unfair.' It turned out that James Caan, Elliott Gould and Ryan O'Neal were all on higher salaries than him.

It was Micheline who read in the press about the figures the others were getting. Sean was disturbed. He rang Joseph Levine, the producer, and asked bluntly: 'What is this newspaper crap?' Levine was equally blunt: he needed Redford for the American market but without two million, Redford wasn't going to appear. Telling Sean he was a much nicer guy wasn't exactly likely to soothe the pain and he knew it. Nor did the fact that Sean's agent had accepted it so readily help much. In the end, Connery settled for doubling his original fee of $250,000.

As Dennis Selinger told me, 'It was simply a case of justice. Sean saw that he was not getting a fair deal and demanded one. He didn't have a violent row, but just calmly said what he thought was right and you couldn't really argue with that. The company had to accept what was true.'

He got the money without having to go to court for it, but it was, nevertheless, the beginning of a heavy litigation season for Sean. Early in 1978 he announced he was suing Allied Artists for allegedly cheating him of money he ought to have got for *The Man Who Would Be King*. He said they owed him more than $100,000. Michael Caine sued for the same amount.

For what they paid him, said Sean in a phrase reminiscent of a line from one of the better Bond movies, all Allied Artists deserved to get was *The Man Who Would Be Prince*. He said that his contracts specified a share in profits that didn't come his way. What he was alleging could be summed up in that phrase which, as we have seen, was part of the agents' vocabulary: 'creative book keeping'. Quite suddenly, it appeared he was being made responsible for 'overheads' which had already been charged to other people.

In return for his demand, the studio organisation countersued. They now demanded twenty-one million dollars – because, they alleged, he had libelled the company. In an interview about Allied Artists with the *New York Times* Sean had said: 'I have been robbed. I think they should be in jail.'

He was now spouting to the press as though it came as naturally to him as asking for a cup of coffee. Quite suddenly the man who had given reporters their marching orders was treating newspaper people as confidants, knowing they were going to report what he said.

In another interview, he suggested that the game Allied Artists played was the kind of sport practised all over Hollywood. It was, he said, 'just the tip of the iceberg'. Then he made his now celebrated comment: 'I've never cheated or stolen from anybody in my life and I would be quite happy to stick anyone who steals from me in jail.'

They were fighting words, and Allied Artists were about to call for the legal equivalent of pistols at dawn. What they may not have realised was that they were embarking on a duel to the death, either Sean's financial demise or their own. Given their own status, the fortune they had made out of *The Man Who Would Be King* and the fact that they had another blockbuster, Harold Robins' *The Betsy*, all ready to bring in the cash, it would not have been unreasonable for the moguls to puff on their cigars and wait for Connery to buckle.

The duel was on. Their seconds were some of the best lawyers in the United States, a commodity that didn't come cheap. As Connery said: 'I said one sentence and it cost me $37,000 in lawyers' fees and I got sued for twenty-two million.'

Having turned their backs for a few months, the studio's 'seconds' advanced into the courtroom, pointing their guns straight at Connery. Sean's allegations, they said, 'seriously prejudiced' their client in 'its efforts to obtain new product, in its negotiations with third parties and in its dealings with suppliers, dealers, employers, exhibitors, bankers, other lenders ...' The list went on like a catalogue, detailing all the people who would now be rushing away from doing any deals with Allied Artists: publishers, authors, almost everybody but their laundry. They complained not only of defamation but also of 'malicious interference' and said they had already paid both Caine and Connery $320,000 each. The libel action was against Sean alone, but he and Michael Caine were also sued ten million dollars each in punitive damages.

This was the supreme test of whether Sean really was assuming litigation as his right, as he constantly said, or whether he would simply take refuge in an out-of-court settlement. Nobody would have predicted it would go further than, at the very furthest, the courthouse door. But none of those who doubted would have known much about Sean Connery and his attitude to the law. As far as Sean was concerned, it was there to serve him, not to intimidate. Others thought he saw it as a game. If it was, he played it with the highest possible stakes and even more seriously than any on the golfcourse.

In fact, the fight was fiercer than anything Sean had experienced in the Arnhem film. But it would be worth it from his point of view. Eventually, it was indeed settled out of court. He and Caine won their money and their opponents lost their defamation action – and promptly went out of business. In the final analysis neither Sean nor Michael got more than their honour satisfied by it all. They were left with their legal costs to meet and, because the company went into bankruptcy, without the damages the court awarded them. The best they could get as far as that was concerned was to be featured in the most imposing castlist since *A Bridge Too Far* – the tally of Allied Artists' creditors. Unfortunately, in that list, neither of them got star billing. As Sean joked, they weren't even featured alphabetically – which, in other circumstances, might have led to another law suit. But once again, it was the principle that counted.

'I am proud to be the cause of them going bankrupt,' Sean said when it was all over. The 'assholes' at Allied Artists had to be stopped because they treated actors as 'performing monkeys'.

Now, though, he was going to be much more careful about what he did. He would look over contract deals more cautiously and if he didn't understand what was on offer, he knew that the smell in his nostrils came from a rat lurking somewhere in the undergrowth.

A year later, he was back on screen, playing someone without his own particular respect for law and order. Wearing a stovepipe silk hat and a checked cloak, he and Donald Sutherland were conspirators in *The First Great Train Robbery*. The second great train robbery, of course, was the one in August 1963 when two and a half million pounds, never subsequently found, was stolen from the London-to-Glasgow mail train. The first robbery supposedly happened in the 1850s during the

Crimean War when there was a heist of the London-to-Folkestone express which was carrying bullion to be shipped to the front. Later it would be used for the pittances paid to British soldiers. Sutherland was the safe robber and Connery, naturally enough, the brains behind the operation and the love interest for Lesley-Anne Down, who had recently made her name in the popular television series, *Upstairs, Downstairs.*

He joked when the time came, kissed when that was called for – which was frequently – and ran along the roof of the moving train when he had to do that. This was the 1970s, and old-fashioned back projection wasn't even going to be considered. Certainly, he wasn't in the mood to see stunt men do his dirty work for him, so when a bridge came in sight, he ducked. Even though the train was travelling at fifty-five miles per hour, he kept moving. 'Did 'em all myself,' he said, recalling those stunts. 'Wouldn't want to ask anyone else to do it. The way it was done? I measured the distance between the bridge and the train and figured that – with my lying on the train, my head on my hand – that if my hand didn't move lower than my ear, I was all right. Quite safe, actually.'

The cameraman was less easily convinced. He was lying in front of Sean on top of the train all the way. Every time a bridge came up, he ducked and closed his eyes.

Later on, Sean said that a double would have been too easily spotted by audiences. So would the use of a safety net. 'In retrospect, it was a very silly thing to do,' he confessed to Steven M. Silverman of the *New York Post.*

Connery never had reason to complain that he was being ignored. Unfortunately for him, his first 1979 film was noticed by too many – and too many critics in particular. *Meteor* might have been a happier experience had the *Guardian*'s Derek Malcolm, for instance, not had cause to write about a film which he maintained 'would lose to a firework display on a very rainy night'. This tale about a space scientist, played by Connery, falling in love with a Russian translator (Natalie Wood in one of her very last roles) while a five-mile-wide meteor was paying a visit to earth did neither Sean nor anyone else concerned with the project any good at all. 'Talkative disaster movie with occasional moments of interest,' wrote Leslie Halliwell in just about the best review it got. The director Ronald Neame probably regretted making it just as much as did Sean.

The trouble with this particular disaster movie was that it was a disaster itself right from early on in the filming. Part of the script called for the flooding of a subway, which was simulated on the set by pumping gallons of nasty, cold, sticky mud into the MGM swimming pool. 'Trying to supply as much mud as possible without actually killing Sean Connery' was how one of the technicians described it.

Connery, like all the actors, found himself playing mudpies without wanting to do so. He and everyone else had to rush their lines in an effort to recite a whole sentence before either slipping onto their backsides and drowning in the stuff or having it thrown up into their mouths. Maybe that alone didn't justify the sort of fee Sean was getting, but it was ready proof that film-making wasn't always a picnic.

It wasn't worth the effort, that was for sure. Even worse, as the decade ended, a question had to be asked: What *was* Sean Connery doing? Sean had now left Dennis Selinger – not because of dissatisfaction, but because, the veteran agent told me, 'He just thought he needed a change.'

Selinger had tried to package him as well as he could, and at least the decision to keep working managed to keep the Connery name in the newspaper film pages and in the women's magazines, in particular. That might have been all right for those actors who believed that any publicity was good publicity, but Sean, on the other hand, still lived by the maxim that all publicists were parasites and every inch they managed to get into a newspaper represented the blood they were sucking from him. The only thing to do, he and Selinger agreed, was to keep working. Unfortunately, just before the break with Selinger's ICM agency and Sean's moving to the Hollywood office of Creative Artists, he worked on a film called *Cuba* about the last days before Fidel Castro's takeover of the island. That didn't at all prove the wisdom of keeping going. On the contrary, it was the best case imaginable for throwing in the towel.

The film was dreadful from the word go. Everything that could go wrong did go wrong, it seemed. They needed a B52 bomber for one of the important scenes; it made one flight for a rehearsal and crashed. Fortunately, there was footage of the rehearsal and Richard Lester, the director, made do with that. Filming was at Cadiz, handy for the Spanish army division that had been promised as extras for the movie – except that the promise was withdrawn after one of the little local difficulties that seemed to be happening regularly in Spain at the time, like the assassination of a political figure in Madrid. Instead of the division, other extras were brought in, and in place of the tank regiment, pride of the Spanish Army, cardboard cutouts were hastily made. Sean threatened to walk out, but in the end stayed – as much out of sympathy for the director, whose fault none of this was, as because of his contractual obligations.

After seeing the picture, Margaret Hinxman, without actually saying so, found herself thinking twice about Sean getting better all the time. The film, she said, was 'ludicrous'. As for Connery, he walked around 'looking perplexed'.

Strangely – and maybe this did say a great deal about the sort of actor he was now perceived to be – even this fiasco failed to harm his image, even if no one was now saying he was the best actor on screen. Man Watchers Inc., an American women's organisation (could it have been anything else ?), declared he was among the most attractive males around – 'intriguing, smooth, urbane with *savoir faire* and class,' they declared. No one asked them if they knew what either urbane or *savoir faire* meant.

Perhaps they were referring to the way he disposed of his various law suits. Now he was facing one that was almost as big as his dispute with Allied Artists.

This one concerned a financial adviser – and confirmed his decision to make most of his money decisions himself now. He had said about this time : 'I've never had a confidant. I've never needed one.'

The new legal action, however, proved just how much he *had* actually needed that help. After all, in a somewhat contradictory statement after the Allied Artists *débâcle*, he had noted : 'I fall into two traps. One is believing things people tell me ; the other is finding the people who are really good at business are betting with their bookies' money.'

Sean was paying the price of betting with his own cash. The subject of his ire was now one Kenneth Richards, his financial adviser. The fact that this dispute came to court was thanks to Micheline, and due, on the surface, to the most mundane of events : she couldn't understand why a new washing machine she had bought had failed to be delivered at the Marbella house. She asked Richards, who was responsible for such things, and he replied – quite reasonably, he thought – that since it wouldn't work on the Spanish current, he had given it on behalf of the Connerys to his own son as a wedding present.

Now, despite whatever reasonable explanation they may be given, ladies who buy washing machines for themselves don't very much appreciate not receiving them. They also tend to want to give their own wedding presents, and not find that someone else has saved them the trouble and presented something in their own name.

But there was more than just a washing machine involved. In fact, she discovered that her desk had been turned upside down. What was more, letters had been removed. They were later photocopied and replaced – a fact that came to light when Richards produced those

Xeroxes at a court hearing two years after the originals had been destroyed. How, therefore, did Richards get hold of them if they were no longer in existence?

Micheline said that it was her 'feminine intuition' that started the Connerys' investigation. Richards, by then living and operating in Switzerland, had been entrusted with the task of moving all their furniture from London to Spain. At the same time, there was the little matter of Sean's money to which he had been given access. A mere three million dollars had been put by Richards and a Swiss property developer named Jean Canela into property negotiations of which Sean not only knew nothing but from which he was not going to extract any benefit. He wasn't exactly broke, but even in terms of the Sean Connery coffers that was digging very deep indeed.

All this was now discovered by Micheline who went to Switzerland on Sean's behalf because he himself was working on a film. She asked Richards to show her the books. He said he didn't have any and knew nothing about any property deals.

Legal proceedings were instituted in the Swiss courts. Richards went AWOL from Switzerland and was sacked – and then began what he considered to be the best form of defence: he attacked, and made his own countercharge against Sean, claiming two per cent of his former client's earnings from some thirteen films, which he said was owed to him under his contract.

Sean then took his own protective action. A new charge was added: he alleged negligence in the handling of his affairs.

It would all rumble on for another seven years – years of anguish for both parties. But nobody had any reason to believe it would be easier for the wealthy and highly successful Sean Connery than it was for his former employee.

Sean kept on working, if not always at the pace Dennis Selinger would have wanted. It was a time for newspaper speculation once again – reasonable enough, considering the fact that he was saying different things to different writers. To the *Daily Mail* in London, he was all ready for a new Bond film. To the *Sunday Express*, he announced that plans for *Warhead*, the revamped *Thunderball*, now were definitely off.

He was still bored with Bond. One night he got back late to his Beverly Hills hotel, turned on the television to see that *Dr No* was playing. He watched it – and fell asleep in the process.

But even he had to confess that it was 007 who had brought him his fortune and, despite what Mr Richards had done to him, he still did have a fortune. The fellow from Fountainbridge had done very well for himself. On the other hand, if you could take the man out of Fountainbridge, taking Fountainbridge out of the man wasn't so easy – the memories were always there. 'I remember when you didn't call the doctor to your house but went and sat in a freezing waiting room instead, because calling the doctor out cost fifteen bob. I'm still not entirely used to having money. I still go around the house putting out all the unused lights.'

A new decade had now begun, and Sean had new plans, although, with hindsight, many of them needed to be treated with a pinch of salt. At the time, he hoped something would come of them – like starring as Daddy Warbucks in the film version of *Annie*. He even took singing lessons for what would have been his first musical since *South Pacific*. But in the end, he lost interest. He said he was 'bugged' by the producer Ray Stark ringing him every day to find out how he was doing and when would he be ready to sign the contract. What really worried Sean was the thought that he could be spending all this time on his voice lessons, to say nothing of the practising involved, only to find – such things had been known before – himself dubbed. No producer was going to guarantee that that wouldn't happen unless he submitted to an audition, and Sean Connery couldn't be expected to audition for anyone. So he backed out and Albert Finney got the role.

As 1980 came and went, people were beginning once more to worry about this unpredictable actor called Sean Connery. His ever-thinning hair was now receding at almost the same speed as a Bond Aston Martin. What there was left was a silvery grey. Women still found him stunningly attractive. And yet for the first time in a decade, a whole year went by without a single new Connery film. It was clear he still hadn't found his niche. In his determination to avoid typecasting, he was travelling too winding a road, and you didn't know in which of the bends to find him. That was how unpredictable he was. But there was nothing at all unpredictable about the quality of his acting. The trouble was it was usually in a different class from the films he made.

It was still necessary to ask where he thought he was going. But wherever it was, Sean knew that he was not going there alone. Micheline was with him all the time, and stayed with him whenever he went away on a film – except when she deemed it judicious not to do so.

11

THE SECOND
MRS CONNERY

People still weren't sure who this man was. Even the London *Daily Mail* thought its readers would have difficulty. They captioned a picture of tired Sean sitting in a deckchair, 'Guess who?' The answer wasn't calculated to have Sean popping the champagne corks: 'It's 007 looking so OO-OLD'. Next to the shot was a smaller picture of the Connery they thought everybody would recognise – as James Bond.

If some people *were* now advising Sean Connery to settle into the kind of role that only he could play, he was not paying much attention. There was nothing anyone could point to and say, 'This is a Sean Connery role.'

Dennis Selinger before Sean left him might have had something to do with that. All that advice to Sean about making three films in the hope that one of them would be a winner didn't seem to have paid off. But he was his own man – up to a point. As Selinger told me, 'I don't think Sean would ever do anything he didn't want to do, but by the same token he is bright enough to take important advice when it's given.'

By now, nobody should have been bothering very much about Sean Connery. Most middle-aged actors without a recent hit film should be getting the old stars' equivalent of 'Don't call us, we'll call you.' Yet they were calling him all the time, offering more and more roles. Nevertheless in 1980 it was difficult to work out why he rejected some pictures while he accepted others.

The literary agent Swifty Lazar knew he could get a million dollars for Sean's memoirs. But Sean wasn't interested. 'I could certainly write some strong stuff but I don't think afterwards I would feel too comfortable in my own skin. You can't write those private things without other people getting hurt.'

Sean's first picture of the new decade was, like those directly preceding it, disappointing. *Time Bandits*, made in 1981, was described as a comedy for children. It included names like Ian Holm, John Clease, Sir Ralph Richardson (playing God) and David Warner (playing Satan). Sean played King Agamemnon.

The picture had as its premise the idea of a schoolboy being taken through time. There was as much violence as there was fantasy. Sean was brought into filming late in the game because the director Terry Gilliam thought it needed some extra weight. His part, though, was so brief that John Cleese, who played Robin Hood, told me he didn't even meet him.

Gilliam always said he was glad to have Sean along – he even put up with Connery's habit of calling him either 'Boy' or, even worse, 'Quasimodo' for no discernible reason.

Outland, which followed later in 1981, ought to have been more important than it actually was. It was a *High Noon*-type story into which a great deal of work and money was fed. But somehow it seems to have got stranded in outer space, which was where it was set – on one of Jupiter's moons called Io, where there were beings who not only looked very much like humans, but did the things humans did, too. They made love – in brothels as well as in more salubrious surroundings; they went to shows featuring writhing couples; they had fights. That was not surprising since they *were* humans, people who worked wearing spacesuits. The reason they were there at all was the titanium being mined on the moon; they were employed by an inter-planetary organisation. And they had illegal drugs that improved their output but then drove them insane.

Sean played the marshal who is sent to clean up the town and ends up fighting a duel. Leslie Halliwell described it all as 'ludicrous' and 'heavily coloured'.

Heavily coloured could well describe Sean's language during much of the making of the movie. He felt he wasn't treated quite as delicately as he should have been. Some of the technicians at whom he shouted might have been quite happy to see him in one of his on-screen predicaments – left stranded weightless in mid-air, hanging from a near-invisible rope and wearing a spacesuit. At one stage during the filming of this scene the wires got twisted and Sean showered the men below with a whole series of obscenities, including the choice phrase, 'Get me down and get everything ready before that harness goes round my balls.'

The film was shot at Pinewood studios – for sentimental reasons as much as anything; he hadn't made a movie in Britain for years and wanted to do so desperately. The trouble arose because the film shooting schedule went over its allotted time and he had other things to do thereafter.

Not all the problems showed. The *New Yorker* critic Pauline Kael said of it: '*Outland* has a great look.' But, she declared ultimately, it was 'full of missed opportunities'.

But what about Sean Connery's marshal? He was one of the few people who made what she called a strong impression. But the real comments were left to the film itself, a picture so big the star appears to be lost. 'This could be the Dolby movie of the year,' she wrote. 'The noise rises to Gotterdammerung level.'

Sean, however, had only good to say of the picture. 'I have done more than my fair share of films which didn't succeed at the box office. *Outland* is unlikely to be one of them.' That was wishful thinking that would turn out to be unrequited.

He said that the response in America had been marvellous, which was a kind exaggeration. 'I think it's one of the first space films I've seen where I could understand what it was all about without getting into all those jet packs and ray guns and what have you. *Star Wars* and *The Empire Strikes Back* were a complete mystery to me. I saw *Outland* in New York and the interesting thing was the identification with O'Neil [the marshal] was total.'

He was sure it would be the same when the movie had its British première in Edinburgh – with all proceeds to the educational trust.

It was said that he had to ration his trips to Britain now. The tax laws allowed him to spend only ninety days a year in the country without the Inland Revenue having their say. In 1993 he insisted again that he had always paid all his British taxes, just as he had those on his earnings in America as well.

But there was another reason besides the première of *Outland* for his visit to Scotland in 1981. Effie had had a stroke and was lying serously ill in hospital.

He stayed at Gleneagles, which not only is one of the finest hotels in the country, it also gave him the chance to indulge in a little golf.

He also did unexpected things – like use a public pool. He not only used it for swimming, but also as a venue for arguing with people he didn't like or whose opinions he respected even less. After one confrontation with a gentleman of military background, he ended the conversation with the solemn words, 'You're such a prick!'

Scotland was always a place to reflect, which is why he took Micheline, his son Jason, then aged eighteen, and Micheline's son Stefan, a year younger, to Fountainbridge.

Micheline, who, unlike Diane, had not known Effie in the happy days before Joe's death, was shocked by the poverty she saw. Could this be where Sean Connery of all people once lived?

He said afterwards of the boys' impressions: 'My problem was poverty. Their problem is being the sons of a film star. It is something they will have to negotiate and learn to handle.' He thought that taking them to his poor origins would help them put it all into perspective.

And in that he deserved their thanks. Sean provided trust funds for his children. Jason said he wouldn't be touching his any more than he intended cashing in on the Connery name when he finally achieved his ambition to become a professional actor like his father. He knew that Connery senior regarded money as a kind of insurance he had never had himself as a child.

There have always been two ways of looking at one's poverty-stricken past – either ignore it and invent in its stead much more prosperous origins, or milk it. Sean had the integrity to accept his youth as a reality without attempting to take any great advantage from the situation. It was part of his 'private' life and he wanted to keep it that way.

The strange, almost inexplicable, thing about him was that he still thought he could escape from public attention. He still couldn't grasp that there was a price to pay for his success. I remember James Stewart, a superstar of a previous generation, once telling me he gave interviews and spoke about himself because it was 'part of the ballgame'. Sean Connery still thought that sort of ballgame was out of bounds. He didn't ask himself how producers would still want Sean Connery if people stopped hearing or reading about him.

He had, however, the right to keep anyone with whom he didn't want to spend his time far away. He was a citizen and had citizen's privileges. He still seemed able to exercise them most at the house in Marbella, which, because it was the place where he relaxed more easily than anywhere else, he called 'the hospital'.

There was no 'hospital' in London now. He had sold the house on Chelsea Embankment for £60,000. It wasn't a very good deal for him. A year later it was worth £150,000.

But there were other deals that worked out better – particularly the 1981 settlement of the first of the hearings in the Kenneth Richards affair. When the High Court in London turned down Richards' suit for two per cent cuts in his films, Sean was close to tears of joy.

There had been three and a half days of cross-examination – after which Richards decided not to continue with his case and withdrew his claim. Mr Justice Talbot told the court: 'I have never witnessed a party's case so destroyed by cross examination to the extent the plaintiff's case was destroyed.' Richards' claim was 'wholly without merit'.

Sean was more than just delighted. 'I am absolutely thrilled that eventually justice has been done,' he declared. 'If I had lost, I would have had to pay him more than £100,000 and continue to pay him. But the truth came out. It was certainly an ordeal I don't want to go through again. It's much better on the film set.' Since 1978 the case had been a constant nightmare.

Not only did Richards lose his suit, he conceded Sean's claim that he had been negligent in handling his business affairs. He was ordered to pay the Connery costs of £100,000 and damages which would be worked out later.

How did a star deal with a situation like that? He cried properly this time. In a way, it was the best way Sean could be seen. Better than all the interviews he didn't want to give, the man who hated exhibiting his private self appeared natural and human in a very private moment that was witnessed by the world.

'I was betrayed by a man I trusted,' he said afterwards. 'What made matters worse was that when the case eventually came to court, the man I had thought of as a friend tried to blame my wife and make her the villain of the piece.' It was not going to be the end of the matter.

But then in 1982 he was planning a new film at Elstree Studios. It was going to be called *Never Say Never Again*, which was a less than coded message to people like himself and had absolutely nothing to do with the subject matter – the plot of *Thunderball* revamped, which was at last to happen.

The title had been suggested by Micheline. Sean was so pleased with it that he thought she should be given a credit. But not even that little bit of nepotism met with general approval and when the film was released, no acknowledgement of her contribution appeared on screen.

The idea of the film had come up while Dennis Selinger was still representing Sean. The agent hadn't been keen. 'I didn't want him to do it, but once he had made up his mind, I didn't try to stop him.' Selinger says he had never had a row with Sean before and was not about to have one then. 'But we did have arguments – usually about something in a contract which he thought I shouldn't have allowed to go through.'

Now Sean was determined to make the most of it all. 'He originally
wanted to write the script himself, but when that went by the board
he still persisted with making the film. But I thought that once he had
got rid of Bond he should lose it. It was probable that he wanted to
prove to himself that he could do it. But it didn't have the famous
Maurice Binder opening sequence and it didn't have the music. And
without them, you didn't have Bond. In my own mind, I'm sure he
just did it out of pique against Broccoli and Saltzman. But I don't
think he has ever been sorry about anything he has done, and he
wasn't sorry about this. He was well enough paid.'

And payment was important. 'Like a lot of people who start from
nothing, the money was important because of the status it gave him,
and like a lot of people from his background, he was frightened of
losing that status. Like a lot of actors, he needs applause. For film
actors, money is applause.'

There had been the legal fights that were predictable. A court was
asked to flesh out the details. Broccoli hoped that even though
McClory had the rights to the film of *Thunderball* he did not have the
rights to make any others. Which would mean, he said, that the
Connery Bond could be nothing but a total remake of *Thunderball*. In
other words, he would be able to reshoot it scene for scene, shot for
shot, but do nothing else with it; make no changes, add no dialogue,
update no situations.

For months, nobody was allowed to say anything. After the earlier
experience with Allied Artists, Sean had been advised 'not to say a
damn thing about it'. He was keeping to it – 'I've learned my lesson
well.' As Sean said, 'We now stand waiting for the lawyers to straighten
out the bloody thing.' Before they did, nothing could happen. In the
meantime, Paramount had advanced Connery and McClory a total of
fifteen million dollars (a third of it for Sean himself) to make the
picture that might never be.

A judge, however, decided that it should go ahead – and when
he did, McClory sold out his interest to Broadway producer, Jack
Schwartzmann.

There were also financial deals to be sorted out. He needed to talk
to Dennis Selinger – whom he traced to the Arctic Circle. 'I was in
Lapland on location. How he found me there, I'll never know,' the
agent remembered for me.

'He phoned me at about 4.30 in the morning my time. He wanted
to know about a meeting that had been set up for that afternoon.
Actually, the meeting had been arranged by my PA in my name. It
was about his trust, but he thought it was about Equity. Sean's mind

immediately turns to lawyers. He instantly started screaming down the phone to me . . .'

All that Selinger really understood were the opening words, 'What the fucking hell are you doing in Lapland?' As he continued: 'It developed into one of those conversations in which he just didn't listen to anything the other man was saying. He was on his great hobby horse, which he was on frequently – how everybody in the business was stitching him up one way or another. He was going on and on and on. I was dying to get back to sleep. Then in the middle of the diatribe, he said, "I've just realised, Dennis, I'm paying for this call. Good night." '

Selinger said he just fell off the bed, laughing. He never did get back to sleep that night.

Before the picture could actually happen, there were three other movies to be made. Again none of them made any impact at all.

Wrong Is Right was the United States title for a picture that in Britain was called *The Man With The Deadly Lens*. The story of a television commentator discovering that the world was being manipulated by the CIA, it could have struck a chord with a lot of people: but maybe too many people suspected that was exactly what was happening and so took the fact for granted. They certainly weren't excited about seeing the movie and it soon disappeared.

Sean's second film of 1982, *Five Days One Summer*, was far better. The picture was based on a story written fifty years earlier by Kay Boyle called *Maiden Maiden*. But really its foundation was director Fred Zinnemann, one of the great Hollywood names, who had always had a fascination with mountain climbing, the joy of his youth. He had always looked for the right story, and when he came upon *Maiden Maiden* he saw the potential.

Sean was Zinneman's first choice for the role of the Scottish doctor. He chose well – the picture was wonderfully photographed and Sean, in a suit, looking every year of his age, was perfect for part. Was he Dr Finlay or Dr Cameron? Older audiences who remembered the television series *Dr Finlay's Casebook* couldn't help noticing the similarity – except that in *Five Days One Summer* the doctor went climbing in the Swiss Alps (new training for the man who thought golf was pretty tough), had the company of a beautiful woman played by Betsy Brantley (an actress who disappeared from view straight afterwards although she deserved to do better), and got himself involved in a taboo sexual relationship.

The role of Sean's mother in the film was played by Isabel Dean, renewing her old *Ransom* connection with Sean. She told me that the cast were so fond of him that when she and another actress realised that the rooms in their hotels had strange names – 'One was called "the Big Bear" ' – they thought they would write and tell him about it. 'One only did that with someone who was very pleasant.'

She told me : 'What I remember is that he was the most attractive, unstarlike person I'd ever met. He's 100 per cent a star on the screen, but he hasn't that aura about him which makes a small actor feel nervous about working with him. Others do do that even if they don't mean to. It's the difference between having to do something in one take and being given two or three times to get it right. They can't afford to spend so much time on small parts. Not him.'

She said : 'I've never found anybody who made us feel so much at ease.' For the first week on the set he went out of his way to have meals with the other actors, 'so we saw him every night. It's a difficult thing to come to terms with, playing a small part, when you do rather more usually in television or on the stage.'

Nevertheless, according to Anna Korda, once more Sean's voice coach, this wasn't the same Sean as of old. 'He was no longer so easy-going,' she said, 'but he was still very likeable.'

Micheline was there with Sean. Anna Korda told me, 'I think it was a mutual admiration society. She plainly adored him and worshipped him and I think he felt the same about her.'

Micheline caused consternation by walking around in a pale-green bikini on the icy-cold Swiss mountaintop. 'She also wore an oriental veil,' recalled Anna Korda. 'I felt she was putting it on and drawing attention to herself. The crew didn't like her very much.'

Unfortunately, yet again, the box office didn't match up to the production itself. Once more, a Sean Connery film flopped dismally.

After these two movies came *Sword Of The Valiant*, which was made in the South of France and earned Sean $600,000. It was a terrible remake of an earlier, equally terrible picture that would have amazed the members of King Arthur's Court had they stepped into a time machine, but did nothing at all for the 1983 audiences who walked into a movie theatre.

But Sean wasn't just aiming for high box office stakes. In 1982 he narrated a short film called simply *Sean Connery's Edinburgh*, a travelogue which included the castle, Princes Street, Holyrood House – and Fountainbridge and the dairy. The final credit was in the form of the brass plate for the Scottish International Educational Trust. Perhaps making a film of a subject that was so close to his heart made it easier for him to risk charges of compromising his artistic integrity by making *Never Say Never Again*.

If people were wondering what was going wrong with the Connery career – for all the money he was making – *Never Say Never Again* did not, remarkably, provide the obvious answers. Right from the beginning, he maintained he really was saying 'never' again. There wouldn't be another Connery Bond film after this one.

That didn't mean, however, that he should not now go into it as though *Never Say Never Again* had been a life's ambition. He planned everything to the minutest detail, including his fight routines. One of his various adversaries fought a little too hard for comfort and Sean broke an arm.

But the new Bond picture looked as though it were going to work out well enough. Like *Thunderball*, it dealt with the theft of nuclear warheads by SPECTRE. The principal difference was the updating of technology since 1965. It was a film that had a huge sense of *déja vu* about it, as though for twelve years an impostor had been wearing Bond's clothes and had stolen his identity papers, but now the real man was back.

Yes, he looked a lot more mature than the Bond of old, but then that was the film's principal charm. He certainly didn't have a paunch, and the women still found him devastatingly attractive. More than ever before, in fact.

The only part of playing Bond that worried him was that old problem of his hair. They matched Sean's toupee to his new silvery hair, as the black hairpiece the 1960s Bond had worn was no longer appropriate. 'When I put it on,' he said, 'it looked like a balaclava.'

So what else was new about this reincarnation of the original Bond? Certainly not the kind of Bond Girl with whom he shared beds. This time, she was Kim Basinger, who later lost a celebrated law suit for refusing to strip in another movie. Once this picture had been cleared for action, there were few inhibitions on *Never Say Never Again*.

Micheline kept away when he was doing his love scenes. She didn't want people to second guess her reactions. She knew she had been right about that the day she turned up on the set during one of the steamier moments. She had made a mistake with the shooting schedule and came just when she had planned not to do so. It was a very hot day and she thought about leaving. But she stayed. As she explained, had she left, it would have been thought she did so in a huff – and she desperately wanted to convey her philosophy that anything which was all in a day's work for her husband was all right with her.

Later she would say that if she were the jealous type she would have been dead long before then ... 'Pooof!' She was concentrating on what was now commonly called *TLC* – she used the phrase constantly – tender loving care.

Desmond Llewellyn, who had played Q in all Bond movies to date except *Dr No*, was staying loyal to the Broccoli regime, and his slim attache case was placed in the care of Alec McCowen, 'Algy'. Similarly Blofeld was now played by Max von Sydow.

There were still the sharks – many more of them, which Sean said he didn't enjoy very much – and still plenty of underwater activity. There were more helicopters and there was also a video game with a new villain named Largo (Klaus Maria Brandauer). By comparison, a session in the electric chair would have seemed a novel kind of entertainment. And there were all the usual Bond gimmicks. More significantly, there were the usual Bond crowds to see it.

There were also the usual rows with the producer. Schwartzmann moved to the Bahamas during filming without leaving his phone number. Sean thought it was intolerable that he had no contact with the man. He said it was 'like working in a toilet'.

He still hadn't forgiven Broccoli and Saltzman either. A story published widely at the time had him being informed of Cubby having a stroke and quoted him allegedly saying: 'Fucking good. I hope he's paralysed down the other side tomorrow.'

It wasn't calculated to make him appear happy to the world. Perhaps what really was wrong was that Sean, who had never enjoyed playing Bond was going through motions he still resented – even though he was acting as well as he ever had before, and certainly much, much better than in any of the early Eon versions. Quite plainly, he wanted something more of life than playing a character he didn't believe in.

The resemblance to *Thunderball* was in the story line, but you could have kidded most people into not knowing there were any similarities at all. What it most closely resembled was the Bond genre. There was no mistaking it. In fact, *Never Say Never Again* could have been interchanged with *Octopussy* which, starring Roger Moore and produced by Albert R. Broccoli, just happened to be going to open at the same time. Broccoli was alone now; he and Saltzman had finally divorced, and he now blew smoke all by himself at the chutzpah of Sean Connery, of all people, trying to muscle in on the Bond patch.

His reaction in what was being billed as the 'Battle of the Bonds' by newspapers who enjoyed above all the spectacle of 54-year-old Roger Moore going into conflict with the 52-year-old Sean Connery was predictable. At Pinewood, the instruction was to pretend that the Connery version just wasn't happening.

The talk in the film industry was not so much which one of the two was going to win the fight, but would each one cancel out the other. Said an executive : 'I doubt if many people will want to see them both. They just might wipe Bond away for good.' The more cynical among us might have thought that was Sean's idea in the first place.

But Connery didn't see any problems in that direction. 'We are not in competition. I'm sure the public will not go to the cinema just to compare the two.' That was a not terribly educated guess. Of course they would go to make the comparisons, as well as to enjoy the proceedings, and he knew they would.

Roger Moore apparently thought the whole thing was very funny and muttered something about it being no more damaging than Olivier and Gielgud playing Hamlet at different theatres but at the same time. Cubby Broccoli, predictably, was said to be 'fuming'.

Sean himself did not think it was all particularly funny. The 52-year-old said he had never worked harder in his life. Now he was virtually playing producer of the picture, writing the script, helping the director Irvin Kershner (he was the first American ever to direct a Bond movie and had previously worked with Sean in *A Fine Madness*).

'I wound up being involved in every aspect of the picture except the music.' But it was his own choice. 'I could have refused. But that would have been rather silly.'

He had money in the film – a great deal of money – so had to take on much more than his usual acting role. Actually, he even had a *dancing* role – doing the tango with Kim Basinger. For that, he took ballroom dancing lessons from Peggy Spencer, who had been a judge on the BBC *Come Dancing* programmes and had actually given Nureyev ballroom dancing lessons for the film *Valentino*.

So how much was he getting ? 'I admit I'm being paid well, but it's no more than I deserve.' After all, as he also said, he'd been screwed more times than a hooker.

This time he was in charge of what would happen. He wasn't going to screw himself. 'I just wanted to see if I could still do it. Nothing more than that.' He wanted once more to play it straight, the way he had done more than two decades ago. He always thought that Roger Moore was more of a parody of the authentic Bond. 'I just wanted to make one more Bond movie, so I could go out with a splash'. And he wasn't referring exclusively to what he and Kim did in the water.

Sean was playing hard too – organising golf tournaments that both benefitted the Scottish International Educational Trust and allowed Sean Connery to play with his pals – increasingly including British comedians Bruce Forsyth and Jimmy Tarbuck.

He played the game wherever he was. Once, it seemed he was also going to take part in a tennis championship. He enjoyed the game but nobody thought he was of tournament standard. Then in 1983 a showbiz tennis marathon was organised at the Royal Albert Hall. He was asked if he would compete. It was to raise money to help fight muscular dystrophy, and was an occasion when, like many of the other big theatrical events, show business liked to show its own muscle. Sean was announced midway through the evening as '007'. When it was realised which 007 this was, the hall, which had seen a few riotous occasions in its time, erupted. Sean bounced on to the arena, wearing a tam-o'-shanter and carrying his golf clubs. It was pure showmanship. He didn't do any more and indeed he didn't need to do more.

Soon after *Never Say Never Again* there was a new Connery film. Not a Sean Connery film but one featuring Jason Connery.

The influence of the father on the son was palpable. He had always wanted to act and now he landed a role in an American movie called *The Lords Of Discipline* about life at West Point.

Sean was pleased. 'He used to say that I didn't want him to be an actor,' he recalled. 'But that was never true. Why would I object? His mother is a good actress, too. So why not? Had he been hopeless, of course, it might have been another matter.'

Later, the younger Connery would say that his relationship with Sean only started to get really close when he did decide to become an actor – not just because he was simply following in his father's footsteps but because he had set his mind on a real goal.

Jason had tried and failed before. He had gone into acting after failing to get a university place when he left Gordonstoun. 'His marks weren't good enough,' Sean said bluntly. When Jason announced he wanted to follow in his father's footsteps, Sean had got him a small-time job on *Five Days One Summer* as a gofer 'running around helping, to give him the feel of things'.

Jason had really wanted to go to RADA, but Sean talked him out of it. Far better to *do* than to *learn* in a classroom, he thought. Jason has always said that his father was right and that his experience on the film set was a good apprenticeship, but it didn't help much when things went wrong. 'When I fail an audition, I can get terribly depressed,' he said at the time. 'But if there's one thing my father's taught me, it's not to be soft.'

The trips round Fountainbridge *had* tended to indicate that. 'If you want something, you go out and get it.' Sean had gone out and got superstardom. For the moment, Jason was not aiming quite so high, but friends noted the younger Connery's intense desire to prove to the older one that he could make it on his own.

Jason had auditioned for both the Bristol Old Vic – alma mater of Peter O'Toole – and for the Traverse at Edinburgh. Finally, he had gone to Perth and worked in rep. Sean denied having any part in it. 'Nepotism I abhor. There's no question that the situation in Perth was helped because of who I am, but once he got there, it was clearly up to him.'

Sean had always determined that if he had opened any doors for Jason – and certainly their relationship was strong and fond enough for there never to be any suggestion of his slamming them in his face – it was up to his son to actually go through them on his own.

'I always felt a little sorry for Jason,' one of Sean's friends told me. 'He and Sean spent so much time apart that you felt both of them wanted to be especially nice to each other. But I never doubted they always felt for each other and I know that if he had any trouble, Sean would have found a way to be with him.'

For his part, Jason treasured that very fact about his relationship with Sean. Not that they always agreed. 'He has never hit me, but he has come close. My temper is just as short as his.' He said it almost as if he were glad they had more than just acting in common.

'I know he is just being constructive when he criticises me and says, "You must do this, you *have* to do this,"' he told Judy Wade in the *Sun*. 'The best thing Dad has given me is a sensible attitude to life. I respect him and want to be like him, except as an actor where I want to go my own way.'

The junior Connery could also be reflective: 'I know a lot of superstars' sons end up committing suicide [one of the most notable was Gregory Peck's eldest]. It isn't easy measuring up to my father. But no way am I going to jump under a train.'

Victor Spinetti, for one, would be surprised if he did. 'They get on terribly well, but then they would. Sean and Diane shared him equally from the beginning and I suppose in a way Diane made him what he became. But both she and Sean are very strong personalities and they have combined to exert both of themselves on him – with only good results.'

One example of their influence was plainly Jason's own career. For two years, he starred in a television series that had its Connery roots, playing the lead in *Robin Of Sherwood*. (After its cancellation for financial reasons, Jason said: 'I thought the series had a quality about it from start to finish. There was plenty of action, the characters were developing, the actors were good in it and there were strong stories.')

Later, Jason would make a film about the life of James Bond's creator, Ian Fleming, an idea which Sean would find peculiarly satisfying. The film itself – *The Secret Life Of Ian Fleming* – never got anywhere.

Jason insists he doesn't discuss his acting with his father. 'I'm a little too close.'

Sean and Micheline now had a home in the Bahamas as well as in Marbella, and a small comfortable apartment in Los Angeles. There was another in Monte Carlo, an address at which he was legally registered as spending most of his time. Dennis Selinger saw them at home in Marbella. 'They had a very nice home there. Very nice indeed.'

If anyone doubted the kind of love that existed between Sean and Micheline, seeing her painting her favourite subject was enough to put an end to such thoughts. Sean was there for the asking, and when she asked, he obeyed the command. Wearing a loose-fitting dress – frequently exposing more than mere cleavage – she painted while he sat, and there was obviously more than an artist–model relationship between them.

There was no question of Sean trying to squash her career or her individuality as Diane claimed he had tried to do with her. Like Diane, Micheline was a free spirit. The fact that she didn't have a similar career clearly helped – there was no rivalry. But she wasn't about to be subdued and the changes she made to the Spanish house made this very clear. The paintings – by other people as well as by herself – and other decorations were visible indications that she was making her stand. As indeed did the very fact that she was painting at all.

However, would a psychiatrist seeing one of her Connery portraits have drawn any interesting conclusions? She featured him with two sets of eyes. Was she suggesting a two-faced Sean? She wouldn't allow the thought to enter her head. But then Sean seemed to be much too comfortable with Micheline in the Marbella house to argue. The very fact that he put up with the smell of paint and the mess it caused – both things he previously would have barely tolerated – seemed to say a lot for their relationship.

'Until I met Micheline,' Sean once said, 'I never bothered with possessions. But this is like a hidey-hole for me. What little stuff I have, I have it here.'

The house, actually just outside Marbella on the beach at San Pedro de Alcantara, a one-time fishing village which had long before succumbed to the temptations of the money brought in by celebrity residents, was now the place he considered to be home, the others mere – if luxury – pieds-à-terre in places he visited frequently.

But wherever he was living, Micheline was living there too – unless for some reason she had to stay in Spain or perhaps visit her family in France or Morocco.

People describe her as 'iron-willed', so it would perhaps be difficult to do anything to upset her. 'I am a very determined woman,' she often says. 'And I admire other determined women, like Mrs Thatcher, with the persistence to do what they want.' However even the woman who is now Baroness Thatcher couldn't hang on to power; a fact that might explain Micheline's determination not to allow anyone else to usurp her place in Sean's life.

'Women adore Sean,' she says. 'He has charisma. With those marvellous eyes and dancing eyebrows, I find it absolutely normal that women desire him.' But she also adds: 'A lot of women are after Sean and if he gave me reason to be jealous then I would react very strongly – which for me would be by walking out.'

But there appears to be no risk of that happening. Both seem to be far too happy staying at home, Micheline wearing whenever she can nothing more than a bikini and Sean a brief pair of shorts and a sports shirt, and wanting no more than to live a domestic life between films – and golf games.

That is so different from the man she first knew. 'Everything about Sean was dramatic. My first job was to calm him down. It was like undoing a knot. He was, and still is, a very emotional man because he is an artist. But I can see things very clearly and I am not fooled by promises or flattery. He was surrounded by people who wanted to take from him. It flattered him that people were saying how fantastic he was. But I would say, "Sean you *are* fantastic. A fantastic actor. The rest? Forget it."'

He appreciates that and, in turn, tries to protect her. When he went into hospital, he banned her from following him. No matter how scared he himself was, he wanted to spare his wife any trauma.

The enviably loving feeling between them was carried through to a second generation. Jason would always say that his relationship with his stepbrother Stefan was a close one, much closer than that with his own half-sister, Giovanna. They became good friends the moment that Micheline entered his father's life. They were about the same age and together they started doing Connery things . . . like going to Spain and playing golf there. (And playing to win. Jason likes to quote his father: 'There's no such a thing as a good loser. Show me a good loser, and I'll show you a loser.')

The friendship also helped to cement his own relationship with his stepmother. 'I am very lucky because I love my stepmother,' he said. 'Micheline is very Mediterranean, so we have our little arguments now and again. She is a very fiery lady. But I feel very lucky. She has brought me and Dad a lot closer, which is really great.'

He had his own pad in Fulham, London fairly close to Stefan's own flat, but quite clearly, the Marbella house was his family home – as was Diane's in Queensland. 'I am very lucky – two fabulous family homes in sunny parts of the world that I can fly off to and visit whenever I want.'

Sean helped make Marbella a happy family home. But that didn't mean he was without his difficulties. He was settling into a pattern of life that seemed to please him. Occasionally, he got drunk – he loved his whisky and was going back to beer now – but there was nothing hellraising about him. He also had a touch of mischievousness about him. When he had a dinner party at one of his homes, he would try to make sure there was at least one couple who might not get on with the other guests. He enjoyed waiting for the sparks to fly.

And he was a good sport – at least some of the time. He didn't turn a hair when, at a showbiz award ceremony at Cambridge, Massachusetts, he received a big kiss from a transvestite. He smiled, which is what all big film stars are expected to do when faced with unexpected situations.

He didn't always smile when approached by fans. Once, a woman went up to him and said : 'Are you . . . ?' He looked at her, said, 'No,' – and walked away. Another time, while deep in conversation with Micheline, he was approached by, said Mrs Connery, 'a Danish woman with big breasts' who broke into their chat with the words, 'You're Sean Connery,' and asked for an autograph. 'Would you go away !' Sean demanded. 'Can't you see I'm speaking ?'

In April 1985, Sean had a personal sadness to endure – Effie died at Edinburgh's Royal Infirmary. Her two sons stood side by side at the crematorium where they had laid a wreath of pink orchids and red carnations labelled 'Mum'. A card was inscribed 'From Sean and Neil'.

The melancholy that Effie's death had brought him didn't prevent the settling of scores. The extent of the damages Kenneth Richards would have to pay had finally been revealed – a colossal £2,800,000. Sean knew Richards would never find the money. He could either leave matters where they were or bankrupt him. He decided to go for the jugular and took his adversary to the bankruptcy courts. 'If he is bankrupt,' Sean declared, 'he will not be able to do to anyone else what he has done to me.'

If hell hath no fury like a woman scorned, it is run a fairly close second by a millionaire who has been rooked of his money. Sean Connery's fury was like a thunderstorm once the rain has come. It was unremitting. You could all but see the lightning flashing from his head to his toes. All he wanted now was to see the electric charge switch to his adversary.

It had been going on for a long time. In 1982 Richards had been ordered to give Connery an interim one million pounds – although no cash came amid predictable statements from Connery that he would only be happy when he saw the money in his hands. He knew he probably never would.

When it still hadn't yet arrived by February 1984, the final judgment was delivered: Richards had to pay up the full £2,800,000. Sean now knew for certain he wouldn't get that sort of cash, although he maintained that more than three million dollars of his money had gone astray thanks to Richards – money that had been 'invested' with the property man Canela.

Richards said in turn that Sean was going to get all the benefit of that investment. 'I thought what was good for Mr Connery was good enough for me,' he told the bankruptcy court, who were no more sympathetic than the previous judges had been.

Sean wanted some kind of justice from the man who claimed he possessed no more than thirty-six pounds cash and whatever other earnings he had came from teaching English literature in Switzerland.

Richards gave his own interviews to the press – and found ways to make Sean look the villain of the piece. 'Sean rang my wife during the case and told her that I had four million dollars. It's not true – all the furniture is my wife's.'

Then came the statement that really got the headlines: Connery had threatened his life. 'If I had a knife, I would kill you,' Richards claimed Sean had told him.

It fitted in with a slightly less violent comment from Sean himself. 'I'd like to wring his neck,' he said. 'It's very nice to be awarded money on paper but that man should pay in flesh.'

It was the closest Sean had come to playing Shylock. In a less Shakespearean turn of phrase, Sean went on: 'He professes to be broke and there doesn't seem to be much I can do about it. It seems that the law inevitably protects the crook.'

Richards was certainly protected by the law. In Britain itself bankruptcy, despite its social stigma and the limitations it places on a person's freedom – no credit, no political rights among them – is a way of escaping responsibilities, once creditors have been paid with what little may remain in one's possession. Few of the restrictions imposed in the country would apply overseas. As far as Switzerland was concerned, even if British law had warranted it, there was no extradition treaty or any other means whereby a bankrupt could be brought to Britain and made to pay up.

But all that sort of thing had to be a mere diversion from his real work. What Sean would do next remained a mystery. One idea being canvassed in 1985 was that he should co-star in a new film about Queen Victoria – playing her gillie John Brown. It was not an unreasonable idea. He then toyed with the idea of playing the teacher in *The Last Emperor*, as the movie about the child ruler of imperial China came to be called. But in the end, Peter O'Toole took the role.

Two great film ideas and two rejections – along with dozens of other scripts that found their way into the Marbella house. For three years, there was no new Sean Connery movie. That had *never* happened before. Somehow it seemed the experience of playing Bond again had been just . . . well, too much. He left Bondage with feelings not unlike those of prisoners finally released from behind bars.

But there are those who detected something else that would have been familiar to an ex-prisoner: a sense of insecurity. Things weren't going well for him. He had bid farewell to 007 and at the same time had also lost the glamour that went with it. If he couldn't make hit movies, what did he have to offer? Was that the reason that he kept working? Did he worry that one day people wouldn't ask him to read any more scripts?

For the moment, the scripts did tumble in, much to the surprise of a great many Hollywood watchers. But every time he contemplated a new picture, producers began to ask what they had never dared ask before: whether it would fit in with his accent. He still steadfastly refused to alter that, but for good reason: he wouldn't change the accent, he said, 'because I wouldn't know who the fuck I was'. It was a fair point. But the accent when it was heard was turning up in strange places.

Why did he bother to make *Highlander* in 1986? Or rather agree to appear in it, as Ramirez, chief metallurgist to Charles V of Spain who is one of a group of people who turn out to be immortal – like the Highlander in question, played by Christopher Lambert, a man born a mere 470 years earlier who is having a bit of trouble with the traffic in 1980s Manhattan.

It wasn't much of a part in what was not much of a movie although it has now acquired cult status. But he acted in it as though it were another *Man Who Would Be King*. And he made his now conventional demands.

Before filming got under way, cinematographer Alex Thompson told me, the director Russell Mulcahy suggested that it might not be a bad idea if Sean flew up to Scotland to practise his sword fighting. Sean replied that he didn't think it was such a good idea. 'Thanks, Russell, but I don't think so,' he said. 'I think I have enough training in sword fighting.'

He could cope with as much fencing as was required and besides, his old friend from the Bond days, stuntman Bob Simmons, was going to do most of the action.

Mulcahy was adamant, however. He wanted the rehearsal and the practice. 'Right,' said Sean, 'it'll cost you.'

'How much?' the director asked. 'Ten thousand pounds,' Connery replied. They shook hands on it and Sean soon afterwards took a helicopter to the Highlands location, where he found Simmons waiting for him.

'He got out of the helicopter, took the sword and started thrashing about with it,' recalled Thompson.

'One thousand,' he shouted with the first thrash. 'Two thousand' with the second. All the way to 'ten thousand'. At which point, Sean handed the sword back to Bob Simmons, got back into his helicopter and flew off again. It was a good half a minute's work.

There were those who thought it wasn't worth two minutes of viewing time. *The People* said the film was 'a moody combination of *Blade Runner*, *Terminator* and your last really good nightmare'. Which was praise indeed. *Variety* was less kind. 'While there are entertaining moments,' reported its reviewer, 'the total work is a mess.' Perhaps Sean was lucky he was just an also-ran in the film.

On the other hand – and fortunately not only for Sean, who somehow wondered whether he had left his feet behind for good and that they were now past finding, but also for his fans – a film came in 1987 that proved what critics and his most fervent admirers had been saying for years but was becoming harder and harder to sustain: Sean was one of the great actors of the generation.

The Name Of The Rose, based on a novel by Umberto Eco, was not on the surface a commercial-looking movie (and, indeed, in America would turn out not to be so). Seeing it in the cinema, there was a darkness about most of it that could have made audiences confuse what was going on on the screen with what could have been happening in the stalls. You just couldn't see the light. You could, though, see in it the light of a wonderful story, beautifully and magnificently portrayed. If anyone wanted to say, 'Come back, all is forgiven,' they had reason to forgive everything he had done before because of this picture and this performance.

He played a Franciscan monk, a wonderfully intelligent, reasonable Englishman (with a Scottish accent, naturally enough) who, with his young novice (Christian Slater in a performance of innocence and wide-eyed enthusiasm which rivals Connery's own) travels to an Italian Benedictine monastery and finds himself in the midst of a series of seemingly unaccountable murders. His is the voice of brilliance and understanding in a sea of obscurity and superstition. He is the one who opposes the Inquisition, as you might expect.

Improbably, this was a role that was originally earmarked for Michael Caine but casting took a different slant when producers changed. 'It's such a great part,' said Sean at the time, '... Thomas More all wrapped up in a habit.' Sean's monk's habit, although bearing no resemblance to the sharply tailored and glitzy outfits he had worn before, nevertheless had a certain theatricality about it. He dominated the movie as he was expected to do, and whatever he wore, this rose of a performance would have smelt just as sweet.

This actor of mixed Catholic and Protestant parentage who said he hitherto had had no interest in organised religion suddenly steeped himself in the philosophy of faith. 'I had to understand the religious beliefs of the period.' He said he was 'intrigued' by the commitment that so many people had towards God.

So he studied things at first hand. He took himself off to a monastery just outside Madrid to ask questions of the monks who, hardly surprisingly, had never heard of Eco's book. More surprisingly, some of them told Sean they had seen a few of his films.

Once prepared, he started active work on the movie.

He was now looking his age – even more than his fifty-six years. But he said that it didn't matter and he was right. 'Celibacy is no great problem at my age,' he added. But more seriously, he did have a definite approach to the role. 'There are two different modes of acting old. One, which is wonderful, is where you get someone like Lillian Gish, and everyone says isn't she marvellous, she's ninety-two or whatever. The other way is to acknowledge your age and the approach of death, and incorporate it in whatever you do.'

His age went with him – like his accent. But it was a matter of generation in more ways than one. 'This whole era can hardly come to terms with death. Even the simple technical details.' It was like when he went to register his father's death – no one ever told him what to do. Nobody told him how to act older, either. It came naturally, perhaps even more naturally in that bleak, wintry landscape.

The film was shot on location at a real monastery – actually in Germany – in the middle of a bitterly cold winter. This was not an easy film to make. Sean said that he had never been colder. He wore his scratchy monk's habit over thermal underwear. But even that was not enough. 'My feet were like solid lumps of ice with open-topped sandals. Then they would shave my head every day on top and around the ears.' As he said, that was the other extreme after all those years of having to put up with toupees of various designs.

But as unappealing as was the setting, some of the extras looked even less pleasant: they were the most grotesque, ugly men seen on film since *The Hunchback Of Notre Dame.*

It could have been a Gothic horror story. Instead, it was a mystery yarn told with the delicacy of a love poem that faces the fact that life can be a pretty terrible experience. Sean Connery made it a wonder to see. It was a much bigger success than most people would have expected, and better than some of the critical reaction would have indicated.

What has been hard for Sean over the years has been living down the hard, crusty image he has made for himself among some groups. To be fair, he hasn't gone out of his way to rectify that image. But there are any number of people with personal experiences to refute it.

It was while making *The Name Of The Rose* in Munich that Sean once more bumped into Jerry Juroe, publicity man on the early Bond films. He remembered him, joked with him and asked how life was treating him. 'Most stars would forget you just as soon as you are no further use to them,' he told me. 'But he knew who I was just as well as I knew who he was.'

He added: 'I do feel that there was a real friendship between us – not good friends – but we had a good professional friendship. I think that if Sean came to trust you, it was a complete trust until you did or said something to break that trust. I think in my case, I was fortunate that that trust was built up before he became much more famous.'

Variety thought the American–German film was 'sorrowfully mediocre', which is probably what should have been said of its critic. *The Name Of The Rose* made money in anything but a mediocre way – but not in America. Sean said the reason the Americans weren't so keen was that the distributors didn't know how to market it – the obverse of an otherwise profitable coin now that Coca-Cola and the Japanese conglomerates had got themselves involved in Hollywood.

'The sales equations are very clear and honest. You know how much a bottle of Coke costs and you know the profit margin and so on.' He had never used the word 'honest' when referring to a studio before. But against the honesty he had to put the lack of marketing knowledge.

On the other hand, the chief executive officer of Twentieth Century-Fox, Barry Diller, was quoted as saying that Sean himself had 'fucked it up' by being responsible for rushing its release. Diller also objected to the cartoon drawings being used to advertise it.

It was being suggested that the failure of the film in America was responsible for its failure to earn Sean an Oscar. By any standard, his performance was certainly worth one.

But he had to be happy with the European scene. The Germans loved the film and brought fifteen million pounds into the box office. It made seven million pounds in Italy in its first week, despite weather almost as cold as that Sean had to put up with on the set. In that week 600,000 went to see it. According to the original agreement, Sean was on a percentage of only the American takings, which meant he would have got next to nothing, but the producer, Bernard Eichinger, behaved in a way that Cubby Broccoli never had. Eichinger thought he owed Sean something, and after the event put him on two per cent of the huge $100 million European box office just the same.

That in itself was something. *The Name Of The Rose* had flopped in America but it was more obviously an acting triumph than anything that had gone before it bearing the Connery name. But there was something else about to happen that would confirm the very select position that Sean now held in the film business. *The Untouchables* showed that he was, as an actor . . . untouchable.

12

AT LAST, AN OSCAR

Quite suddenly Sean Connery had found his feet. Or rather, new feet. In *The Untouchables* he was allowing himself to follow further the furrow he had carved in *The Name Of The Rose*.

The Untouchables was different from *The Name Of The Rose* in every way. Except for one factor: Sean was improving even on his own performance. In *The Rose* he had to be bald – having hair would have been out of character and even he needed to have his pate shaved. Now, though, his head looked the way it did to Micheline in the morning.

He had found a vehicle that allowed him to appear to be – and the word 'appear' is important – not just balding, but middle-aged and grandfatherly, broad, mustachioed and wearing a battered cardigan. His weight went down 28 pounds to 199 pounds for the role, but even so, four years after *Never Say Never Again*, he had rarely looked so unglamorous. Or acted so well. Or so bravely.

It was the film that won him his first Oscar – for best *supporting* actor – as well as the Golden Globe awarded by the Hollywood Foreign Press Association and the prize of the British Film Critics Circle (which was also for *The Name Of The Rose*, a movie that had already won him the Federal Republic of Germany's Film Prize for acting).

Of course, it was that Oscar which really set him apart from almost every other actor in his fee bracket. He had played cameo roles before. But now Sean Connery was supporting Kevin Costner, breaking one of the most important and cherished rules in Hollywood: like eschewing the idea of playing opposite children or dogs, a top actor of long-standing should never take second billing to the much newer Big Star of the day. In 1987, they didn't come much bigger than

Kevin Costner. But Sean was – that word again – untouchable in his performance. As Costner said: 'When you're with Sean, you learn pretty quickly what your own place in the galaxy is and it pales.' Somehow, nobody thought these were mere pious words of a new-comer who could afford to be generous to a veteran.

Another top star had a secondary role in *The Untouchables*: Robert de Niro played Al Capone, a cameo that had always been acceptable. But despite the trademark white suit and the turned-up side brim on his white fedora, he was no competition for Costner's character, who succeeded in laying to rest the ghost of the 1950s highly successful black-and-white television series of the same name, starring Robert Stack. Compared with Sean, de Niro, one of the most powerful actors of the era, barely featured in the movie.

Connery played a tough, ageing Irish cop named Malone (with a Scottish accent, of course, but Americans weren't supposed to know the difference any more now than when he made *The Molly Maguires* eighteen years before; they were told he was Irish and that had to be enough) fighting alongside Eliot Ness in his war against Capone and his gang. Sean was sympathetic, human and totally believable as the cop who seemed destined to pick up nothing more complicated than his pension – only to suddenly find himself recruited as one of Ness's squad.

Sean ran away not only with his own role, but with the whole movie. As much as anything, it was because he knew his role so well. Again, he had put his own marks on the script – particularly the part where he meets Ness for the first time as he patrols the Chicago bridge. The investigator, in desperation, has just thrown a rolled up piece of paper into the river. Malone, the cop, chastises him for dropping litter.

'I decided to be quite nit-picking,' Sean said later. 'I decided to have an unnecessarily strong go at this guy. So I talk to him like a child or an idiot. And that creates humour, because the audience knows he's a police investigator who's just had a terrible day – but after all I don't know that and *I'm* in a job I'm not happy or satisfied with.'

It was the down-to-earth philosophy with which he invested the role that struck people: 'You want to get Capone?' he asks Ness. 'Here's how you get him. He pulls a knife, you pull a gun. He sends one of yours to the hospital, you send one of his to the morgue. That's the Chicago way.' A new rule had just been invented: actors ought now to be wary of playing with children, dogs ... and Sean Connery.

He had to ride a horse in the picture, just as he had in *The Name Of The Rose*. The difference was that in the earlier film, he rode at a gentle trot; in this one he had to go fast – so fast, in fact, that he was thrown and damaged his knee. He had to have instant surgery.

It was a moment of confession for him. He told the doctor that this man who had carried a gun in a dozen or more movies – indeed who had held a licence to kill – who had the power to recover from what appeared to be instant death, and who packed a punch that sent a score of men (and not a few women) reeling, was afraid ... of injections. 'I faint at the sight of needles,' he told the doctor, 'and can collapse having a blood test.' Fortunately, Blofeld never knew that.

The operation involved the use of lasers and the insertion – by needle – of miniature television cameras. Sean was terrified. The doctors invited him to watch it all on the monitor, but he admitted he had other ideas of small-screen viewing.

'I'll have the full anaesthetic,' he told the surgeon.

'But it's not necessary,' he was told.

'It is for me,' Connery replied. 'I don't want to see a thing.'

The fact that the picture was set in 1930, the year of Sean's own birth, somehow seemed to heighten the poignancy of the fellow still described as the sexiest man in films playing a superannuated hero whose motto in life was, 'Make sure when your shift is over, you go home alive. Here endeth the lesson.'

The real lesson of *The Untouchables* was that Sean Connery had now *totally* ditched Bond and had finally created a new image for himself: now producers could stop playing lucky dip. There suddenly arose the notion of what felt right as a Connery role.

Connery knew it himself. 'There's nothing I like better than a film that really works, provided you don't have to deal with all the shit that comes afterwards in terms of getting what you're entitled to.' And this was a film that *really* worked.

Pauline Kael in her *New Yorker* review said that Sean was showing all the signs of being the new Olivier. Certainly, from this movie on, critics, other actors and the more informed members of his audiences had good reason to make use of a new saying: as he gets older, Sean Connery gets better and better. *The Untouchables* was the picture that allowed them to forget the indifferent things he had done before or any of the jokers in the packs of cards he was to deal himself in years to come. This was like Olivier's *Hamlet*. Nobody was going to remember *The Betsy*, which Sir Laurence made, he said, along with a whole series of trashy films 'to put something in the larder'.

And now there was no reason for an acting triumph not to be good box office, too. Sean did *The Untouchables* for a share in the profits. 'I agreed to do a piece and go for a shot at the film working,' he explained in an interview to the London *Mail on Sunday*'s *You* magazine. The director Brian de Palma had seemed to be someone on whom it was worth taking a risk. 'I'd seen his films and he has a marvellous technical sense, a nice sense of style and he is quite fearless.' Which was exactly what Sean's cop, Malone, was. It was a picture that felt right.

Just before *The Untouchables* was released, Connery's fearlessness got him into an embarrassing situation – with the British Royal Family. It was a moment when that institution was seen as unable to do wrong – or at least very little wrong. Princess Anne's marriage had come to an end, but the Prince and Princess of Wales did still seem to be deliriously happy and the Duke of York was engaged to Sarah Ferguson. They, too, were in the midst of a fairy-tale romance.

Sean met the future Duchess at a summer function. It was so hot that day that she felt the need to fan herself – inserting her hands in her pocket and waving her skirt around to create a breeze. Sean whispered to her: 'If I did that in these trousers, I'd be arrested for indecency.'

The only thing that was cool in the room was the icy stare that Fergie gave Sean before walking away from him. A somewhat rich reaction from the girl who became the tearaway member of the Buckingham Palace set.

Nevertheless, everything felt right at about this time. Partly, it was because of where he now stood in the show-business pecking order. Looking back on that time totally dispassionately now, Dennis Selinger told me: 'Making *The Untouchables* without any doubt put Sean Connery firmly back in the marketplace from the American end.'

And because it had, he was being even more adventurous, doing things he wouldn't have dared approach in the less secure days. In August 1986, he had even appeared in a BBC Radio 3 play, *Barnes People III: After The Funeral*. He wasn't the star. He just shared billing with John Hurt and Donald Pleasence. He sang in the play, too.

Sean wanted to do it so badly, he came to England specially for the play, which paid him peanuts – it cost far more to make the journey from Spain than his actual fee. But he had never done radio before and the idea of the tiny but prestigious Radio 3 wanting him was too tempting to resist. So he flew to Heathrow, took a taxi to the BBC's Maida Vale studios and then, when the recording was all over, caught another cab back to the airport.

It also fitted in with his previous love of performing the classics at Oxford, as well as with an aspect of his life that he very successfully kept to himself and his family – Sean Connery is an enthusiastic poet, although he never allows anyone to see his work.

Possibly it was this enthusiasm for the classics that made him agree in principle to play the lead in the German-inspired fantasy, *The Adventures Of Baron Munchausen*. Terry Gilliam who had directed *Time Bandits* was raising twenty-five million dollars for the project. But after months of talks, Sean lost interest in the project and decided he didn't fancy being one of two people living on the moon. The part went, instead, to Robin Williams.

It was a pity for Sean's enhanced 'new' reputation, that *The Presidio* didn't go the same way. It was a none too spectacular film about a murder at a military base in San Francisco, although the strength of the Connery of *The Untouchables* was visible even in this.

Sean played the head of the military police at the base, a widower who has as much trouble with his sexually promiscuous daughter as with youngsters who don't really want to be in the Army. The daughter was played by the then 27-year-old Meg Ryan, who said that Sean made her hate him.

'It had to be so full of hate ... I walked right through Meg to make her really resent it,' he admitted. 'That really got up her nose. No one gave me much assistance when I was starting out, so I thought I'd help her. I think it worked.'

Once again, nobody tries to explain the officer having a Scottish accent, but with his bald head – shaved even more than it was in *The Name Of The Rose* – he looks menacing enough to have been given the job on fear factor alone.

But really it was his sex appeal – or so he may have thought. For $2,000 a night, he was accommodated at the Hyde Park Hotel in San Francisco. So was Mark Harmon, the 32-year-old who had second billing in the movie. Harmon had recently been voted the world's sexiest man. One evening at the hotel, he faced a group of near-hysterical girls. Harmon was delighted – until he realised that the women were shouting for Sean, who happened to be standing behind him.

Connery loved it. Later on, he teased Harmon: 'Hello, ducky,' he said sidling up to him. 'God, you are sexy! How about dinner tonight?'

But it wasn't his sex appeal which necessarily attracted the critics. 'Like a patriarch,' wrote Stephen Schaefer in the *New York Post*, 'Connery at fifty-eight evokes moral authority, physical strength and rugged maturity.'

Sean told Schaefer that he thought it was time to show 'the human side of the American soldier, that in a funny way got lost since the Vietnam war. That fellowship was what we really wanted to examine.'

246

It also examined the violence of the American soldier. Sean is shown to be quite nifty with his thumb : with that digit alone he overpowers a hoodlum at a bar who seems to weigh at least 100 pounds more than he does himself. It was a matter of putting the full force of the body behind the thumb. He learned how to do it from an *akido* wrestler – a man weighing no more than 110 pounds faced by a man twice his weight. 'But he could reduce that big guy to his knees.'

Even so, that wasn't Sean's biggest problem. He said that came when he had to march in formation. 'It was very difficult not to march like a British sailor,' he explained.

The film was dreadful, but it did have the Connery touch.

Indiana Jones And The Last Crusade certainly had it, too. But it was appreciated more.

Here, once again, Connery ran away with a movie in which he had no more than a supporting role. In a way, taking it this time was even braver than playing the cop in *The Untouchables*. For here he was not just accepting subsidiary billing to that of the star Harrison Ford ; he was playing his father. Now that broke *all* the rules.

'I admire him for that tremendously,' Dennis Selinger told me. 'It took a lot of guts to play Harrison Ford's father at his age. Michael Caine, for instance, or Roger Moore would never have done it. I thought that was wonderful.'

The director, Steven Spielberg, who claims to have been a Connery admirer since he saw *The Hill* at the age of seventeen, thought Sean would 'give Harrison a run for his money'. He gave him a gallop.

Harrison Ford was one of Hollywood's most popular actors and had been so ever since the first Indiana Jones picture, *Raiders of the Lost Ark*. But there was no doubt who the audiences were watching as they settled in their seats for the third in the *Raiders* series.

But plainly it hadn't been the simplest thing to arrange. The producer, George Lucas, had few hopes of it coming off in the first place. He doubted that Sean would want to play Harrison Ford's father. So did Spielberg. 'Obviously, Sean had his trademark on the James Bond movies and we are a kind of James Bond movie ourselves,' he said at the time. 'I'm not quite sure I'd be interested in being in James Bond's rival motion picture.' But the real problem had to be the one Lucas envisaged – the notion of playing father to one of the most popular *middle-aged* stars of the day. After all, the vanity of most actors is one of their principal qualifications for the job.

Sean had his own reservations. Not really because of the age problem but because he didn't think there was 'any jazz' in the role. It was all too serious. But then he thought he found the key : the senior

Jones was from the mould of the nineteenth-century explorer Richard Burton, crusty and intolerant.

He decided it wasn't something to worry about. 'But it would cost them,' he said. You bet it would.

Lucas agreed – and the money Sean got would have been fairly good compensation for anybody. Tom Stoppard, who wrote the script, was called in to make the alterations. There would be others. It was the start of a somewhat taut relationship between the two men. John Boorman had brought Sean to dinner at Stoppard's home, the writer told me, but they didn't actually 'work together'. Each had his own job to do and they performed them in isolation from each other.

As it was, he got on exceedingly well with both Lucas and Steven Spielberg. 'I've stayed friends with most directors I've worked with,' said Sean at the time, giving every impression that there wouldn't be any change now. 'And I never have a problem with any other actors, unless they're assholes.'

The hardest thing about filming was once again the weather – although not in the same way it had been while making *The Name Of The Rose*. Temperatures now were 110 degrees and Sean was wearing a three-piece tweed suit. However, for scenes in which only the Connery head and torso were on show, he just wore the top half of the suit – nothing, apart from his underpants below the jacket. 'Harrison didn't quite appreciate it at first,' said Sean. 'Then when his face was dripping in perspiration, he realised it was quite clever.'

In the Indie Jones film, there was every reason to believe most of the things on screen. Now you positively knew that the bald pate was real and the white beard hadn't been any other colour for a year or two. You also believed it when Professor Jones Senior told his son about the women he had been sleeping with. He was a sexy old rogue who managed to get involved in Spielberg-type adventures with no more difficulty than had the film been made all those years before and was in fact *Dr No* first time round. It also has to be said that a number of the sequences wouldn't have embarrassed the Bond team. Some left them standing.

The difference was that the story was more subtle and in many ways a great deal funnier than anything Broccoli and Saltzman's writers had devised. This was a Bond who looked like his own father, who wore in addition to the tweed suit a porkpie hat and rimless glasses, and was cantankerous and caustic where James had been casual – casual about sex and casual about killing, but careful about the right clothes and the right drink. You understood that the archaeologist Sean now played wouldn't have known a shaken Martini from a crème de menthe and if he had, would have regarded them both as a trifle too pretentious.

The impact the role would make was not wholly predictable when Sean signed to make the movie. It really did seem 'supporting', which could easily have been seen as an unpleasant term. What was more, he wasn't supposed to be introduced until about the seventieth page of the script. 'But,' said Spielberg, 'he kept coming up with so many extra scenes that we put him in twenty pages earlier.' They also added scenes with him towards the end of the movie. As the director said, 'When he gets a good idea, which is about twenty times a day, he's such a child; his face lights up.'

In the picture, Indiana berates his father for never talking to him. 'You left home at nineteen just when you were becoming interesting,' retorts his father. That was pure Connery, inserted by Stoppard.

The interesting thing was the way it compared to a 007 script. Talking about his 'son', Indiana, Sean himself saw the similarity and for once wasn't afraid of mentioning a Bond connection. 'Aside from the fact that Indiana Jones is not as well dressed as James Bond,' he said, 'the main difference between them is sexual. Indiana deals with women shyly.' Of course the old man, Professor Dr Henry Jones has few inhibitions in the sex department, although he doesn't do much more than talk about them in the movie.

But he and the junior Jones got in and out of the same sort of impossible situations as Bond, and it came as a certain relief to know that their rivals were a gang of real Nazis competing with them in the search not for something so everyday as nuclear warheads, but as exciting and realistic as the Holy Grail.

Perhaps *Never Say Never Again* had given Sean a self-confidence on the Bond issue not to worry about it any more; *The Untouchables* had proved for all time that the new Connery was even more successful than the old one had been.

The movie also broke all the records. It took in £24 million on its first weekend and then proceeded to get close to the all-time record of £500 million held by Spielberg's earlier movie, *ET.* (Four years later, Spielberg broke it again with *Jurassic Park.*)

In the spring of 1988, he won his Oscar for *The Untouchables*. His fellow nominees were Albert Brooks in *Broadcast News*, Morgan Freeman in *Street Smart*, Denzel Washington in *Cry Freedom* and Vincent Gardenia in *Moonstruck*.

'My name is Connery,' he said as he got to the microphone that night in Los Angeles, 'Sean Connery,' a twist on the old Bond introduction. The lights and the shouts from the audience underscored the words. Then he added: 'I first appeared here thirty years ago,' referring, presumably, to the time he spent in Hollywood making *Darby O'Gill And The Little People*. Now he was holding his own Oscar, like a boxer clasping his hands on high after finally winning the title he has sought for years, and said: 'Patience is a virtue.'

Sean later explained: 'I was never that interested in the Academy Awards. I used to watch them thirty years ago, but I never knew how to join. I thought you had to put your nose in the door to be considered. Guys like Jack Nicholson and Dustin Hoffman are entrenched in that scene, but I'm not. I don't know. I don't suppose all the lawsuits helped.'

But now that his nose had prised open that door, he was as excited as a schoolboy who had walked off with the mathematics prize.

Two things were notable about the Connery win. The first that he was nominated at all – it had never happened in thirty-two years of film-making. The second was that he worked very hard to get it. For the first time in living memory, he engaged a press agent and gave a whole series of interviews he might have been reluctant to subject himself to at any other time. In short, he campaigned.

There was good reason to do so. The money he could command thereafter rose higher than even he had ever dreamed possible. His earlier demands to Broccoli and Saltzman now seemed like requests for lunch allowances.

The following year, he was back among the celebrities *presenting* the awards, which some would say was worth even more than the money.

The week of the win was a very happy one. A few days later, Jason made his own West End debut in a new version of R.C. Sherriff's play *Journey's End*, at the Whitehall Theatre. Sean went to all Jason's first nights by way of a family tradition. (It was not a mutual arrangement since Sean himself never went to his own, although when he went to Australia Jason made it his business to see Diane at work at her own theatre in Queensland.)

Sean had arranged for Jason to have an agent whom he had used himself in the early days – Joy Jameson. He also protected Jason financially – the vast trust fund was gathering interest like harvesters picking up corn. But while he was acting, Jason still vowed not to touch what he regarded as his father's own cash. 'I know he thinks his money is a safety net – which he never had – to catch me if I fall. But I am determined not to use it.'

He was less reluctant to 'use' Sean's advice on professional matters, although Sean did not offer it all that regularly in any case, expecting his son to rise and fall by his own efforts and ideas. 'You have to make that kind of decision yourself,' Jason agreed. 'Then if you are right, it is *you* who is right and if you're wrong, it's *you* who is wrong. There's no two ways about it.'

But Sean was a critic of his son's work, nevertheless. 'He always tells me what he thinks of my performances. I was really pleased when he came to the first night of *Journey's End*. He even sees things I have done before I see them. People send him my work to look at, which is great.'

Occasionally, Jason went to see Sean at work. But it could be an unnerving experience. As he explained: 'It was weird to go on to a film set and hear someone else call my father "Dad".' It had been even more weird when Harrison Ford was called 'Son' by Sean.

Meanwhile, amid endless references in the press to Sean's sex appeal, all that Jason says is that he hopes it 'runs in the family'.

What does run in the family is a lack of fear of the practice of litigation. When the *Sun* newspaper alleged in 1992 that Jason was too scared to fight for his country, he sued – and collected £35,000 in libel damages.

It is possible that in doing that Jason was happily aware that he was merely doing what his father would have done – although writers were warned not to dwell too much on that relationship. 'Don't talk about Sean,' one press agent cautioned a newspaperman about to interview Jason – only for the journalist to then find out that all Jason wanted to talk about was his father.

The older man's advice is ever with him. At one time, Sean told a friend: 'What that boy's got to remember is that life isn't going out to lunch every day; it's having a bowl of minestrone on the back burner.'

Another piece of advice for his son was: Watch out for the sharks. Jason in return said that it was not impossible he could eventually pass his father by – perhaps *à la* Michael Douglas. 'Then,' he joked, 'they'll call me 008!'

It was by all accounts a happy relationship between father and son; even less traumatic than that between Indiana Jones and his old man. 'I think I'm a wonderful father,' joked Sean at the time, 'but Jason might not agree. In fact, I think we get along very well.' But he accepted that there could be a certain lack of perfection there: 'I can be as contrary and difficult as most fathers are, and lacking in understanding.'

After all the problems of the early years, the relationship between

Sean and Jason is more satisfying than it has ever been. When Sean won his Oscar, the first thing he did was phone his son to tell him.

Diane, too, has shown similar consideration. Jason went to Australia and made a film with her there, *The Boy Who Had Everything*. 'I learned such a lot from mom,' he said afterwards.

Of course, people still wanted to encroach on Sean's private life, some more seriously than others. There were still girls wanting to sell stories of how he would make passes at them when the occasion arose – like, as one suggested, at country weekends. Sometimes, the papers played up stories that amounted to no more than a paragraph or two of printed space and which nobody took very seriously. The Sean–Micheline marriage was much more important and probably much more true. They weren't going to give any details, but as far as anyone knew, it had become one of the most successful showbiz relationships.

For her part, Micheline knew how to deal with him. She didn't like people who said that everything he did was turning to gold. As she recalled: 'He is good at making money but not so good at keeping it. Not that he is stupid – just too open and honest.'

As for his public life, the founder of the Scottish International Educational Trust was getting dangerously close to becoming an academic.

Somehow, the trust was now even more than before a sort of substitute education for him. The boy who left school at thirteen was a great believer in the value of what he himself had been denied, which was why, when in 1988 St Andrews University awarded him an honorary doctorate, Dr Connery D. Litt. couldn't have been happier – unless, that is, he was nominated for another Oscar.

It was his second award from a Scottish university; seven years earlier he had received the same degree from Heriot-Watt. He had also been named in France a Commandeur des Arts et des Lettres.

But the trust remained his main educational interest. John McLellan, the director of the trust, told me: 'He had been so impressed by the scenes of dereliction in his native Scotland and the industrial waste and unemployment, that he wanted to do all he could to try to change it.

'It has continued since then on the basis of twin objectives to help both individual young Scots and Scottish projects.'

McLellan advises on these. But Sean still participates with the other trustees in discussing the awards. 'He wants to help people who have no other means of funding for a place at, say, the Massachussetts Institute of Technology or a young musician who wants to study at a conservatoire somewhere. The normal funding bodies are not going to do that, so we want to look at it sympathetically.'

About thirty people are helped every year.

Sean recommended a theatre company in a small Scottish town for consideration by the trust. Other ideas dealt with have ranged from an accordionist who wants to study at a music school in the United States to the funding of an 'educational pack' for children visiting the reconstructed Clyde town of New Lanark, a matter which in particular had his personal support. But that doesn't mean he goes to every meeting. 'In the eight years I have been in this position, I think he has been to a meeting once. But he is often in touch with me on the phone and I ring him, too. I think he regards the trust as a buffer against the attacks on his generosity. He sends us people who want to milk him for funds so that I can work out whether this is a genuine appeal to Sean for funds at his own discretion or should come from the trust.

'It is right that ideas from the trustees who have given so much of their time and money should be given a little favouritism. As far as Sean is concerned, it's a means for him to demonstrate his love of Scotland. I believe in drawing a distinct line between Sean as a Scottish nationalist and Sean as a Scottish benefactor.'

The trust is not the only educational hobby horse that Sean has been riding. Assisting the National Youth Theatre was a means of helping youngsters get a chance in the profession which had been so good to him himself. The NYT needed £100,000 to get through its year's activities when Sean made the gift of precisely half the target amount in April 1988.

It was hoped that the Arts Council would provide the balance of the money. Sean, on the other hand, thought successful actors had a duty to help a cause like this – particularly those actors who had got their own start through the organisation.

'I think in future there should be some kind of scheme where actors and actresses who started with the NYT and become successful can help ensure its future.'

As he said, 'British actors and actresses, writers and directors are among the best in the world. We come second to none. The NYT is one source of this talent, a source that everyone should be proud of. It shouldn't have to go cap-in-hand for money.'

If he thought struggling actors needed help, his own relationship with producers hadn't exactly been easy either. About this time, he began legal proceedings against Cubby Broccoli, alleging non-payment of royalties, but litigation was dropped before long.

But he remained unhappy with the Hollywood system. 'There's no way you can be in bed or in business with Los Angeles unless you're prepared to accept that these guys are gonna take it from you.'

There were, however, happier Bond connections that he was content not to sever. When Ursula Andress celebrated her fiftieth birthday, he flew to Rome as a surprise guest to toast the girl who had stepped out of the water with the dagger at her hip. Honey Ryder wouldn't have minded looking the way Ursula Andress looked that evening, the grey-bearded Sean might well have noted.

At about this time Craigie Veitch happened to be in Marbella, and quite casually bumped into his old schoolfriend on the golf course, where his in-laws had come to play. 'I had no idea I'd see Sean. I was very pleased to see him.'

Sean seemed as happy himself. 'I didn't know how he recognised me,' Veitch remembered for me. He fixed me with his beady eye and said, 'I recognised the suit.' It was the sense of humour the journalist recalled perhaps best of all.

Sean asked him how long he was going to be in town. Veitch told him two weeks. 'Look,' Sean said, 'here's my phone number, give me a ring and let's get together.'

Actually, Sean croaked it. He was in the midst of a series of throat problems which were going to plague him for months. 'There was no way I was going to impose on him, yet it was so nice that he thought of me and gave me his number,' said Veitch.

Sean's family were still happy with him. Neil was managing to scratch a living as a bit-part actor now that he could no longer work as a plasterer (a few years earlier he had fallen eighteen feet from a ladder). He lived in a small bungalow in Edinburgh where, because of his relationship to Sean, he was something of a celebrity. He played golf with his elder brother whenever Sean returned to Scotland, and when Sean was in Hollywood filming, Neil was given charge of the Connery Mercedes, which he happily drove round the streets of the Scottish capital. Sean thought it was better for the car to be driven than to lie idle in a garage for months on end.

Neil himself still got the odd television part, like playing a policeman in the series, *Taggart*, but he insisted he wasn't jealous of Sean. Every time there was a new Connery film showing in Edinburgh he was first in the queue to see it.

'I'm not James Bond,' he said once, 'I'm Brooke Bond,' after the tea company of that name.

As for Sean himself, there were people who said now that he should be given an award for ageing gracefully. Actually, there was no graceful, gradual change in his appearance – it happened suddenly. But to many women that was the charm of the man.

His friends were aware of that charm. So were other people – and it came expensive. Michael Winner was due to have dinner with Sean at the Plaza Hotel, just about the swankiest of New York eateries; the kind of place where men needed jackets – which presented a problem for Sean, who didn't have one.

Winner was staying at the hotel and said he could have one of his. They weren't exactly the same build, but it would satisfy the maitre d' who was not prepared to make exceptions for Sean Connery any more than a couple of generations before he would have done for Clark Gable.

'We went upstairs,' Winner told me, 'but when I got to the room, I realised I'd left the key behind.' It didn't bother Connery one bit. He just pretended he was making a movie.

'He just stood at the door and kicked it down. We went in and got the jacket. One kick and the door had gone.'

'I just want you to know, Sean,' Winner told him on the phone later that evening, 'I've just spent an hour picking up pieces of door from the floor and flushing them down the toilet, so that the hotel might not notice it.'

In fact, had the director told them the door had been knocked down by Sean Connery, the management of the hotel might even have put a plaque outside the room. He was that sort of celebrity and people were happy to accept him for what he was, sex symbol or Harrison Ford's father.

On the other hand, was he ready to play a grandfather on film? Not just a grandfather, but the grandfather of a grown-up young man? In *Family Business*, released in 1989, he did just that – the grandson was Matthew Broderick, born in 1962. The son was played by Dustin Hoffman which really did stretch credulity – Hoffman was born in 1937, and therefore would have made Sean a seven-year-old father. To deal with this the script said he was in his seventies, which could not have flattered him.

Sean suggested that perhaps his role would have been more suitable for someone like Burt Lancaster, then really in his seventies, but Sidney Lumet, again working with Connery as the director, was adamant. Eventually a compromise was worked out to make it all more acceptable to Sean – the grandfather was a 'young' man in his sixties, not a septuagenarian.

Lumet had always had a good relationship with Sean and took advantage of every opportunity to work with him. 'Most people think of him as a legendary star,' he said. 'I don't, but only because we go to the toilet together.'

Having sorted out Sean's part in it all, there were other difficulties in this story of a three-generation crime ring out to achieve the robbery of the century of a top-security laboratory: the grandfather was Scottish (surprise, surprise), the father was Sicilian and the youngest member of the trio Jewish. All it lacked was a meal of haggis and spaghetti on a bagel.

Broderick went around impersonating Dustin and Sean on the set. Connery wanted to know why he never allowed him to see the impression. 'I think he's afraid,' said a technician. 'He should be,' said Sean.

Both Hoffman and Broderick said they had found a lot to learn from Sean. 'The character I play is very physical,' said Dustin, 'and Sean showed me ways to get that across. I liked him genuinely as a person.'

Family Business was a failure but that did not prevent more offers flooding in and his continuing to accept the ones he liked best – including a story involving the Soviet Union, *The Russia House*. Another film with a Russian theme, *The Hunt For Red October*, was already in the process of being filmed when *Family Business* was released.

But before *The Hunt For Red October* could get under way, Sean was involved in what could have been called 'The Hunt For Red Throat'. All over the world, there were stories in splash headlines which all said the same thing: 'CONNERY IN CANCER SCARE'. In London, the *Sun* newspaper led its front page – 'Another *Sun* Exclusive' – with the 'news' that the Connery career might be ended. He had been told not to use his voice: doctors were afraid that initial tests were proving he had a malignant growth.

The rumours were immediately denied, but it made a sensational story just the same. The *Sun* thoroughly enjoyed a doctor's thoughts that a major operation 'for the removal of cancerous tissue' would be needed. A French radio station broadcast the news that Sean was dead. Apparently, that was nothing more than just the kind of story that big stars had to expect.

He was told not to speak for a month. 'The effect [of not speaking] on me was awful,' said Sean. 'And I still didn't know what the outcome would be at the end of the month.'

The outcome was diagnosis of nodules on his vocal chords and minor surgery to remove them. While he was resting his voice, he wore a sign round his neck saying: 'Sorry, I cannot speak. I have a problem with my throat.' But people then asked him, 'What's the matter?' which he thought was pretty idiotic. 'It showed me that the world was full of idiots,' was how he put it. So he then started carrying a pen and pad (actually some old scripts, which might have shown just what he thought of them) on which he would write his explanations.

He sought three opinions before deciding to have the surgery and which surgeon to go to. 'The terror returned,' he told the British writer Garth Pearce. The operation showed that the nodules were, as they had anticipated, benign.

When it was all over, he wrote a cheque for £46,000 to the Royal National Throat, Nose and Ear Hospital where he also had treatment. It would go towards buying a laser machine to treat throat cancers.

He then set about learning how to use his voice properly with Dr Lillian Glass, a Beverly Hills voice specialist and, as a former Miss Miami, quite the most glamorous medical practitioner in America.

Sean called on Dr Glass as a result of a personal recommendation. 'It was word of mouth,' the doctor said without being conscious of the pun. 'He was one of the loveliest human beings I have met in my life. A truly elegant gentleman, warm and personable,' she said.

She never told him not to use his voice : 'I told him how to eliminate the vocal problems he had. I told him how to use his voice properly, to use his abdominal muscles. He was going to do that permanently.'

It all had an effect, she said : 'Quite a bit. The voice became richer and eliminated glottal fry, the creaking sound. It didn't make him less sexy. It made him more.'

Most of the fear had gone by the time he started going to Dr Glass's office. 'Although I can't be sure about that and it would make me less of a professional to get into that,' she told me.

One of the things that he did say was that he regarded her 'as a godsend'. 'I think,' she told me, 'I was able to put his mind at rest. It is after all something that most actors and singers have, because they use their voices more than other people.'

Sean had treatment for an hour each day – based on her own ideas which she had put into a book – just so that he could get to work on *Red October* . There was what she called 'vocal hygiene – they have to drink liquids, keep the throat lubricated, not talk over noise, use abdominal muscles. You need to project your voice, and not have a lot of milk products, which make more mucus.' It was, in fact, simple voice training, a training that was originally prescribed for three months and, although there have been stories of more recent recurrences of the troubles, the regimen continues.

'It was all due to bad habits,' Dr Glass told me. And the habits she had in mind had nothing to do with women.

She was referring to the things he said in his movies – and how he said them: 'When he said, "My name's Bond ... James Bond," it sounded sensuous but it was very damaging.'

What had already gone by the board was his plan to do yet another new film, *Rosencrantz And Guildenstern Are Dead*, based on the Tom Stoppard play.

Connery and Stoppard had just one meeting to discuss the plan. 'I went up to St Andrews to discuss *R And G*,' Stoppard remembered for me. 'He was playing golf.'

Sean said he liked the material. 'I thought it would be a terrific thing to do.' Tom had never directed before. Then, just before filming began, Connery dropped out. Stoppard was offended and it took a long time for him to get over his disappointment. 'He became rather unpleasant,' Sean remembered, 'maybe thinking it was over the money, which it wasn't.' The deal had been that Sean would work for $75,000, which in his world really was nothing.

The writer-director flew to Los Angeles 'with one object – which was to tell him that we would wait for him.' Sean didn't want to meet Stoppard. He let it be known it was because of his throat condition. Since he couldn't speak, there was no point in meeting, he thought.

So Tom conveyed his thoughts to Micheline, who then relayed them to Sean, who then wrote down his replies. His responses amounted to one thing: he didn't want Stoppard and the producer John Boorman to wait for him.

Connery paid to be released from his contract – $300,000, although he said that if he had taken the matter to court, he was sure he would have won. 'I've put lawyers' kids through school. And I wouldn't have lost this one, but life is too short.'

That comment came in what was only one of several interviews that Sean gave about the matter. Stoppard was incensed – particularly about the statement in an article in *The Times Saturday Review* that the matter had been settled out of court.

'I have never been in litigation with Sean Connery,' he wrote, 'and therefore there is no question of his settling a dispute with me in or out of court. The producers of the film *Rosencrantz And Guildenstern Are Dead* sued Connery and he settled on terms which, I understand, each side agreed not to divulge or discuss. Connery has forgotten this and at the same time maligned me.'

Stoppard then went into the detail of the affair. 'When Connery let me know, a month or so before shooting, that he might have a problem with his throat, I told him in so many words that a film was only a film and he must put his health first. A few days later he confirmed that he would not be fit to film in February.'

He wrote about the Los Angeles meeting-that-never-was: 'I explained that if there were any chance of his working later on (we only needed him for three weeks) we had little choice but to wait, since, on his signing his contract, we had committed ourselves to delivering "a Connery film" and had accordingly been spending much of our budget in preparing it. Connery then got cross (on paper, read out by his wife) and that was that. Next day I was told that I had "harassed" him. Happily, he recovered sufficiently to make *The Hunt For Red October* in the spring.'

And he added: 'Meanwhile the producers of *Rosencrantz* had an obligation to substantiate the reason for their being unable to deliver the Connery film as contracted, and it was their unsuccessful attempts to get Connery's co-operation on this which he now characterises as "they thought I was on some dodge".'

There was one final dig in the letter: 'Connery says that but for his throat, "I would have sued Stoppard out of the country". He is confusing different parts of his anatomy. Connery paid up because he didn't have a leg to stand on.'

Stoppard had said it. They had prepared a 'Connery film'. That was the status the man had.

In May 1989 Sean failed to turn up at a gala dinner at the Cannes film festival despite the fact that he was expected as the main representative of what remained of the British film industry. He pulled out because he had unexpectedly gone to Hollywood. For a reputed fee of four million dollars – which showed just how much more clout he wielded since the Oscar – he had replaced his old Bond adversary, Klaus Maria Brandauer as a Soviet submarine commander in *The Hunt For Red October.*

Not only did a replacement for Sean at the gala dinner have to be found in a hurry (Sir Peter Ustinov agreed to step in) but all sorts of other arrangements were changed at the last minute. Thames Television decided that without Sean, they weren't going to televise the dinner and, as a result, the listings magazine *TV Times* changed their Connery cover.

It was alleged that Sean offered neither an apology nor an explanation. Not true, said Sean. 'This was not a whimsical decision,' added a spokesman for the film company making *Red October*. 'Sean feels terrible about the situation. He made extensive efforts to rearrange his schedule, but it proved impossible. Sean wanted to go. If there was any way he could have been on both sides of the world on the same day, he would have done it.' But even a brief shutdown would have cost thousands of dollars.

His explanation did not appease his would-be hosts. He was due to receive a lifetime achievement trophy at the dinner, but his name was now removed from the award and it was not presented that year.

On the whole, however, the British film industry were proud of Sean – there wasn't a great deal else that could be said of what was no longer an industry at all. The few studios that still existed were mostly idle, and those in business were letting out their sound stages to foreign, mostly American production – when they weren't being used for television commercials.

Steven Spielberg announced loud and clear in 1990: 'There are only seven genuine movie stars in the world today and Sean is one of them.'

In *The Hunt For Red October*, Sean proved it yet again. The movie was based on a novel by Tom Clancy. Sean's performance was as immaculate as was his attire: the heavy blue overcoat and fur hat of a submarine commander who takes his ship over to the West. He says he does it because he is Lithuanian, not Russian. The Allies smell a rat: unless there are some really devious deeds afoot, why should a commander of impeccable credentials give away not just a submarine, but the prototype of a new nuclear vessel which runs so silently nothing would pick it up. When the movie came out, the Soviets admitted that it was based on fact: there *had* been a mutiny on board one of their submarines and a deputy commander had taken the ship out to sea. But the plot had been foiled, the ship stopped and the officer involved had been shot. That didn't happen to Sean.

The movie started off with the distinct advantage of being based on a very filmable book. But there was no guarantee of its becoming a worthwhile film. With any other actor, it might never have been so; Connery made it work largely because of who he was and what he did with it.

Neil Norman wrote in the London *Evening Standard* that Sean was 'not actually called upon often to do anything. So he stands around looking like Sean Connery in a fetching uniform and a silver wig.' The wig, it has to be said, was used not because Sean's own hair wasn't the right colour. There just wasn't enough of it. By now, however, audiences had come to realise that he changed his hair for every film he made, which was more than could ever be said about his accent.

Another thing that changed was Sean's fee. It was while he was making the film in America that Sean had seen the way the value of the dollar was plunging in relation to European currencies. So his agents, Creative Artists, renegotiated the deal taking account of the new situation. Nobody had ever done that before, but Sean made history in doing so to the extent of £150,000.

It might have been difficult to argue with him. He was now boasting that he had sued every major studio apart from Paramount, and anybody making Connery films had to bear that in mind. The film was given a royal première – in the presence of the Prince and Princess of Wales before the breakup of their marriage.

The Russia House saw Soviet life from a different angle from *Red October* – and was worth five million dollars to Sean. It was now the time of Gorbachev's spring – an era when the Soviet Union looked a lot better to the casual observer than Yeltsin's Russia would do. St Petersburg was still Leningrad and there was no rubbish on the pavements. The film was based on John le Carré's story, with all the intrigue and complications one would expect from the author. It also contained a message that was proved to be true soon after the Iron Curtain came tumbling down – there wasn't much substance in the Soviet threat; it was sustained by Moscow lies.

In this picture, Sean plays a British publisher visiting both Moscow and Leningrad who gets caught up in a romance with Michelle Pfeiffer, something that should ease the pain of most of the other things in which he is involved – including spying in the last days of the Cold War. (Was it surprising that almost every newspaper report on the picture would be subheaded, 'From Russia With Love' – especially when stories surfaced that he had managed to get an exit visa for a woman interpreter working on the set?)

Sean said that he admired Michelle Pfeiffer. She was a new breed of leading lady. As he told the *Daily Mail*'s Baz Bamigboye: 'They seem to be very serious these days. Very dedicated, which I think is terrific. Michelle Pfeiffer is exceptional and really worked hard with me.'

He thought she set a good example. 'I do think a lot of American actresses' indulgences are permitted by some producers. Somehow all their neuroses, or whatever they are, come out. They think nobody but them has problems.' But there were, on the whole – and in comparison with some of the earlier films – few problems with *The Russia House*.

Klaus Maria Brandauer, after giving away a role to Sean in the previous Russian film, was now one of his co-stars. He played a Soviet scientist with the information to prove his country was no threat to the West (Hollywood still believed that accents didn't matter and that no one would be bothered by a Russian who spoke like a German, so long as he sounded 'foreign'). Brandauer smuggles out a manuscript that makes the point about the Soviets' real power and leads the publisher to investigate things both for himself and for the CIA. It goes against the grain, because the publisher loves the Russian people in general and one Russian person in particular (Michelle Pfeiffer).

Sean said that at first he found his role quite boring but, as usual, he made his suggestions and, as usual – after paying him five million dollars, studios can't afford to do much arguing – he got his way. It didn't look as if he had made many mistakes.

The script was once again by Tom Stoppard, who obviously had now made things up with the star. Sean wanted to see how he had adapted the novel to the screen and said he would go to Los Angeles to discuss it. 'But,' said Sean, 'by the time the plane had touched down, the answer to the whole project was a definite "yes" because the story is so good.'

What the director of the new picture, Fred Schepisi, might not have realised was the involvement Sean had in his films. There weren't many actors around with his power. But he said he needed it – because until a picture went into the theatres (and the video stores) he could never be sure of the way it would turn out. For this film, Sean had approval on casting and had suggested both Michelle Pfeiffer and Roy Scheider (as the CIA chief) as well as Klaus Maria Brandauer himself. He said he made changes to the script, and, having made them, he watched every detail of the filming.

Tom Stoppard, however, told me he had doubts about those changes. 'I am not aware that he reworked the script,' he told me, 'I don't think he did.'

Observers on the set would note that if he could, Sean would beat Schepisi to his canvas chair – so that he could study the videotape of the work done (the 1990s version of 'the rushes') on the six-inch screen monitor.

That was something the director was willing to tolerate. After all, he said that Sean was the only choice for the role of Barley Blair the publisher, and it is not difficult to see why.

'As an actor,' he said, 'it's much more interesting to play a character like Barley Blair than it is to play James Bond, but you know, the Bond character in actual fact is not really as easy as it appeared, because the essence of Bond's character is to appear effortless. If it looks in any way as if he's struggling, it loses the whole flavour of what the movie's about.'

Tom Stoppard was very pleased with the Connery performance.

He told me he was 'tremendous – yes, a very good actor'. But why did women still find him so attractive ? Michelle Pfeiffer said it was to do with his 'real charisma' in *The Russia House.*

The unit filmed on location for five weeks – the first major American film ever to be shot in the USSR, which said a great deal about Gorbachev and the pragmatic approach of the secretary-general of the Communist Party to American dollars.

Sean, incidentally, said that he liked the look of the Soviet President – 'an extraordinary combination of intelligence, serenity ... and baldness'.

That from the balding fellow who had just been voted by *People* magazine 'the sexiest man alive'.

He said that all sorts of other men of his age were now expressing their gratitude to him. 'They told me I had done wonders for their morale. I think my sex appeal lies in my voice. Lots of women have told me they think the Scottish burr is very sexy and that's why I never want to lose it.' Dr Glass could have told him as much.

As he said, 'Luckily, women seem to really go for it.'

Micheline had more than once put her mind to that matter and every time she did, decided not to worry. 'I knew the situation right from the start, so I wasn't going to be bothered by other women throwing themselves at him. But if Sean were giving me any real reason to be jealous, I'd probably kill him.'

The Russia House received some fairly good reviews all over the world. The London *Daily Express* couldn't have been better: 'As Barley, Connery proves he is in a class of his own as a screen actor and produces the best performance of his career.'

Clearly, the British Film and Television Academy thought so in 1990, even if they hadn't yet seen *The Russia House.* Sean was the obvious choice for the year's BAFTA award, presented to him by the Academy president, the Princess Royal, for his contributions to world cinema.

Everybody who had been anybody in his public life – as well as Micheline and Jason representing his private life – came along to pay him tribute at the Odeon Leicester Square where extracts from his career on film were shown to a packed house.

Roger Moore, Honor Blackman (recalling the romp in the hay in *Goldfinger*), and Michael Caine were among those present. Sir Richard Attenborough, vice-president of BAFTA, said: 'It is surely no accident that Sean Connery is one of the most admired screen actors of his generation. He is wry, rugged and forthright, yet brilliantly able to convey the most subtle and complex of emotions.

Not content to rest comfortably on his laurels as the suavest of secret agents, he has continually sought challenges of the highest order in his career and, in triumphantly surmounting them, has created an extraordinary range of compelling characters to delight audiences.'

Gina Lollobrigida, Stefanie Powers and Robert Wagner, Jill St John and Jane Seymour were all on hand. Ursula Andress was there, too – minus her dagger. In addition, almost anyone who had ever played golf, including Nick Faldo, Bruce Forsyth and Jimmy Tarbuck did their best to denigrate his game, rather in the fashion of Hollywood's famous roasts.

Sean himself used the ceremony – as had Dirk Bogarde, Peggy Ashcroft and Julie Andrews who had all received similar awards in previous years – as an opportunity to speak up for what was still allegedly the British film industry and was still all but dying. 'It's a sheer waste. We have all this brilliance in Britain, with the quality of technical achievement and direction you won't see anywhere in the world. Yet we are putting the brakes on it.'

It was also an opportunity to attack the Conservative government – which, in the year of Margaret Thatcher's resignation, was having enough problems of its own. 'This government has been devoting its energies to shaking off restrictions on talents in every other industry but the film industry,' he said. 'I applaud their efforts in other directions, including the new tax reductions. But when are they going to do anything for us?'

He talked of the idea of leading figures in the film industry – like David Puttnam and Richard Attenborough – setting up a think-tank to discuss their problems with the government. (Everybody thought it a great idea, but three years later, the film business was in an even worse state; even Elstree studios were earmarked for closure, only to get a last-minute reprieve from the local council.)

Sean went on: 'We neglected to put up our own funds, left it to the Americans, so the money is American. But don't tell me that *Indiana Jones* is an American movie – or the Bond films. The Americans colonised the place. We weren't smart enough to do something about it here. It should be an apolitical part of the country. It should have its funding. It should be structured.'

Sean himself was structured now to maintain his role as the leading light of that same industry he was taking to task – except that he wasn't doing any filming in Britain either.

Problems of the industry apart, the ceremony was a wonderful occasion. Britain's only remaining superstar had come home (at least to Britain; he still maintained that England had nothing to do with Scotland) and was delighted to be there.

The producer of the event, Steve Minchen, told me Sean couldn't have been easier to deal with. But then, that was part of the job of the star – not to be difficult.

The publicist for the occasion was one of the most experienced in the business, Judy Tarlow. She has more misgivings about Connery.

She flew down to Marbella with Minchen. 'Sean wanted to meet us at the Marbella Club, where we checked in. We had the day to discuss various things. When you have people come to pay tribute to a star, you want that star to feel comfortable with who they are going to be.'

It wasn't her first meeting with Sean. She recalled working on a film at Shepperton at the time he was making *The Hill*. 'I remember everybody said, "What a fool! It would never work! People will only think of him as Bond." And there we were arranging a tribute to him by BAFTA!'

She said that even on that mission to Marbella, it was 'difficult to get close to him.'

She had the feeling, she said, that Micheline was watching over him all the time. 'She's very canny and was picking up things he might have missed. If we started to discuss something, a name might be mentioned, and she would step in. Her memory of how right that person would be was strong. She was more attuned to how useful that name might be to him than he was himself. But I am sure that he then made up his own mind.'

And she added: 'I think he tries very hard to catch up. He works hard at it. He really cares about reading and art. But I think it's an effort. It doesn't come easy to him.'

But the rapport between Tarlow and Connery worked. 'I was very lucky. He looks at you straight in the eye and he judges you immediately as to whether you are trustworthy and whether you know what you are talking about.'

He asked her direct questions: What is going to happen? What do you want me to do? How long is it going to take? He was not going to waste time for publicity. 'I told him I needed four and a half hours to do what I wanted to do. He gave me four and a half hours. We wanted David Frost and Selina Scott. Because of the set-up, I needed another fifteen minutes. I showed him the schedule and all he said was: "I said four and a half hours. You take that fifteen minutes from somewhere else." '

'I think that was a security blanket on his part. He needed to know precisely what was happening. It wasn't ego. I actually admire him for that.'

Of course, publicity and Sean Connery have never been good bedfellows, but just as he always agreed to a certain number of interviews for a film, he was agreeing to do them for the BAFTA presentation, too.

He also agreed on things that no public relations expert would have dared to suggest. Minchen had the idea that an acrobat dressed like Sean should begin the show doing cartwheels and things, followed by a fade out in which the real Sean would appear. 'I said, "You can't expect Sean Connery to do that." But he liked the idea and it was done.'

Indeed he liked the idea more than he did a photographer appearing on the scene for their meeting at Marbella – almost immediately after a waiter had spilled drinks on their table.

Sean saw the cameraman and then saw red. 'Is he with you?' he asked the BAFTA party. They said that he was not. 'We died. We were frightened what he was going to think.' It turned out that the photographer had been retained by the club who saw it all as a great publicity opportunity. Sean saw it as nothing of the kind.

Sean spoke to the man in Spanish. 'I'm sorry,' he said, 'I do not want photographs taken. Please go. Go now.'

He wasn't rude. 'I think,' said Judy, 'that if he had agreed to have the pictures taken, he would have been charming and polite. In this case, he wasn't rude; he was icy cold.'

That was roughly the way Judy Tarlow feels she was treated by Connery – although he not only never told her to leave, he took her advice.

'But there was a feeling of freezing me out. Although he was very polite and professional with me, I didn't get an iota of feeling that he liked me or cared about me. I never got any kind of thank-you or appreciation for what I did. I never got any letters from him.'

Even though she often sends on to him letters or invitations that have come to Sean care of her office, there is never an acknowledgement. 'If there's something urgent, I'll fax him in Spain. But even if I scribble a note, saying, "This came for you. I hope you are both well. Love Judy," never have I ever got a note of thanks from him. In the years since the tribute, I have not once seen his handwriting. Even Dirk Bogarde, who can be extremely difficult, always writes to thank me if I have done the same thing for him. I think Sean only comes into his own when he's working.'

She thought that was apparent the night of the tribute. 'When he

266

was in the company of Michael Caine and Roger Moore, they were laughing – but I had the feeling it was still scripted. There couldn't be anything natural about him. It's almost as if there is something missing in his natural development. I don't think he knows how he got from point one to point two in his life.'

But that question of the British film industry was one with which people had more sympathy. He raised it with Margaret Thatcher when they met at the Salzburg Festival. 'And she gave me a look as if I was asking for a job.' All he got from her, he later remembered, was 'some shit. And that was it! End of story.'

There was no doubt where Sean Connery stood now that the 1990s had settled down. He could do all that he wanted, although once again there was the feeling that perhaps he didn't really know what that was. Micheline tried to be helpful. 'If Sean wanted to give up acting tomorrow and move to Scotland, then of course I would support him.'

He couldn't afford to move to Scotland. And, apparently, he didn't want to give up acting either.

13

TIME FOR TRIBUTES

Quite remarkably, the sexiest man alive had become an elder statesman among superstars. The cantankerous Connery, who everyone knew was one of the finest actors on screen, was now being feted as someone to cherish. In Marbella they not only welcomed his living among them, they named a street after him: the Avenida Sean Connery.

The BAFTA tribute had had a lot to do with the way he was being treated, but now Sean was more than just a performer. The award came in the year of his sixtieth birthday, which is a milestone in anyone's life. In his case, it was reason for people to start speaking of him in the way they had once talked about Olivier.

Except that Olivier had never been elected the 'sexiest man alive' – a title which, after Sean's birthday, prompted more references in the world's press to *People*'s tribute than he might have welcomed. He managed to deal with it fairly laconically – noting that there weren't many sexy men who were dead. One writer got all she deserved when she asked if 'sixty-year-old men are more virile,' and he replied that he didn't know because 'it's years since I've been to bed with a sixty-year-old balding guy.'

Knowing his attitude to suffering fools, it was an exceedingly polite riposte. But he would allow this: 'Being comfortable in your own skin is more important than anything else, and I feel pretty comfortable in mine.'

But because he was now so important – and perhaps so aged? – everything about him had a magnitude it hadn't had before. His operation was being referred to as 'major surgery'. His golf was spoken of as 'championship standard' – and Sean liked to think it was. He admitted he was 'highly competitive' because 'it's a complete revelation of all my shortcomings – temper, ego, feeling, thinking; it almost gives you a philosophy, which is a great help to somebody like myself who doesn't have a religion.'

What was more, even the studios were being more deferential. 'It's funny, but I'm treated differently now,' he said at this time. 'They play it straight down the middle and I like it that way.' Putting it in golf terminology was paying them a compliment indeed. They, for their part, also knew what would happen to them if they didn't 'play it straight down the middle'.

Roger Moore at the BAFTA award hadn't thought there was any-thing unusual in the way Sean was now being regarded. 'Class will out. Why shouldn't he be at the top? He's younger than me.'

And then there was Ursula Andress: 'I adore Sean and I am very proud of him.'

If there was one person who didn't have Sean in his good books – any more than Sean had him in his – it was the former television talk-show presenter, Michael Parkinson. Sean alleged he welched on a ten-pound bet on a football game, which was why he never agreed to go on one of the Parkinson shows.

Certainly he stayed loyal to his friends, and they liked him for it. 'I may not see him for years,' Ronald Fraser told me, 'and then we meet and it's like we were last together yesterday.'

Michael Winner feels much the same way. This was the time Winner himself had gained a spot of notoriety over an affair with a girl, even though he had a live-in lover. The press had had a field day over it. 'I was standing with Sean and Michael Caine at a party that week when Sean quite suddenly said, "This'll give the press something to talk about." ' 'This' was suddenly cupping Winner's head in his hands and giving him a huge kiss on the lips.

What did seem remarkable to some people was the continuing love affair between Micheline and Sean. Through his second marriage, Sean had become a grandfather twice over. Sean and Micheline were as loving with each other abroad as they were at any one of their homes. At the Grosvenor House Hotel in London, Micheline called down to reception to ask if there were any messages. 'Just one from your husband,' the man on the desk said promptly. 'It says "You're the best." ' It was all she wanted to hear. There was no need to send a reply.

'It's incredible to think of him being sixty,' she said. 'He still looks and acts much younger and is so full of energy. He is also a wonderful husband. There are so many advantages being married to Sean, but I always remember who I am: MRS Connery.'

He wasn't over-romantic. He never told her she was gorgeous. 'The most I am going to get is : "You look very good tonight." ' There were no surprise presents. 'Flowers from Sean ? It would be like, my God . . . like a miracle.'

Nevertheless, he constantly left messages for her saying '*Je t'aime*'. And spelt badly, she noted.

But there was one thing about women that caused a problem or two. His old 1961 statement that he didn't think it a bad thing to hit them occasionally raised its head again – in an interview with American television hostess Barbara Walters. It was as though he had just said it for the first time : it caused an international furore.

There had been a television programme about battered wives. He said that a man could do worse things than give his wife a slap – 'a slap as opposed to a hit'. Later he explained to the London *Sunday Express* : 'I was talking about the kind of relationship where a man can destroy a woman without laying a finger on her by taking away her dignity, her integrity.' And he was not recommending that either.

But it led to a mass of hate mail – more than he had ever received before. For the first time, women deliberately cut him dead instead of swooning. The letters described him as 'a sexist pig' and worse. The day after the show went out, he pulled up at some traffic lights in America and, unfortunately for him, happened to glance at the woman in the car stopping alongside his. He smiled. She gave him a V-sign – but not the kind that Winston Churchill had used.

But there were worse worries. A week after the 1990 BAFTA award, Sean was again suffering from a sore throat and this time booked into the London Clinic – terrified yet again. But once more a biopsy revealed that there were no problems and he was ready to go back to work.

Highlander II resurrected Sean's 1986 character Juan Villa-Loboss Ramirez. Sean looked slightly older, although the pearl earrings he wore first time round were there again. But Sean made only a brief appearance in this fantasy set in 2024, although his Spanish grandee was from a different age altogether. So were the jokes. But it didn't seem to matter : you didn't complain about appearances by elder statesmen. Sean didn't complain, either – he got two million dollars for two weeks' work in Argentina.

But he said there was more to it than the money. 'I've always taken parts that attracted me. The age factor has never been a consideration. "Is he young or old ?" I just ask : would playing this character be stimulating for me ?'

What attracted him about *Highlander* was the same opportunity that

Robin And Marian had offered. 'I love roles that take the idea of the hero and re-examine it.'

Even so, the money had to be a factor. The initial two million dollars was not all he received: he was called back to reshoot a scene, for which he was paid another £350,000 – which worked out at £3,000 a minute. The director, Russell Mulcahy thought it was worth it. 'When you have a costly star for a small period of time,' he said, 'it's unfair to shortchange the audience.'

It didn't worry his audiences. Somehow, every time he made a film it was an event to be savoured – as if you couldn't be sure how many more were to come.

But were they being 'shortchanged'? *The Times* thought so. The picture was 'dismal'. Sean himself 'briefly injects humour ... but genial moments are swiftly swamped by special effects trumpery and mindless action'.

There were only *just* moments of Sean in *Robin Hood, Prince of Thieves*, although everybody knew from the billing he was there. Kevin Costner was Robin. Sean – now you see him now you don't – was Richard I. If the audiences hoped this would be a sequel to *Robin And Marian* they were disappointed. Sean wasn't. For the four lines he spoke, he got a million dollars – an even better deal than *Highlander II*. The educational trust found itself a million dollars better off.

If Sean could afford his generosity, he could also afford to join the world's most expensive golf club, the Lake Sherwood Club in Los Angeles. The privilege cost him £150,000. But then, the club did boast Rolls Royce golf carts – and made available to him a locker with the number 007. Somehow, in the 1990s he wasn't embarrassed by those James Bond associations any more.

As he said, 'I care about Bond and what happens to him. You cannot be connected with a character for this long and not have an interest ... All the Bond films had their good points.' He didn't even object to people talking about his 'licence to thrill', which was how the London newspaper, the *Independent* headed an interview with him in 1991.

He was, though, fascinated by some of the thrills he was claimed to have given. He had a call at about this time from an Italian inviting him to Rome to publicise his new film of Christopher Marlowe's *Tamburlaine*. Sean said he would love to do so, except for one little problem: he hadn't made a film of *Tamburlaine*. It turned out that the producer had begun to believe his own propaganda – he had raised the money for the film by saying Sean was going to make it and now wanted to prove the point.

Sean never failed to surprise. A television producer came to him with the idea for a sit-com. Nobody would have expected a man earning the sort of money he was making to accept such a commitment – with all the work and time it would take. But he said that if the offer came a little later, he could be interested. 'Ho Ho Seven' said *Today* newspaper (ironically, he was also now saying he would even do a new Bond movie if the money was right). 'Right money', it was fair to assume, now had to be close to eight figures.

But what was clear now was that other things in life mattered to him. The occasions that brought him honours but no money now seemed to be the ones he prized most. Could there be anything more gratifying than being awarded the freedom of the city of Edinburgh? That came to him in June 1991. He might have reflected that he was the only known milkman from St Cuthbert's, or the sole local coffin polisher for that matter, to be given such a tribute.

The Lord Provost, Eleanor McLaughlin, declared at the Usher Hall ceremony that Sean had 'walked with kings and millionaires, but at all times he is still that boy from Edinburgh'.

He might have most enjoyed this tribute from fellow Scottish-born actor Tom Conti: 'There are good actors who will never be stars. There are some stars who will never be actors. There are very, very few who, like Sean Connery, are both.'

The night before, there was a celebratory function at the Edinburgh Press Club, which awarded Sean honorary membership. Craigie Veitch, who remembered 'Big Tam' at school, saw the irony of that. 'It must have pleased him no little bit.'

Sir David Steel, the former leader of the Liberal Party, was among the guests at the ceremony, although he had to rush back to London for parliamentary business. 'I think Sean was thrilled by the people who came,' Craigie Veitch recalled for me. 'Many of them had known him since they were lads and he was among his peer group. There were girls who remembered dancing with him and lads who remembered weightlifting and swimming with him at Portobello.'

Indeed, Big Tam certainly had come home and received tributes he could never have imagined on those rides to the baths at Portobello. But it was a wealthy Tam who wanted to put the record straight. It wasn't true he didn't pay tax in Britain, he kept emphasising now. 'I pay full tax in Britain and America where I work without the benefits of living in the country.'

The ceremony was not the standing-room-only occasion these things usually are. Conservatives on the city council boycotted the evening, because Labour members had voted against a similar honour going to the Prince of Wales the year before. It wouldn't have done much good for Sean to point out that he himself didn't think much of the Labour Party.

He even went to one of his old schools, now called Bruntsfield Primary, where he said he was impressed with the way children are taught today. But he had some advice for the headmaster, David Strachan. 'They should teach law, so the bandits out there do not take advantage of you.'

There was no doubt how much Edinburgh had taken their favourite son to heart. They even arranged a special showing of the Connery film of the city, now released on video as the Scottish capital's principal means of drumming up tourism.

But certain parts of the visit were kept secret – like his visit to an Edinburgh hospice where he cradled a baby dying of Aids. There were reports afterwards of tears streaming down his face. They probably did, but it was one of those 'private' moments.

What he really wanted for Scotland was independence. That old line of his was given new force in the April 1992 general election campaign. He didn't stand for Parliament himself as the Scottish National Party candidate many of his fellow supporters would have wished to see – had he done so and won, while waiting for a new Parliament to be set up in Edinburgh, he could have sat a few places away from Labour's Glenda Jackson, who won the Hampstead and Highgate seat in London – but he did lend his voice to the SNP election broadcasts. He couldn't actually appear because of his film contracts, but the five-minute voice-over was partly written by himself. He recorded it while attending a golf tournament at St Andrews.

Explaining why he was taking politics that seriously, he said : 'People are enthusiastic about Scotland all over the world. The sooner they get to grips with finding out if they can govern, the better. They should be allowed to make their own mistakes and pick up the tab for whatever it is.'

The party leader, Alex Salmond MP, said that Sean had 'shaken, stirred and panicked' the other parties.

'Vote for Scotland,' declared Sean on the broadcast. 'It's up to you.' He thought that if the Baltic states could go it alone, so could the Scots. 'This will happen when you make it happen,' he said.

The SNP thought things would start to happen after the broadcast. They had a bank of telephones ready to take the offers of support which inevitably came during the campaign.

He wasn't the only showbiz personality to do party political shows. In addition to his and Glenda Jackson's broadcasts, John Cleese did one for the Liberal Democrats. 'It's so much easier if you live in the same country. It's very difficult for me to get on top of things from here,' Sean said in a call from Spain.

He joined a new group, 'Artists For An Independent Scotland' and declared: 'Let them tell us why Scotland can't be independent when San Marino with about 25,000 people has a seat at the United Nations.'

As for Prime Minister John Major and his fellow Tories, they were 'verbal terrorists' because they kept Scotland in chains.

But not everything was going perfectly for Sean and his Scottish connections. His own trouble came a month later with an advertising campaign. His television commercial for Japanese whisky – which most SNP members would regard as a contradiction in terms, if not downright sacrilege – led the Scottish Whisky Association to issue a statement saying: 'It certainly shows where his loyalties lie. Considering his strong pro-Scottish stance, he might have had second thoughts and put patriotism before commercial greed.' On the other hand, it was a clever move on the part of the advertising agency to lead their commercials with the best-known symbol there was for the place where the real stuff came from. And, in any case, the commercial was only going to be shown in Japan.

Sean might have felt happier had that been the case with his next film, *Medicine Man,* the story of a doctor who thought he was on the trail of a cure for cancer. Later Dr Wilburn Ferguson, aged eighty-seven, claimed that the story was based on his own researches in the Amazon jungle and said that he had tried to sell his autobiography to the Creative Artists Agency in 1988. CAA represented the author Tom Schulman as well as Sean. Ferguson said he would sue.

Sean's efforts didn't provide him with a cure for hating the work he did in the movie, even though the ten weeks he spent working on it in the Mexican jungle earned him six million pounds.

He was asked who his co-star would be. 'Trees,' he replied, 'fucking trees.' In fact, his co-star was Lorraine Bracco. He made no secret of wishing she was not. He complained that she forgot her lines and when she remembered them had the habit of breaking into fits of giggles.

He might even have complained about his current hairstyle. He had to wear a pony-tailed wig provided for £800 by a Mayfair speciality salon. Bond might have been an exceedingly tempting prospect by comparison with this film.

Despite the riches it brought, he said making the picture was 'horrible, probably the worst experience of my life'. He drank, he said, 'gallons of vodka' to try to fight mosquito bites. As he told *Premiere* magazine 'It was a disaster from start to finish. The conditions were appalling. I hate the heat and most days the temperature hit 115 degrees by 6.30 a.m. When you combine that with 98 per cent humidity and swarms of mosquitos that eat you alive, you can imagine what it is like – hell.'

The critics didn't go that far to describe the picture, although *Variety*'s Tod McArthy did venture that 'these are not two of his better hours'.

His relationship with Lorraine Bracco didn't escape notice. 'It certainly shows,' declared the *Sunday Telegraph*'s John Preston, 'with nothing apart from a kind of dark watchfulness between them on screen, culminating in one of the most half-hearted declarations of love one ever witnessed.'

Sean's character 'swings rather more towards Weissmuller than Schweitzer in the pantheon of jungle VIPs,' he declared.

It was something of a jungle in Spain, too, at times. Once, driving home in Marbella with Micheline in the front passenger seat and his two grandchildren in the back, he was cut up by another car. Sean caught up with the man at the lights, forced open his car door and punched him. 'I didn't knock him out, I just gave him a real thump on the jaw,' he explained.

There were other problems for him at this time. He complained that a woman was plaguing him with hate mail. When he discovered her identity, he threatened to throw her personally into the Mediterranean. 'She was trying to blackmail us and was looking through our bins,' explained Micheline. 'She did it for two months and she was sending threatening letters. She was saying we loved the devil and things like, "You kill a chicken and you drink the blood."'

The woman was American. Sean reported her to the police and she was deported from the country.

Women still got him into trouble – even for things he said three decades before. In 1992, he was asked once again about slapping women. He said to Australian *Woman's Weekly*: 'A guy lives in a tenement, three children, works all day, and he's got a problem with his wife. Nobody's perfect, so if someone in those circumstances is intent on a physical confrontation then it's going to happen.'

Once more, it was reported as though he had just said it for the first time. People were so incensed about it that Labour MPs Dr Norman Godman and George Robertson, both fellow Scots, were among those who decided to censure him in a House of Commons early-day motion.

Maria Fyfe, another of the Members who signed, said she was 'appalled at the views expressed by Sean Connery in an Australian magazine that giving a woman a smack in the face is acceptable conduct'.

The motion dragged up two points that had come to haunt Sean. It declared: 'The original James Bond is a member of the Scottish National Party and was given prominent billing in its election campaign. The SNP should immediately disassociate itself from these remarks.'

Said Dr Godman: 'For a big man like Sean Connery to slap a small woman across the face with anything approaching force could easily break her jaw or knock two or three teeth out of her mouth.'

The good doctor couldn't avoid making political capital out of it all. 'I thought it was a stupid observation to make, perhaps typical of the fervent members of the SNP,' he said.

For the moment – and a very brief moment it turned out to be – there the matter was allowed to rest.

Meanwhile, Sean, now aged sixty-two, told the *Daily Express*'s David Wigg that he hadn't any anti-feminist prejudices. 'I like women. I don't understand them, but I like them. Maybe that comes through. I've always loved women.'

By then, he had come to terms with his position in general. 'I've been very fortunate and have never had any real problems with people. But I've also had the guts to tell them, "You're a bore."'

That was certainly not something people said about him – which was why he was still making films. In the summer of 1993 he reversed what a lot of his countrymen had thought about Japan. A year after his commercials for Japanese whisky, he starred in *Rising Sun*, based on the Michael Crichton bestseller, which was seen almost as a racist attack on Japan and Japanese control of industry. It was as if he were trying to make up for the whisky indiscretion – except that he denied the movie was an exercise in Japan-bashing. That would be a 'dangerous precedent'. Instead, he told Zoe Heller in a *Vanity Fair* article that it was about 'what is happening realistically in the United States'.

Co-starring with the black actor Wesley Snipes, Sean played a detective investigating a murder in the Los Angeles boardroom of a Japanese company run entirely by Japanese executives.

Sean was executive producer of the movie and as such had approval of much that went into the making of *Rising Sun*, including the selection of Philip Kaufman as director. Naturally, he contributed to the script, too, the most obvious instance of his input coming in one of the many confrontations in the film.

One of the men he is investigating, tells him: 'You should know that

I'm a black belt.' 'Of course you are, dear,' says Sean as he slams his fist into the much younger man's stomach. James Bond never said it better – or much differently.

He said of the picture: 'It has got all the interesting things I like about a movie, and that is characters, a culture clash, talking about something of some significance, and it's a detective story.'

In a way, discovering the real Sean Connery is always something of a detective story, too. He was always laying new clues as to what he was and what he did. There were plans to play another Scottish doctor in Africa in a movie, and before that there would be a new film about King Arthur and his Round Table.

He might have hoped that his film work was all people would now be concerned with. 'I'll go on for as long as I find it interesting and stimulating and want to be part of it,' he said.

Michael Winner for one hopes Sean continues for a long time – and that one day he will make a movie with him. 'I hope it happens before we both pass on,' he told me.

'You see,' he said, 'Sean has danger about him. There's a roughness and an integrity and it shows through in whatever he does. He's real in real life and real on the screen and you can't say that about every actor. When you see him, it's always a delight. He's so bright and giving, and is an immensely popular person.'

Except among those who think he is a male chauvinist. When *Vanity Fair* published their interview in June 1993, it dragged up yet again the question of his slapping women. And again, again, again, it was reported as though he had just said it for the first time. Micheline was asked for her comments: 'It's very simple,' she said. 'I am French and I am not the slave type. I would not take anything like that. I am a woman and wouldn't take a slap from him and he knows that. I'm his wife and if he slapped me, I'd kill him.'

Golf remains one of the ways he has of bridging the barriers that some might consider inevitable between a star of his stature and less lofty people – and yet his golf partners also worry about risking his ire. In Marbella, one of his regular fellow players is the Italian-born former singer Toni Dalli, who wrote an article in a London magazine about 'My best friend Sean.'

He told me: 'I don't want to talk about Sean because he might think I am trying to get publicity out of him. He is a wonderful human being.' When Dalli, who now owns a restaurant, was ill in hospital, Sean regularly phoned to ask about his progress, and when Dalli came home, Sean was among the first to see him. It would be a tribute to Connery to say that he didn't think it was any remarkable thing. His friends, though, like to stress his ordinariness, which by its very nature they see as extraordinary.

Playing golf is now much, much more than either a pastime or a social thing for Sean. It is what this man's man chooses for his male-only occasions. He said: 'I mean, I like playing golf with men, right? At the club where I play there's a men's bar and there's a mixed bar. Women don't go into the men's bar. I think that's perfectly normal ... I like a men's bar where I can sit and talk only with men. It's harmless really. Usually, you've come in from a round of golf and you're talking about the shots you missed, the shots you made. It's just camaraderie.'

But he wasn't into the idea of male bonding. 'I can't see me dancing with some hairy-arsed guy with a beard in the woods.'

Much of his success, of course, had to do with coming to terms with all the changes that had occurred in his life, and reflecting upon it all. 'I was a keelie,' he once said, 'and that's Scots for a tough little kid. I didn't have any money. I didn't have an education. All I had was broad shoulders and a broader chip on both of them.'

Was that chip still there? Probably. There can be no other explanation for the fact that he was constantly making sure there wasn't someone out there ready to get at him. Perhaps even when 'getting at him' was nothing other than a marvelling at his success and the talent that brought it.

How do you explain Connery's sexual magic? People go on trying to do so but the real answers only come with the evidence. Interestingly, unknown to each other, people make the same comparisons. Ken Hyman told me: 'When he started out with James Bond, Sean was a young Clark Gable. Today, he *is* Clark Gable. He has a wonderful presence on camera. Women think he is the most sexy thing they have ever seen and men think he's wonderful, too.'

Michael Winner also has thoughts about that. 'He has that wonderful twinkle and that zest for life. He's quite the best actor around.'

The publicist Jerry Juroe remembers how recently, the grey and now virtually bald Sean walked into the White Elephant Club in London's Curzon Street. 'Everything stopped as people looked at him. I think the only time I have ever seen anything like it was years and years ago once at Paramount when Clark Gable walked in. It was something very special. But he just ignored it.'

In Gable's day, of course, the stars were more remote. In the years before space travel, getting to the stars was beyond imagination – which is perhaps why famous actors were called stars in the first place.

Jerry Juroe has seen the conflict. 'I think it is very difficult to tell at what point an actor still enjoys the fame but removes himself from it in relation to the public.'

Maybe that was Sean's achievement – achieving his place in movies while removing himself from traditional starlike activities. Or was it more the surmounting of obstacles? Dennis Selinger put it succinctly to me: 'The Americans don't really accept British actors. I know they win Oscars and other awards, but in the long run they are always second-best cousins and never quite there with the Americans. You know that from the money they get.

'Sean is the only exception to that. He gets the same sort of money as an American. Roger Moore or Michael Caine get good money, but never the sort of money they could command if they were American. It's due to the fact that Sean has an extraordinary star quality. There are an awful lot of women out there who say they would like to go to bed with Sean Connery. But equally he has a very great appeal to men.'

What was not so easily explained was the movies' appeal to him. Sometimes, bearing in mind that colossal output, the impression was that he worked for the sake of working, but not because he enjoyed it particularly. He complained about conditions while making films. With rare exceptions, he wasn't the life and soul of the set; he got his work done and went home to Micheline – and his golf. To most people those were his priorities.

He demanded for each film more money than most people would expect to earn in two lifetimes. Why? He didn't need it.

'An actor,' says Dennis Selinger, 'thinks that unless he works, people are going to believe he's dead – and every actor goes into a film wondering if he'll ever work again. They all think that and they *need* that to keep them going, and I don't think Sean is any different from anyone else. He needs the money and he won't give up until he's six feet under.'

His old colleague, Kenneth Griffith, last saw Sean when they had lunch together in 1990 with Dennis Selinger. After lunch all three walked down Piccadilly. 'Sean was wearing his checked golf trousers. He had no worries about walking in the street with people all around him. You don't forget walking with Sean. It takes a little discipline.' But people didn't go up to him or demand his autograph. 'People don't, you know,' said the actor. 'They never do. Not the English.'

But what he admired about Connery was not that so much as something on a more professional level; something for which he's earned the thanks of his fellow actors: 'I think he has done for all of us what nobody else would do. He's had the guts to stand up to producers – and I and every other actor have been robbed by producers in our time. I thank him for that.'

So why is he doing *so many* films these days? His friends and old colleagues wonder why he isn't satisfied, if not to rest on his laurels, then at least to cut down the output and perhaps confine himself to one new movie a year.

Certainly, he doesn't do it for the cameraderie of Hollywood. He goes to the film town to work and lives in his own small, elegant apartment in Century City. The moment the filming is over, he is on the plane back to Marbella. He doesn't go to the parties. They don't interest him. He doesn't indulge in the small talk and 'schmooze' of the movie set. He wants no part in it.

Letizia Adam says she has found him changed in recent years – more reserved than ever, less willing to play one of the 'chums'. 'He's not as warm as he used to be, as he would have been twenty to thirty years ago. It's his wife and his new lifestyle. Certainly, it's not success that has spoilt him. We don't get together any more at each other's homes – not just Sean and us, but nobody does.'

Her husband has an explanation: 'It's all those very long hours we have to work – never less than a thirteen hour day.' But that's the work that got him where he is today, and earned him the admiration of both fellow actors and fans.

And those fans and admirers are as many and as loyal as ever. Particularly in Edinburgh. Shelves in at least one of the local libraries are devoted to Conneralia, boasting a virtual collection of icons. A photograph of him in his old haunts is featured in a history of the area.

His video, *Sean Connery's Edinburgh*, is still in pride of place at the local tourist office. But of course it would be, for in Edinburgh they still call him Big Tam, something he obviously enjoys greatly. He certainly likes it a great deal more than some of the things he is called by strangers who may be well-meaning but annoy him dreadfully. Few address him as 'Mr Bond' these days, but he can't take much of the fawning that goes with the fat cheques.

As Ken Adam noted for me: 'There is nothing more difficult than being a star. You almost have to be born into it – like royalty. But he enjoyed talking about the fact that he was not born into it, about his humble origins.'

Charlton Heston, the veteran American film star, still wishes he had worked with Sean and gave me an interesting interpretation of the way Connery avoided typecasting with Bond. As he told me, 'He spent his early years with his career focused on one role and so didn't get used up in anything else. On the other hand, most actors who do one part become chained to it. Not Sean. He went on to other things. I admire him as an actor and as a fellow Scot. I have a great pleasure in his skills and his talents. He is a very good actor.'

Everything appeared to be just about as perfect as it could be. Until, that is, early in 1993 he was back in hospital in England with the old throat problems – this time at the Royal Marsden in London, which specialises in cancer treatment. It was revealed he had been receiving radiotherapy. What was not revealed at the time was how he was coping with the treatment, a wearying, worrying ordeal for anyone faced with it and plainly not a happy experience for the man who even hated having a needle puncturing his arm. Yet he faced it in the way he always faced his challenges and his work.

As every producer knows, he still has his accent. He still gets passionate about the Scottish National Party. In fact, as those women who elected him the sexiest man on earth would be pleased to hear, he is still passionate. Period.

He won't forecast the future any more than he will say he will ever make another 007 movie. But the recipe for his success remains as it was more than three decades ago: Leave 'em shaken – and stirred.

INDEX